CAMBRIDGE LIBRARY COLLECTION

Books of enduring scholarly value

Literary studies

This series provides a high-quality selection of early printings of literary works, textual editions, anthologies and literary criticism which are of lasting scholarly interest. Ranging from Old English to Shakespeare to early twentieth-century work from around the world, these books offer a valuable resource for scholars in reception history, textual editing, and literary studies.

Shakespeare and Stratford-upon-Avon

A detailed account by the secretary to the festival committee of the extensive Tercentenary celebrations of Shakespeare's birth held in Stratford-upon-Avon in 1864. The jubilee, inspired by Garrick's of 1769, included performances of several of the plays in a specially built pavilion on the Paddock in Southern Lane. There were also a banquet, a ball, fireworks, church services, a pageant and several concerts. Planning was fraught with difficulties and disagreements such as the committee's refusal to provide the pageant (organised in the end by the townsfolk) and walked a financial tightrope. The event nevertheless was a success and paved the way for the Shakespeare Memorial Theatre, opened in 1879. A short biography of the playwright, with an assessment of previous biographies, a topographical narrative of the town and description of the three previous jubilees held there (especially Garrick's) provide context and the perspective of the time.

Cambridge University Press has long been a pioneer in the reissuing of out-of-print titles from its own backlist, producing digital reprints of books that are still sought after by scholars and students but could not be reprinted economically using traditional technology. The Cambridge Library Collection extends this activity to a wider range of books which are still of importance to researchers and professionals, either for the source material they contain, or as landmarks in the history of their academic discipline.

Drawing from the world-renowned collections in the Cambridge University Library, and guided by the advice of experts in each subject area, Cambridge University Press is using state-of-the-art scanning machines in its own Printing House to capture the content of each book selected for inclusion. The files are processed to give a consistently clear, crisp image, and the books finished to the high quality standard for which the Press is recognised around the world. The latest print-on-demand technology ensures that the books will remain available indefinitely, and that orders for single or multiple copies can quickly be supplied.

The Cambridge Library Collection will bring back to life books of enduring scholarly value across a wide range of disciplines in the humanities and social sciences and in science and technology.

Shakespeare and Stratford-upon-Avon

A 'Chronicle of the Time'

Robert E. Hunter

CAMBRIDGE UNIVERSITY PRESS

Cambridge New York Melbourne Madrid Cape Town Singapore São Paolo Delhi

Published in the United States of America by Cambridge University Press, New York

www.cambridge.org
Information on this title: www.cambridge.org/9781108001625

This edition first published 1864
This digitally printed version 2009

ISBN 978-1-108-00162-5

Shakespeare's Monument,

STRATFORD ON AVON CHURCH.

SHAKESPEARE

AND

STRATFORD-UPON-AVON,

A "CHRONICLE OF THE TIME:"

COMPRISING

THE SALIENT FACTS AND TRADITIONS,

BIOGRAPHICAL, TOPOGRAPHICAL, AND HISTORICAL,

CONNECTED WITH

THE POET AND HIS BIRTH-PLACE;

TOGETHER WITH

A FULL RECORD OF THE

TERCENTENARY CELEBRATION.

BY

ROBERT E. HUNTER,

LATE SECRETARY TO THE STRATFORD-UPON-AVON COMMITTEE.

"It should not be overlooked that the Stratford authorities have undertaken an onerous and costly scheme in deference to the public voice of demand. It is also to be remembered that the matter will be discussed a hundred years hence, with sharp curiosity, to discern what the appreciation of Shakespeare really was about the year 1863."—*Daily News.*

LONDON:

WHITTAKER AND CO., AVE MARIA LANE.
STRATFORD-UPON-AVON: EDWARD ADAMS.

1864.

PREFACE.

THE "paragon of all patience" thought he should hear of something to his advantage if his enemy would write a book. Book-making in all forms has been a serious undertaking at all times—never more so than at present; but I am in this work free from many of the anxieties of authorship. I have not written a book: this is only a compilation. The confession will strike the intelligent reader, who may have dipped into these pages before glancing at the preface, as less necessary than that of the very "old master" who, having painted a model specimen of the feline tribe, attached the celebrated inscription—"This is a cat."

To the making of some record of the celebration at Stratford in 1864 I felt myself bound. The festival had no ordinary purpose, neither was it of common magnitude. It appealed to the sympathies of the nation, and sought support from the entire country. The object was one which engaged the attention, and, to some extent, aroused the enthusiasm of all classes of the community. A very considerable sum of money was involved in the undertaking, and in the carrying of it out an amount of labour, mental and physical, was expended which cannot be over estimated. Without much exaggeration, it may be said that for nearly a year the inhabitants of an entire

town devoted all their leisure, and not a few of their
business hours, to what was commonly called "tercentenary
affairs; " and as a very praiseworthy result was achieved,
some history of their labours and the fruits thereof—
beyond that contained in the newspapers of the day—
appeared desirable and due to the Stratford Committee and
to the public.

Accordingly, as no one else indicated any intention of
making such a "chronicle of the time," I undertook the task;
but in the performance of it have travelled considerably
outside the boundary to which I originally thought of
confining myself. In the first place, some account of the
old jubilees appeared requisite, in order to show the more
comprehensive character of the tercentenary celebration;
then a history of the four festivals in honour of a poet's
memory, without any description of the town in which
they took place, or memoir of the man to whom these
repeated triumphs were voted, appeared to me likely to
prove unsatisfactory. Hence the extent of this volume. I
would have willingly avoided the biography of Shakespeare
had I thought that the facts in relation to his life and
character which have been ascertained were sufficiently
known to the public; but I had found such startling proofs
to the contrary as forced me to venture on a work much
more likely to result in censure than applause to the
author.

In detailing the labours of the Committee, reference to
documents and public correspondence became unavoidable;
and I have preferred reproducing these documents *in
extenso* rather than giving abstracts, epitomes, or descriptions
of them which might engender unpleasant discussion hereafter. To the general reader they may not appear very
interesting, but to all who have been connected with the

festival they will possess some degree of importance. A "Blue Book" may not be a very amusing volume, but it is generally a valuable one; and that occasionally more for future reference than for present information.

But whether diverting or instructive—both or neither—this volume owes its existence to the encouragement and assistance I received from Mr. William Greener and Mr. Edward Adams, of Stratford, whose kindness I can never forget until the "warder of this brain shall be a fume, and the receipt of reason as a limbeck only."

I have only, in conclusion, to express a hope that *this* "chronicle of the time" will be received amongst readers and critics on the principle laid down by *Hamlet*, for the reception of "the abstract and brief chronicles" of his time—that is "after their own honour and dignity : the less it deserves the more merit is in their bounty."

London, 1st June, 1864.

CONTENTS.

SHAKESPEARE:

AN OUTLINE OF HIS LIFE,

WITH REFERENCES TO

HIS FAMILY, HIS FRIENDS, AND HIS CONTEMPORARIES;

ALSO,

HIS BIOGRAPHERS.

———◆———

It may be safely asserted that the prince of British biographers could not, under any circumstances, have written a life of Shakespeare that would have been comparable with that wonderful achievement of personal history which stands unique in our language, the life of Johnson. Gentle, modest, and retiring, "the great heir of fame" would have been no hero after its eccentric writer's heart. But the man who could have worthily played the Boswell to Shakespeare, might have placed himself for ever amongst our principal literary creditors, and performed a work "which the world would not willingly let die."

We are, however, so far from possessing such a treasure that we know, directly from his contemporaries, nothing of Shakespeare's biography. Strange, indeed, that in an age of great men, "when learning triumphed o'er her barbarous foes," no one seems to have troubled himself to place on record any account of the man whose immortality they foresaw, and whose genius they confessed—

"To be such
As neither Man, nor Muse, can praise too much."

And the strange circumstance is the more deeply to be regretted as we ponder on the treasury of wit and wisdom which might then have made us rich indeed.

Without supposing that Shakespeare was in his day distinguished as a mighty conversationalist, or given to display, in or out of the social circle, it is easy to believe that maxims of religion, politics, philosophy, and worldly prudence "came mended from his tongue;" that the grandly serene "star of poets" must have been in his serious hours the most sagacious of mentors, and in his lighter moments the most charming of companions. Old John Aubrey, who gave the first brief memoir of him, says, "He was a handsome well-shaped man, very good company, and of a very ready and smooth wit;" and afterwards adds that he heard Sir William Davenant and Mr. Thomas Shadwell ("who is accounted the best comedian we have now") say Shakespeare "had a most prodigious wit." Amongst his family and guests at New Place, in the circle of his professional *corps* at the Globe, or taking his ease in his inn—"At Bread Street's Mermaid," or elsewhere, it may be readily imagined—

> " Aged ears played truant at his tales,
> And younger hearings were quite ravished,
> So sweet and voluble his discourse."

But the records of his life are so meagre, that of what he was or did we know little, and of what he thought (apart from his composition) or said, nothing.

The literary men of the time would appear *prima facie* to have been guilty in this matter of most culpable negligence, and himself strangely reckless, touching the name, which things " standing thus unknown should live behind him," Campbell says, " The Genius of Biography neglected him in his own day. She gave records of men comparatively uninteresting and said nothing about the paragon of nature. She embalmed the dwarfs of our literature and left its colossus to be buried in oblivion. Perhaps our baulked curiosity can fix on no individual more strangely responsible for this than Shakespeare himself;" and Dr. Johnson asserts that "no author ever gave up his works to fortune and to time with so little care." "So careless," the same author remarks, "was this great poet of future fame, that, though he retired to ease and plenty, while he was little declined into the vale of years, before he could be disgusted with fatigue or disabled by infirmity, he made no collection of his works, nor desired to rescue those which had been already published from the depravations that obscured them, or secure to the rest a better destiny by giving them to the world in their genuine state." "Of all trusters to futurity," writes Dr. Warburton, "commend me to the author of the following poems (Shakespeare), who not only left it to time to do him justice as it would, but to find him out as it could."

Now, if he left time to find him out as it could, may it not be that time is doing him great injustice in this matter. That he wrote some thirty-seven wondrous plays we know; and that he carried on business and correspondence we feel also assured; but the mystery that transcends all others, and one of the most unaccountable facts in the whole history of literature, is that not a single scrap of this vast mass of manuscripts has ever been discovered. The whole has vanished and left not "a rack" behind. "All," says Mr. Hallam in his "Literary History," "that insatiable curiosity and unwearied diligence have hitherto detected about Shakespeare serves rather to disappoint and perplex us than furnish the slightest illustration of his character. It is not the register of his baptism, or the draft of his will, or the orthography of his name that we seek. No letter of his writing, no record of his conversations, no character of him drawn with any fulness by a contemporary has been produced."

How, then, knowing this extraordinary disappearance of all Shakespeare's papers—all the MSS. of the plays he wrote, all the letters he received (with one exception)—how can we reasonably charge him with total carelessness of his reputation with posterity? May he not have kept a commonplace book? or written an autobiography? Some of his many admirers may have written his life, and that manuscript being lost, was for anything we know destroyed by the devouring element which may have robbed the world of his own precious writings. No man valued more highly the precious treasure of a goodly reputation than he did. He took heed for to-morrow in worldly affairs ; made hay while the sun shone, and put more money in his purse than any poet who went before or came long after him ; and he who was so careful of that "which has been slave to thousands" was not likely to forget entirely "the fame," which he says, "all men hunt after in their lives."

Nearly all his heroes—*Macbeth, Hamlet, Othello, Brutus, Harry V., Richard III.*—look to future ages with hope or fear, according to the deeds done in the body. The terms of his will indicate a desire to have his name carried down honourably to future generations. And respecting the condition in which he left his works, it may be in some measure accounted for by the shortness of his life and the suddenness of the attack, which, in a few days, and at the comparatively early age of 53, carried away into "the undiscovered country" the greatest genius "that ever lived in the tide of times ;" and it is here worthy of remark that his professional associates, John Heminge and Henrie Condell, who published the first complete edition of his works seven years after his death, ascribe to this cause— his sudden death and too brief candle of life—indirectly the fact of his not being the editor and publisher of his own works. "It had bene a thing," they say, "we confesse, worthie to haue bene wished, that the Author himselfe had liu'd to haue set forth, and ouerseen his owne writings; But since it hath bin ordain'd otherwise, and he by death departed from that right, we pray you do not envie his Friends, the office of their care, and paine, to haue collected & publish'd them." I therefore hold that there are not sufficient grounds for the opinion that he left no record of his life and character, and that he designedly trusted to those who might come after him—such doubtless loving, if not able editors, as Heminge and Condell to do justice to his works.

Despite the disheartening account given by Mr. Hallam of Shakespearian explorations, a number of clever, earnest labourers have gone forth into the unfertile field in late years, and have returned not altogether empty-handed. It cannot be denied that Mr. Halliwell has added much to our stock of knowledge, however little the whole may be, in relation to *the* genius of our isle, and given to the public the nearest approach to a satisfactory biography of him we can yet have. Others think there is yet much to be found. "There are possibly in existence," says Mr. Bellew, "many documents, which, if discovered, would throw a flood of light upon the business of his manhood and his authorship that remain for the present shrouded in obscurity."

It is needless for me to say that I do not profess to have found any one of these precious documents, or to be able to lay before the public one truly original fact touching the subject of this memoir. I am indebted for all I know of him to the researches of others. Neither do I purpose, however I may have amused myself by theoretical speculations anent the matter, to trouble the reader with a congeries of surmises and conjectures in lieu of positive information ; and as for rhetoric or fine writing, I have no pretensions to either. The plan of this record requires me to give some account of the man to the honour of whose memory these national triumphs have been voted, with a view of showing that our information concerning him, scanty though it be, is sufficient to prove he was as a man no less worthy of these demonstrations than as a poet he is universally admitted to be above the possibility of undue appreciation by anything that jubilees or monuments can manifest.

The earliest skeleton of a memoir (it cannot be called anything better) of Shakespeare as yet discovered was put together by John Aubrey many years after the poet's death, 1680. The author states—(1.) that William Shakespeare was born at Stratford-upon-Avon, in the County of Warwick; (2.) that he was the son of a butcher; (3.) that he was inclined naturally to poetry and acting ; (4.) did act exceedingly well; (5.) that he began early to make essays at dramatic poetry, which at that time was very low, and his

plays took well. As a proof it may be of the truthfulness
of his remark touching the condition of poetry at that time,
Aubrey gives us the following taste of Shakespeare's quality,
" One time," the biographer says, " as he was at the tavern,
at Stratford-upon-Avon, one Combes, an old rich usurer
was to be buried; he makes there this extraordinary
epitaph: "—

> " Ten in the hundred the devil allows ;
> But Combes will have twelve, he swears and vows.
> If any one asks who lies in this tomb,
> ' Ho ! ' quoth the devil, ' 'tis my John o' Combe.' "

Having given a deliverance on the poet's personal
appearance, and the quality of his art as above quoted,
Mr. Aubrey informs his readers that Shakespeare was wont
to go to his native county once a year, and that he understood Latin pretty well, for he had been in his younger
years a schoolmaster in the country. And thus ends the
bald disjointed chat of Aubrey, which passed for a " Life of
Shakespeare."

Of the statements it contains the first may be taken as
unquestionable ; the second as possible but improbable ; the
third is doubtless ; the fourth is very questionable, and
positively contradicted ; for Rowe says his highest performance was the *Ghost* in his own " Hamlet," a part certainly
calling for considerable innate dignity and elocutionary
power, but one which may be played well by an actor devoid
of the energy, the enduring flexible voice, feeling, facial
expression, and graceful gesticulation essential to the true
tragedian. That he began early to make essays in poetry
is most likely, but that he wrote the doggerel epitaph for
John o' Combe is very doubtful. There are more than one
version of the lines. They are very dull and ill-natured,
and Shakespeare was neither. I do not believe the gentle
and the good Shakespeare ever wrote a line calculated
" to make one worthy man his foe," and John Combe
appears to have been anything but the foe of his alleged
libeller, for he bequeathed him a legacy of £5, and Shakespeare in turn left his sword to Thomas Combe, John's
nephew. The next statement has more truthfulness about

it. One can readily credit the old *gobe-mouche*, when he says Shakespeare visited Stratford annually, for here were all his early old associates, and here was his heart with his treasures of wife and children. In conclusion, Aubrey says he knew Latin pretty well; thus discrediting the *dictum* of worthy Ben Jonson on this point.

Naturally dissatisfied with Aubrey's account of Shakespeare, and unable to find out anything more satisfactory about him in London, Thomas Betterton, the most gifted and accomplished tragedian of his age; and, according to Pepys, "the best actor in the world," travelled to Stratford-upon-Avon to ascertain further particulars. Whatever Betterton learned there when he arrived, towards the end of the seventeenth century, he communicated to Nicholas Rowe, a scholar and gentleman—poet laureate to George I., but better known by his contribution to our dramatic literature. Rowe worked the materials into what he modestly enough calls "some account of the life, &c., of William Shakespeare," published in 1709.

Now, one would have expected from the devoted zeal of Betterton and the literary ability of Rowe a respectable biography ought to have been compiled; but the work deserves no better title than the author bestowed upon it. Its merits have been variously estimated. Johnson, not a rash or lavish dispenser of literary reputation, says, "I have borrowed the author's life from Rowe, though not written with much elegance or spirit, it relates however what is now to be known, and therefore *deserves to pass through all succeeding publications.*" No publication of Shakespeare's works or life has certainly ever been since given to the public without some degree of obligation to Rowe; but the astute critic was singularly—yet—duly liberal in his judgment on such a production. If, however, overrated by the critics of the past age, Rowe appears to me to be unduly depreciated by those of the present. Mr. Malone confines the information of the life to eleven facts, and in these he asserts that only "two truths are told," not

> "As happy prologues to the swelling act
> Of the imperial theme;"

but as " the be all and the end all " of the certainties to be
found in " The Life," by Rowe—namely, the poet's birth
and death.   One he says is doubtful (his recommending of
Ben Jonson and his writings to the public) and the other
eight are altogether false.   Adopting the same view, a
writer in that most respectable periodical, " Chambers's
Journal," a few days ago, says, " The traditions gathered
by the gossiping and uncritical Aubrey or mentioned by
Rowe cannot be depended upon as containing even a germ
of fact."   Here the credulity of Johnson is fully counterbalanced by the infidelity of Chambers.   Truth lies between
them.

Rowe, as it appears to me, may be fairly charged with
giving full credence and unqualified assertion to things
which were in themselves doubtful and utterly without
proof, whilst he places before the public, upon mere hearsay
evidence, facts which might have been established by incon-
trovertible testimony.   For instance, we are told by him
that Shakespeare was obliged to fly from Stratford for deer
stealing.   This indictment is sent up to the jury without
even the name of a witness to sustain it, and there seems
to be no scepticism in the mind of the author upon the
subject.   But when he comes to narrate matters in relation
to which positive proof might have been easily discovered
there is no such confidence in his manner of assertion.
He makes no question of the deer stealing story; but
Hathaway, Shakespeare's father-in-law, is only *said* to have
been a substantial yeoman—a fact of which no one need be
sceptical who visits his house in Shottery even at this day.
Then we have the language of rumour in nearly every
subsequent sentence.   "*He seems*," says the author, "to have
given entirely into that way of life," &c. ; " the ballad on
Lucy *is said to have been*," &c. ; " it is upon this accident
he is said to have made his first acquaintance," &c. ; "Falstaff
is said to have been written," &c. ; " John Combe is said
never to have forgiven him," &c.   Rowe will not even state
positively that Shakespeare resided in Stratford-upon-Avon
for any considerable period before his death.   He tells us
that it was " said " he did so.   Nearly everything he states

is of no more certainty than flying report. It would indeed be difficult to find a piece of biography of the same length so provokingly stuffed with " doubtful phrases."

Could the gifted and accomplished Mr. Betterton find out nothing more of the poet in Stratford ? Dr. Johnson says, " Rowe relates what is now to be known ;" but surely not all that Betterton communicated to him. Did he take any notes of the information he received from the actor ? If so, had he lost them ? or did he attach but little importance to the work ? No one can now give answer to either of the first-mentioned queries, but to the third a reply in the affirmative may be given with safety. He introduces the memoir to his reader with a sort of apology. He " fancied that some account of the man himself might *not be thought improper* to go along with them" (Shakespeare's plays). When he was not certain of the propriety of writing and publishing a life of Shakespeare, we need not be surprised by the barren result of his labours.

Happily for the memory of the poet, there is at least something more now to be known about Shakespeare than in the days of Nicholas Rowe or Dr. Johnson. Mr. Steevens, one of the cleverest of Shakespeare's critics and commentators, despaired of adding an item to the slender stock of facts positively ascertained with respect to him ; but not so Mr. Malone, who laboured with the utmost zeal and energy indefatigable, and if he did not increase our knowledge in a degree corresponding with his efforts, he directed searching and not unprofitable scrutiny into the whole subject. Dr. Drake published two large volumes, with the view of gratifying public curiosity in the matter. Mr. Dyce and Mr. Thomas Campbell have published interesting biographies of Shakespeare, but devoid of any novelty in matters of fact ; and Mr. Charles Knight, who has contributed so largely to popular literature and the information of the people, has devoted a considerable portion of his time to Shakespeare and his works, recording not only all that is known of Shakespeare—all he was—all he said, or did, or knew, but all that he might, could, would, or

should have known in the glorious age of enlightenment
and rapid progress in which he lived; Mr. Payne Collier
too, has laboured long and earnestly to "unsphere the divine
William, and make him known at our fire-sides;" and
Mr. J. O. Halliwell has published a Life of Shakespeare,
of which it may be said with more truth than of Nicholas
Rowe's brochure, that it " contains all that is now known"
of the man who

> " In our wonder and astonishment,
> " Has built himself a live-long monument."

"The vast information collected in this work," says Mr.
Robert Bell, "the variety of documentary evidence by
which its statements are supported and illustrated, and the
vast expenditure of time and toil bestowed upon its production, render it altogether one of the most remarkable monuments of industry and intelligence concentrated on a single
subject in the whole range of biographical literature." Mr.
Howard Staunton, a diligent labourer in the Shakespearian
vineyard, has also given the public some account of the
great man's life ; and many essays, sketches, and lives, and
works of criticism and exposition have been called forth
by this Tercentenary Festival ; amongst the principal of
which may be mentioned "Shakespeare Commentaries," by
Dr. G. G. Gervinus, professor at Heidelberg; and in what may
be called works of detail, " Shakespeare's Home," by the
Rev. J. M. Bellew; "Life Portraits of William Shakespeare:
a history of the various representations of the poet, with
an examination into their authenticity," by Mr. J. Hain
Friswell; "Shakespeare : his birthplace, home, and grave,"
by the Rev. J. M. Jephson ; &c., &c.

I have thus, perhaps, over drawn my space in giving an
imperfect sketch of the work already done by earnest and
erudite men, to gratify the natural curiosity of all readers
to know who and what manner of man this " boast of
nature " was. My object has been to direct the attention
of the reader, if necessary, to more extensive sources of
information than my brief and simple narrative can afford,
and at the same time to acknowledge at the outset my obliga-

tions to the principal authors above named, for the materials of the subjoined memoir. Indeed I may well imitate the candour of Dr. Johnson, when referring to the critics who went before him. "I can say," observes the great lexicographer, "of all my predecessors what I hope will be hereafter said of me, that not one has left Shakespeare without improvement, nor is there one to whom I have not been indebted for assistance and information."

With the orthography and orthoepy too of Shakespeare's name the biographer's perplexities commence. About the orthoepy the public have come to a pretty general agreement. The name is rarely pronounced nowadays otherwise than with the first syllable short, and second long, as Shax-speere; but the mode of spelling it has been for many years, and still remains, a subject of no slight controversy. According to the entries of the Common Council of the Stratford Corporation, in their book A, John Shakespeare's (William's father) name was in his own day spelled seventeen ways, as Shackesper, Shackespere, Shacksper, Shackspor, Shackspere, Shackespere, Shakspayr, Shaksper, Shakspere, Shakspeyr, Shakysper, Shakyspere, Shaxpeare, Shaxper, Shaxpere, Shakxspere, and Shaxspeare. Of the three modes of writing the name which prevail at present, it will be observed that only one occurs in this list, namely, Shakspere; Shakspeare and Shakespeare are not given. But in the records of Warwickshire, where some curious modes of spelling the name will be found, as of Schakspeire, Chacsper, &c., "Shakspere" is to be discovered. The first of the three prevailing ways of spelling it is adopted by Sir Frederick Madden, Mr. Charles Knight and many others; Mr. Malone and Dr. Drake the second; Mr. Collier and the Shakespeare Society the third. "We have now," says the *Athenæum* in a paper on the subject, published in 1844, "the six existing signatures of Shakespeare, copied with all the skill the human hand seems capable of arriving at (the glorious art of photography was not then available). The *first* is from the deed of sale, dated 10th March, 1612, now in the City of London library, already engraved in Malone's

'Inquiry;' the *second* from the mortgage, dated the next
day, commonly called the Garrick autograph; the *third* is
from the autograph on the fly leaf of the first edition of the
'English translation of Montaigne,' by John Florio, in
1603, now in the British Museum; while Nos. 4, 5, and 6
are from three briefs of the poet's will, preserved in the
Prerogative Court at Doctors' Commons. We have seen
the originals of the six several signatures here engraved;
we have stood over them with a curious eye; and recently
as we were from the ingenious pamphlet of Sir Frederick
Madden, we came to the conclusion that if any man had
endeavoured to write his name in six different ways, he
could not have puzzled his correspondent more ingeniously
than William Shakespeare has, in these six signatures,
puzzled his commentators and admirers. In No. 1 and
throughout the whole six signatures the christian name,
William, is written clearly and unmistakably, as if the
poet had made up his mind and new nibbed his pen for the
orthography and caligraphy of that portion of his name.
Now let us come to the name so dear in sound and in any
kind of spelling to every British ear and eye. We have, it
appears to us, in No. 1, *Shaksper* or *Shakspea*, the strip of
parchment on which the signature occurs being unfortunately too narrow for the full insertion of the name.
No. 2 we have apparently *Shakspea* or *Shaksper*: no jury
of twelve would agree as to which it is. In No. 3
(the Florio), we have unquestionably *Shakespere*, but the
genuineness of this signature will admit of more than one
doubt. In the will we have almost anything, the *espeare*,
speare, or *spere*, being a complete jumble of penwork, a
realisation of one of Ben Jonson's comic characters—an
in and out—'in and in medley.' " Doctor Drake is
persuaded that the third signature to the will is William
Shakspeare, and that the intermediate *e* I use was very
seldom used, and more rarely pronounced. How a man
can pronounce so definitely as he does on the pronunciation
of the word Shakespeare three hundred years ago, I am
at a loss to ascertain; and respecting the spelling of it,
the question will probably amuse coming generations of

critics, as it has past and present, and to as little purpose. The spelling I have adopted is, as above stated, that of the Shakespeare Society and Mr. Collier, also Mr. Howard Staunton and the people of Stratford-upon-Avon, who probably use it from an unwillingness to lose even a letter which might have belonged to the name which has to Stratford bequeathed a name imperishable. It directs the mind moreover most clearly to the derivation of the chivalrous old patronymic which, as has been justly remarked, was doubtless present in the mind of rare old Ben when he wrote the lines—

" Look how the father's face
Lives in his issue ; even so the race
Of Shakespeare's mind and manners brightly shines
In his well-toned and true-filed lines ;
In each of which he seems to *shake a lance*,
As brandish'd at the eyes of ignorance."

However spelled, families of the name had been settled time out of mind in Warwickshire. From these families the poet's first became distinguished by services to " Young Richmond," when he undertook to rid the country and the world of the usurper Richard, " one," as Shakespeare describes him, " rais'd in blood and in blood establish'd." The record connected with the grant of arms to John Shakespeare, dated 1596, attests the fact. But the rolls of Henry VII., having been carefully searched, gave no evidence of it. I do not however think the public documents are fabrications which record of the father of William Shakespeare that " his parent and late ancestors were, for their valiant and faithful services, advanced and rewarded of the most prudent prince, King Henry VII., of famous memory." Sundry circumstances go to corroborate the testimony. John Shakespeare was of the third generation succeeding the adherent of Henry of Tudor ; and it is not improbable that his son, the great dramatist, had the traditions of his own family in his mind when he put into the mouth of Richmond the well-known lines—

" For me, the ransom of my bold attempt
May be this cold corpse upon earth's cold face ;
But if I thrive, the gain of my attempt
The least of you shall share his part thereof."

Sharing, it may be by hereditary possession, some portion, however trifling, of the gains of the bold enterprize, John Shakespeare about the year 1556 felt emboldened to woo, and in due course of time, about a year afterwards, felt doubtless blessed in wedding Mary Arden, in the pleasant, quiet, Auburn-like village of Willmecote, near Stratford-upon-Avon. She was the youngest daughter, and, as testified by the father's will, favourite child of Robert Arden, a yeoman, who traced his pedigree in an uninterrupted line to the highest antiquity of any family in Warwickshire.

The worldly circumstances of Shakespeare's father prior to this marriage are thought to have been somewhat depressed; and it has been regretted that the first mention we find of his name in the borough of Stratford is connected with an offensive incumbrance in Henley Street (1552), and in the second place (1556), as a defendant in an action brought by one Thomas Siche for the recovery of £8. But as Mr. Halliwell has discovered that the decision of the court was against the plaintiff, it may be reasonably concluded the claim was unjust, and repudiated in consequence. That he was at this period a well-to-do man may be fairly inferred from the fact of his purchasing house property in Stratford. He is variously described as a butcher, a glover, and a considerable dealer in wool. There is some evidence to show that he was engaged in all of these kindred occupations, and may have been at the same time a farmer. As the heiress of Robert Arden, John Shakespeare's wife brought him a respectable dowry in houses and land, so that we are not surprised to find him rising rapidly to positions of trust and public importance amongst his fellow townsmen. In 1556, he was on the jury of the court-leet; in 1557, an ale-taster; in 1558, a burgess; in 1559, a constable; in 1560, an affeeror; in 1561, a chamberlain; in 1565, an alderman; and in 1568, high bailiff of the town. His education, together with the rise and supposed decline of his worldly prosperity, has formed a subject of controversy amongst biographers. It will perhaps surprise some readers to learn that it has been ascertained he governed the borough without assistance from a glimmering of scholarship ; but those who reason on the Baconian principle, from the known to the unknown, will not be astonished to hear that three hundred years ago the chief magistrate of Stratford-upon-Avon could not write his name.

The thriving burgher knew, however, how to succeed in life, and was perhaps "happy because he knew no more." His respectable wife brought him a respectable family of sons and daughters, who arrived in Stratford, according to the parish register of their baptisms, in the following order :—

Joan, or Jone, "daughter of John Shakespeare," baptized 15th September, 1558.—Died young.

Margaret, baptized 2nd December, 1562.—Died in 1563.

WILLIAM, baptized 26th April, 1564.—Died in 1616.

Gilbert, baptized 13th October, 1566. [Was alive in 1609.]

Joan, or Jone, baptized 15th April, 1569.—Died 1646.

Anne, baptized 28th September, 1571.—Died 1579.

Richard, baptized 11th March, 1573-4.—Died 1613.

Edmund, baptized 3rd May, 1580.—Died 1607.

Thus of these eight children three died at a very tender age. The burial of Margaret is recorded on 30th April, 1563, and that of Anne on 4th April, 1579. The evidence of the death of the first-born is contained in the fact of the baptism of another Joan in 1569. The burial is not entered on the register, and some have asserted that the latter child was not the sister of William Shakespeare, but the daughter of another John Shakespeare. Mr. Knight says "the registry of a second Joan leaves no reasonable doubt that the first died, and that a favourite name was preserved in the family;" and as the only second John Shakespeare known in that age was not married till 1584, he was clearly not the father of the child born fifteen years previously.

It would not be to the purpose to try to trace the lives and fortunes of any of the five children, who survived the death of Anne, with the exception of our subject, the incomparable William. The only claimant to be a descendant of the stock of John Shakespeare is George Shakespeare, a worthy workman resident at Wolverhampton, who, with the assistance of Mr. George Griffith and other friends, has been for a considerable time endeavouring, at much expense and trouble, to trace his lineage to Edmund Shakespeare. His faith is founded on family tradition, and he believes he could in all probability establish it to the public satisfaction, but that some leaves have been torn out of the middle of an old registry at Charlecote, which breaks the line of his recorded pedigree. He has not, however, abandoned his dry and somewhat hopeless labours, and every Shakespearian must wish him success.

We have no record of the birth of William Shakespeare, or of the house at which he was born, but both important facts are sufficiently established to justify the universal belief that the " Star of Poets " first appeared on the 23rd of April, 1564, in Henley Street, Stratford-upon-Avon. The first documentary notice of him is in the parish registry, which informs us in bad Latin that William, the son of John Shakespeare, was baptized April 26th, 1564. No register of birth, singular to say, was kept for ages, and those of baptisms, marriages, and deaths not strictly made until 1558, when, by an act of Elizabeth, due attention was enforced to the matter. Baptisms more closely followed the birth, however, in Shakespeare's than in our time, lest death should step in between the events, and the third day after the birth was fixed for the ceremony. The practice is the more likely to have been observed in Shakespeare's case, from the fact that the plague, which raged that year in Stratford, cutting off in six months one-sixth of the population, no doubt created a general apprehension of sudden dissolution. There was a glorious escape vouchsafed to Shakespeare's family, and a mercy to the great family of mankind, for the poet remained unscathed by the malady.

SHAKESPEARE'S BIRTHPLACE.

The house in Henley Street, which has been shown for generations as the birthplace of Shakespeare, has never been seriously doubted to be the tenement in which he first saw the light. In 1555 John Shakespeare purchased two copyhold houses, one in Henley Street, and the other in Greenhill Street; and as no one has ever disputed the honour on behalf of Greenhill Street, Henley Street has always been the place to which constant tradition has pointed as the residence of John Shakespeare at the time of William's birth. "The best support given to tradition," says Mr. Hunter, "is the entry in the Court Roll of Stratford, by which it appears that, in 1552, John Shakespeare and others were amerced for making a dung heap in Henley Street." And whilst it is thus proved that he lived there for a considerable period before the great dramatist was born, it appears by a document, only discovered at the Branch Public Record Office in 1845, that he had his residence there for many years afterwards. This was the return to a commission issued out of the Exchequer in the 32nd of Elizabeth, 1590, for the survey of the possessions of Ambrose, Earl of Warwick. In that portion of this report which refers to Stratford, the following sentence occurs:—" The street called Henley Street, John Shakespeare holdeth one tenement with appurtenances, for the yearly rent of 6d. and suit of Court. The same John holdeth freely one tenement with appurtenances, for the yearly rent of 13d. and suit of Court." There is no doubt that this was William Shakespeare's father, for the other John Shakespeare was a shoemaker. Shakespeare's father had also some land at Ingon, a short distance from Stratford by the Warwick road, to which, from the amount of rent paid, it was supposed that a house was attached, but it has never been hinted that the bard was born there. " Tradition," remarks Mr. Knight, " says that Shakespeare was born in one of the houses in Henley Street; tradition points out the very room in which he was born. Let us not disturb the belief." To disturb it is impossible, and the author should have said—

" We could not if we would,
And would not if we could."

This tenement, architecturally so humble, but historically so magnificent, long neglected and subjected to mean occupations, has been at last secured to the nation and restored to that appearance which, so far as could be ascertained, it bore in the poet's time. A visit to this old house (of which I shall give a fuller account hereafter) bewilders the mind with "thick coming fancies" of Shakespeare's "mewling infancy," childhood innocence, and studious boyhood; when, under the spacious chimney he pored upon the story of love and chivalry, adventures by flood and field, or read with thoughtful eye "the historic pages of kings and crowns unstable;" for doubtless, like Scott, he devoured all the literature light and solid which came in his way—studying with a mind "waxen to receive and marble to retain."

We have no account of his elementary education, but may fairly conclude that his mother, the favourite of a family of daughters, was not negligent in having her eldest son prepared to take his place creditably in the grammar school amidst the boys of Stratford. That the son of the principal office bearer in the town went to the best seminary there can be no question. He must have been then seven years of age and able to read. Without supposing for a moment that he was an eighth wonder of the world in his family circle, or a prodigy boy out of it, I believe he had read much even before he had reached the age at which he could gain admission to the endowed school of Edward VI., which, according to the assertion of Ben Jonson, he left with "small Latin and less Greek."

This brings me to the question of what pedants would call his classic attainments. It has been long and laboriously discussed by the learned; but the decision is of little moment, for whatever it may be, the poet's transcendent genius and never dying fame remain intact. Johnson and Dr. Farmer have however always appeared to me to under-rate his scholarship. He certainly did not give up his youthful prime, fortunately for his species, to the reading of "words, words, words:" facts, ideas, motives, purposes, the passions, and propensities, and history of mankind; the mysteries of nature, animate and inanimate—these were the studies of his mighty mind. "Those," says Dryden, "who accuse him to have wanted learning give him the greatest commendation." Samuel Johnson thought the testimony of Ben ought to decide the controversy unless some testimony of equal force could be opposed. We know that Ben was a very warm hearted, out-spoken, fearless man of genius, but in this case I suspect him of prejudice probably unknown to himself. Upton, a man skilled in languages, as Dr. Johnson testifies, and acquainted with books, held a different opinion; and speaking of Ben Jonson's testimony, says truly that "people will allow others any qualities but those upon which they highly value themselves." Whatever his attainments in Latin and Greek, most readers will agree with Dr. Johnson that "he was possessed of a stock of knowledge sufficient for a mind so capable of appropriating and improving it;" and with Mr. Theobald, that "the result of the controversy must certainly either way terminate to our author's honour: how happily he could imitate them (the classics) if that point be allowed, or how gloriously he could think like them without owing them any imitation." His general information was marvellously extensive and no less wonderfully exact. Whatever his knowledge of the classics, it may be affirmed that he knew intimately every important work on subjects of general interest to be found in the English language. He lived in an age remarkable for many things, especially studious and learned men and women; and I cannot think that the gifted son of alderman Shakespeare was not in every intellectual attainment quite abreast of his age and the scholars with whom he consorted. His works fully prove that all his life it may have been said of him as Cæsar does of Cassius —

> "He reads much;
> He is a great observer, and he looks
> Quite through the deeds of men."

His religion has formed another question, but one discussed only amongst theological zealots. Shakespeare's father was of the reformed persuasion, else he could not have

held the offices he did.   He made a public affirmation of his
belief, and the writings of the poet ("Hamlet" and the
doctrine of purgatory therein recognised notwithstanding)
fully show that the son was reared in the form of religion
then established by law.   Had it been otherwise he never
would have permitted any of his characters to speak of the
highest of Roman Catholics as *King John* does.   Were I in
any doubt upon the point, his remarkable intimacy with the
text, his appreciation of the spirit, and correct views of the
doctrine of the Holy Scriptures would convince me that he
regarded them as a complete and sufficient guide to mankind
for time and eternity.   His extensive reading and solid judgment, and his prodigious knowledge of the infirmities of
humanity must have prevented him from ever yielding that
implicit obedience to the commands of the Church which
is the first principle of Roman Catholicism.   But whilst I
am quite satisfied he was not a Roman Catholic, his
Christianity was truly Catholic in the highest sense of the
term.   He was no Protestant, as thousands understand the
appellation at the present day.   With the greatest of virtues
—charity, which he truly says, "itself fulfils the law"—he
was probably as largely endowed as any author of any age
or country.   There is no trace of sectarianism or intolerance
about him.   For the adherents of the elder faith he had
much respect, and piously regarded some of the doctrines
and many of the usages and ceremonies of the Church of
More and Fenelon.   There blended in him, in short, the
best qualities of all sections of Christians, forming a
well-balanced character, devoid alike of fanaticism and
scepticism, of extravagance or indifference.

Of the many improbable stories told of Shakespeare,
none is more so than that which informs us he was taken
from the Grammar School about the age of fourteen to
assist his father, who was then in depressed circumstances.
For whether we believe with Mr. Malone, that at the period
in question John Shakespeare was by no means in affluent
or even easy circumstances, or with Mr. Knight, that the
proofs of his alleged social downfall are capable of explanation leading to a conclusion different from the general

beliéf, it is by no means likely that the Chief Magistrate of Stratford had become so reduced in the short space of seven years as to be obliged to withdraw his son—a mere boy—from school to work for the family at home. The story is coupled with a well ascertained misstatement, that John Shakespeare had ten children, when it is known he had only eight in all, and but three besides William at the period we speak of; for Joan (the first-born), Margaret, and Anne, had died, and Edmund was not born for two years afterwards.

It is more likely that Shakespeare remained at school till he was sixteen or seventeen, and that ere he attained the latter age his attention was somewhat distracted from Ovid and Homer by the charms of fair Anne of Shottery, and that when removed from his studies it was to be placed apprentice to some tradesman; or as Malone, Collier, and others believe, and with reason, an attorney. In whatever way he was employed between the period of his leaving school and that of his marriage—whether as attorney's clerk, butcher, woolstapler, school-master, or glover, he had no time to become master of any business, for somewhere about November, 1582, he married Anne Hathaway, the substantial yeoman's daughter of Shottery, who was then twenty-five years of age: this has been proved by a document only discovered a few years ago in Worcester. In May following he gave, with corresponding precocity, a hostage to fortune. On the 26th of that month, 1583, Susanna, his eldest daughter, was baptized at the same font in Trinity Church, Stratford-on-Avon, where he had himself lain in his mother's arms only nineteen years previously. Thus early did he enter upon the most serious responsibilities of life. Hamnet and Judith (twins), his son and second daughter, were baptized February 2, 1583.

About three years after this date the young husband and father is represented by Rowe as flying from his native town and home endearments to the great city of London, that he might avoid a criminal prosecution for deer stealing. I wonder if any intelligent reader now believes this fable? or

if the notion so long indulged in still exists in any addle-
pate, that the fugitive robber was the part which a mys-
terious Providence fated Shakespeare to enact before he
could become the independent gentleman, the favourite of his
sovereign, the idol of his contemporaries, and the dramatist
for all time? That he may have been in some way mixed
up in or accused of deer stealing (in that age a very trifling
offence) at some time of his life I think by no means
incredible, but I totally deny that there is any justification
whatever for the calumnies based on the circumstance. It
is alleged by the narrator that he was the companion of
thieves, and escaped to the city to avoid the consequences
of the malpractices into which they led him. The thief
and profligate of Stratford was not likely to find London or
a London theatre a Noah's ark to save him from the
vindictiveness of Charlecote! If he arrived in London
under such circumstances, the offending Adam must have
been whipped out of him with miraculous celerity.

But can his departure from Stratford and from his wife
and children be accounted for on no more rational and
satisfactory grounds? He was naturally inclined to poetry
and acting. Neither a lawyer's office nor a butcher's stall
was likely to have contained attractions for such a mind
sufficiently powerful to counteract the magnetic influence of
a London stage. It was under the auspices and patronage
of his father when the latter was bailiff that plays were
occasionally performed at Stratford, as in 1569, when the
Queen's players were paid 9s. out of the corporate funds,
and this must be considered liberal remuneration, or the
Worcester players who acted the same year received but
lenten entertainment at the hands of the Stratford Corporation, being only paid 10d. for their services. Be that
as it may, Shakespeare, then five years old, most likely saw
on this occasion the first glimpse of his "field of fame."
He may have seen plays frequently acted in his youth,
and who can tell at what age "Hamlet," "Lear,"
"Macbeth," or "Othello," began to loom on that wondrous
mind. Greene and Burbage had gone from the fertile valley
of the Avon to the busy banks of the Thames, and had

eminently succeeded. I cannot prove that Shakespeare carried a manuscript copy of a play to town as many poor creatures "hungering and thirsting for scribbling's sake" have done; but I have no doubt that at that time some of his early works were in embryo if not fully matured. The dates at which his plays are first mentioned in the books of the Stationers' Company are no guide whatever to the time of their production from the brain of the author.

The absence of all proof for the deer stealing, and its discreditable consequences contrasted with the knowledge we have of the young man's social position and inclination, leads to the inevitable conclusion that it was under a higher and nobler influence than the impulse of fear he quitted Stratford to "catch dame fortune's golden smile" in London. At twenty-two he must have known something of himself, and of his destiny. He had not that passionate and terribly earnest consciousness of his innate greatness which over-mastered every other thought and impelled Kean towards the town; but he looked with a calmer and no less penetrating eye into the seeds of time. He knew it was not for him to live—

> " Dully sluggardiz'd at home, and
> Wear out his youth with shapeless idleness."

He had a wife and children to provide for, he did not " deny the faith " and become " worse than an infidel," but went forth to do his duty; and however he left Stratford there is no question he returned to it an independent self-exalted man.

" He came to London," Dr. Johnson tells us, " a needy adventurer, and lived for a time by very mean employments." How the Doctor satisfied himself as to the truthfulness of this serious statement I am at a loss to discover. He may have been thinking of himself and "Davy," and the circumstances under which they came to London, and thereby became easily convinced that Shakespeare was still less a

curled darling of fortune than themselves. We have however
no positive proof of Shakespeare's object in going to London,
of the year he went thither, or of his employment for some
time after his arrival.   But the motive and object are to
me sufficiently apparent; the time has been closely enough
ascertained (1586), and, as discovered by Mr. Collier, he was
in 1589, then twenty-five years of age, joint proprietor in
the Blackfriars Theatre, with a fourth of the other proprietors below him in the list.   Had he been a dissolute deer
stealer at twenty-two, subsequently a needy adventurer in
London living by very mean employments, "a call boy"
and holder of gentlemen's horses at the theatre door as
asserted (preposterous rubbish!), his rapid elevation in the
social scale would almost suggest that the age of miracles
had not terminated with the fifteenth century.   Whether
Shakespeare acted very well or was only, as has been also
stated, a very mediocre histrion, acting was certainly his
first source of livelihood at the Blackfriars Theatre.   It is
not at all credible that he was ever reduced lower.   He
may have thought himself a gifted comedian.   There is
nothing about which there is so much self-deception as
histrionic ability.   Many literary men have thought they
could have acquired fame and fortune on the stage if their
friends had only let them get the chance in time.   The man
most worthy to be compared with Shakespeare in the history
of dramatic literature is James Sheridan Knowles.   He
considered himself an actor of no ordinary ability.   There
was indeed a period of his life when he was prouder of the
name of "comedian" than that of "author of Virginius,"
although by the latter title he linked himself in reputation
more closely to the author of "Lear" than any dramatist who
went before him or is likely to appear for centuries to come.
Shakespeare and Knowles both understood acting well.
The latter taught elocution very successfully at the Belfast
Royal Academical Institution.   He declaimed with power,
feeling, and effect, despite his Irish brogue; but an elocu-
tionist and an actor are different artists.   Shakespeare was
no doubt a useful member of the Blackfriars Company,

might have sustained a portion of the "heavies," as the actors would say, with credit, but could not have undertaken the leading business. Of his *Romeo* or *Richard*, I can form no notion whatever.

He was connected with the Blackfriars Theatre, and a word or two with reference to the playhouse so highly honoured may not be out of place. It was erected in an area called to this day Playhouse Yard, between Apothecaries' Hall and Printing House Square, where the *Times* office now stands. It was, as contra-distinguished from the "Globe," an enclosed winter house. The foundation was laid in 1575 by James and Richard Burbage and the other "servants" of the Earl of Leicester. It had little of the convenience or comfort of a modern theatre ; no scenery, and perhaps no curtain. Mr. Knight conjectures from the title—"The Curtain"—given to another theatre about that period, that the refinement of separating the actors from the audience during the intervals of a representation was at first peculiar to the latter.

Several of the actors of the company which Shakespeare first joined were authors also ; and the requirements of the theatre, combined with the specimens of dramatic authorship which he witnessed amongst his "fellows," may have encouraged him to throw forth some of the "strong conceptions that he groaned withal."

The profession of an actor at that age, although quite unfixed, as it still is unfortunately in the social scale, and taking precedence of nothing in heraldic honours, was a profitable calling. Richard Burbage died in 1619, worth £300 a year in land, besides personal property. Mr. Collier in his "Memoirs of Edward Alleyn," and in the "Alleyn Papers," has adduced evidence to prove that the founder of Dulwich College was a richer actor at an earlier date. As another proof, if such were wanting, that theatrical speculations were very advantageous during the period that Shakespeare was an actor on and a writer for the stage (from 1590 to 1613), the following was published in the first volume of the Shakespeare Society's papers. It is extracted from a small volume of epigrams printed in

1613, under the title of "Laquier Ridiculosi, or Springes for Woodcocks," and runs thus :—

"Theatrum licentia,
Cotta's become a player most men know,
    And will no longer take such toyling paines;
For here's the spring, saith he, whence pleasures flow,
    And brings them damnable *excessive gaines*;
That now are cedars growne from shrubs and sprigs,
    Since Greene's ' *Tu quoque*,' and these ' Garlicke Jigs.' "

The " Garlicke Jigs " were a sort of petty interlude, and seem quoted here to heap contempt on the entertainment.

The Greene here mentioned was a member of the company of the Blackfriars Theatre in 1581. His name appears fourth on the list and William Shakespeare is the twelfth. He is supposed to have been a native of Stratford-upon-Avon, and to have had the honour of introducing his great townsman to the theatre. He was what is now called a low comedian of considerable ability, like Robson or Toole, and became so distinguished in the " Tu Quoque," that the comedy was called after his name. This successful actor, Thomas Greene, reminds us of the unfortunate author, Robert Greene, who died in 1592. The profits of dramatic literature were not so great in his day as they subsequently became; but it is doubtful whether at any time whatever his talents might have enabled him to accomplish, whether his habits would have permitted him to amass wealth, or attain respectability. Reduced to extremities by dissipation, subsisting upon the charity of a poor shoemaker, and dying as Jonathan Swift feared he would depart, "raging like a poisoned rat in a hole," the ill-starred Greene wrote a pamphlet entitled, "A Groat's worth of Wit bought with a Million of Repentance," which I must refer to here as a valuable proof of the position Shakespeare had at that time taken up in London, and as incidentally drawing forth a more valuable piece of testimony bearing on the personal character of the young actor and author. It is addressed " To those gentlemen, his quondam acquaintances (believed to be Marlowe, Lodge, and Peele), that spend their wits in making playes, R.G. wisheth a better exercise and wisedome

to prevent his extremities." After a lecture not very per-
spicuous, but the nature of which the foregoing sentence
makes plain, the poor disappointed man raves on as
follows :—"Base minded men, all three of you, if by my
misery yee bee not warned ; for unto none of you (like me)
sought those burs to cleave ; those puppits (I meane) that
spake from their mouths, those Anticks garnished in our
colours. Is it not strange that I to whom they all have
bin beholding ; is it not like that you to whom they all
have been beholding, shall (were yee in that case that I am
now) be both of them at once forsaken ? Yes, trust them
not ; for there is an upstart crow beautified with our
feathers, that with his *Tygres heart wrapt in a players hyde
supposes he is as well able to bombast out a blanke verse as
the best of you; and being an absolute Johannes Fac-totum
is in his own conceyte the only* SHAKE-SCENE *in a countrey.*
Oh that I might intreat your rare wittes to be employed in
more profitable courses, and let these apes imitate your
past excellence, and never more acquaynte them with your
admyred inventions. I know the best husband of you all
will never proove an usurer, and the kindest of them all will
never proove a kind nurse ; yet whilst you may, seeke your
better maisters ; for it is pitty men of such rare wits should
be subject to the pleasures of such rude groomes."

The reference to Shakespeare here is palpable, and has
never been doubted. The "upstart crow" who, probably
with "the young the initiate fear" of authorship upon him,
had commenced his career by altering, and we may say of
course vastly improving the plays he found in stock at the
Blackfriars Theatre. He felt keenly the injustice and
spitefulness of Greene's libel. Marlowe also, whom Greene
had called an atheist, was naturally irritated by the insult.
I am not aware what mode of resentment, if any, the
dramatists so assailed adopted, but in the preface to the
"Kind-Heart's Dream," a sort of apology subsequently
emanated from Chettle, who had put forth Greene's
pamphlet, in which he says, "How I have, all the time of
my conversing in printing, hindered the bitter envying
against schollers, it hath been well knowne; and how in that

I dealt I can sufficiently proove. With neither of them that take offence was I acquainted, *and with one of them I care not if I never be :* the other whome at that time I did not so much spare, as since I wish I had for that, as I have moderated the heate of living writers, and might have used my owne discretion, especially in such a case, the author being dead.   That I did not, *I am as sorry as if the originall fault had beene my fault, because myselfe have seene his demeanor no lesse civill than he excelent in the qualitie he professes; Besides divers of worship have reported his uprightness of dealing, which argues his honesty and his facetious grace in writting that approoves his art.*   For the first, whose learning I reverence, and at the perusing of Greene's booke stroke out what then in conscience I thought he in some displeasure writ, or had it been true, yet to publish it was intollerable; him I would wish to use me no worse than I deserve.   I had onely in the copy this share; it was il written, as sometimes Greenes hand was none of the best; licensd it must be ere it could bee printed, which could never be if it might not be read: to be briefe, I writ it over, and as neare as I could, followed the copy, onely in that letter I put something out, but in the whole booke not a worde in; for I protest it was all Greenes, not mine nor Mr. Nashes, as some unjustly have affirmed."

The other, "whome I did not so much spare," is clearly Shakespeare, the description of Marlowe leaving him distinctly alone ; and nothing could be more satisfactory or in accordance with our own notions of Shakespeare than the testimony here borne to his " civill demeanor " and the " excelent qualitie he professed."   What a contrast the modest, prosperous Shakespeare presents to the arrogant and wretched Greene. But, indeed, the life of this wonderful man is not remarkable for anything more decidedly than its difference from the lives of poets generally.   There is a tradition that Homer was a blind beggar—the man to whom he is as a poet most closely related amongst the ancients; and comparing him with poets of our own country his life throughout must be regarded as a singularly happy one.   Milton suffered nearly " the whole catalogue of woes that sting the heart of man." Otway, who wrote the only tragedy ("Venice Preserved") in the English language, with the exception of "Virginius," worthy to be compared with Shakespeare, died of the poet's form of starvation. "Johnson's Lives" is a very melancholy book. Voltaire, in the height of his literary fame, wished he had never been born; and in our own generation hearken to the wail of the very author of the "Pleasures of Hope." "I am alone in the world. My wife and the child of my hopes are dead. My old friends, brothers, and sisters are dead—all but one, and she too is dying. As for fame it is a bubble." And who could have been more wretched than those children of genius, Byron and Burns. To quote proofs of their misery would require a book for the purpose. Shakespeare, I feel assured, became early a steady and hard-working student, subsequently a man of active business habits and indefatigable application to literature, he amassed an ample fortune; he acquired deathless fame; he spent the evening of his life in ease, retirement, and in the conversation of his friends; he died with his children's faces round his bed, and now lies quietly interred in that beautiful sepulchre enshrined in a fame for which "kings might wish to die." But this is anticipating.

The date at which he produced his first or any of his works we know not with any degree of certainty. In Spenser's "Teares of the Muses" (1591) complimentary reference is supposed to be made to Shakespeare; but as he was only 27 years of age then, the date at which some critics believe he commenced the trade of authorship, and but five years at most away from the banks of his loved Avon. The "Pleasant Willy" Spencer speaks of—much against inclination—we believe to be somebody else. It is seven years afterwards that we find he had made his mark indelibly on the dramatic literature of his country.

" If," says Mr. Knight, " the instances of the mention of Shakespeare by his contemporaries during his life time be not numerous, we are compensated by the fulness and explicitness of one notice—that of Francis Meres, in 1598. Short as his notice is, it is by far the most valuable contribution which we possess towards the life of Shake-speare." Meres was a master of arts at Cambridge, and subsequently entered the church. In 1598 he published a book called " Palladis Tamia "—" Wit's Treasury." It is a collection of moral sentences from ancient writers, and it is described by Anthony Wood as a " noted school book." Prefixed to it is a comparative discourse of our English poets. Nothing can be more decisive than this " Comparative Discourse," as to the rank which, in 1598, Shakespeare had taken amongst the most eminent of his contemporaries.

The master of arts aforesaid pronounces judgment as follows :—" As the Greek tongue is made famous and eloquent by Homer, Hesiod, Euripides, Æschylus, Sopho-cles, Pindarus, Phocylides, and Aristophanes ; and the Latin tongue by Virgil, Ovid, Horace, Silius Italicus, Lucanus, Lucretius, Ausonius, and Claudianus ; so the English tongue is mightily enriched and gorgeously invested in rare ornaments and splendid habiliments by Sir Philip Sydney, Spencer, Danial, Drayton, Warner, Shakespeare, Marlow, and Chapman.

" As the soul of Euphorbus was thought to live in Pythagoras, so the sweet witty soul of Ovid lives in melli-fluous and honey-tongued Shakespeare ; witness his Venus and Adonis, his Lucrece, his sugared sonnets among his private friends, &c.

" As Plautus and Seneca are accounted the best for comedy and tragedy among the Latins, so Shakespeare among the English is the most excellent in both kinds for the stage. For comedy witness his ' Gentlemen of Verona,' his ' Errors,' his ' Love's Labour Lost,' his ' Love's Labour Won,' his ' Midsummer Night's Dream,' and his ' Merchant of Venice ;' for tragedy his ' Richard II.,' ' Richard III.,' ' Henry IV.,' ' King John,' ' Titus Andronicus,' and his ' Romeo and Juliet.'

" As Epius Stolo said that the Muses would speak with Plautus' tongue if they could speak Latin, so I say the Muses would speak with Shakespeare's fine-filed phrase if they could speak English."

Thus we find that in the short space of ten years he had climbed from obscurity to the highest position in the literary world ; and in the estimation of men of ability and scholarship rivalled by the splendour of his genius the Greek and Roman glory. He had acquired some fortune too, as well as fame, for in 1597, a year before the above laudation was published, he had purchased for £60 one of the best properties in Stratford—New Place—subsequently his dwelling-house and last earthly mansion. This fact forms one of the many proofs we possess of that beautiful trait in his character—his extraordinary attachment to the tranquil and lovely scenes of his boyhood, an attachment which all the attractions of the city could not sever, the profits of business, nor the allurements of learned or courtly society in any degree abate. That he visited his beloved Stratford yearly is most probable, and in all likelihood was there in 1596 completing the arrangements for the purchase of New Place, which he afterwards ratified. I shall refer to this acquisition more particularly hereafter.

He had another errand and a more melancholy one to Stratford in that year. Extending his fame and rapidly accumulating an independent fortune, he was not so fortunate in his domestic affairs. The death of his only son, Hamnet, which took place in August, 1596, must have been a sad visitation. Hamnet was twelve years of age, and being a twin, his decease gave to the old gossips of Warwickshire confirmation, strong as holy writ, in their superstitious belief that when twins are of different sexes one must die before the age of twenty. The generally delicate constitutions of such children, however, sufficiently accounts for their being short-lived.

Shakespeare was probably present at the funeral of his son, and the event would naturally make a serious impression on the mind of such a father, young as he was. It may have first suggested that withdrawal from " clapping theatres and shouting crowds " which he did not however manage to completely effect for seventeen years afterwards ; but being then a man very little more than in the prime of life (48), the course he adopted shows that he was not one of those worldlings "who think it solitude to be alone." It suggests to me an anxiety to prepare for the termination of his successful life in a befitting manner by keeping himself "unspotted from the world."

An additional link now bound him to his dear Stratford. His father and mother lived there, together with his sister Joan; and as we have no record of his own family ever having been removed from their native town, there also, doubtless, resided his wife and his daughters, and to these ties was added that of his only son's grave. But whilst bound to Stratford by all this family relationship, and no less perhaps by that intense love which he cherished for the beautiful hills of Welcombe and the picturesque valley of the Avon, he slackened not his labours in the only field where they could have been productive. He had had no children for twelve years—his hope of direct descent was gone—his only son was gone; he lived like Burke in an inverted order, but did not give up the pursuits of life in despair or proclaim like the profoundest of statesmen and most persuasive of orators, that "he would not give a pack of refuse wheat for all that is called fame or riches in the world." Shakespeare's mind was cast in a still more philosophic mould. He not only felt his grief like a man, but bore it like one.

He was at this period a shareholder in, and of course one of the managing body of two theatres. The Blackfriars Company, of which he was a member, had built "The Globe," in 1594, on the south bank of the Thames. He was also an actor and author, so that his head and hands were full of business. He had work to do for himself—his family, and the world at large. How well he performed it we have ample testimony. His success was great. In the race for fame and fortune his competitors could not be placed. Shakespeare was first and the rest nowhere.

> "When learning's triumph o'er her barb'rous foes
> First rear'd the stage, in mortal Shakespeare rose."

And as he ascended the British stage rose with him in popularity. "The people of his age," says Rowe, "who began to grow wonderfully fond of diversions of this kind, could not but be highly pleased to see a genius rise from among them of so pleasurable, so rich a vein, and so plentifully capable of furnishing their favourite entertainments. Besides the advantage of his wit, he was in himself a good-natured man, of great sweetness in his manners, and a most agreeable companion; so that it is no wonder if, with so many good qualities, he made himself acquainted with the best conversations of those times." Queen Elizabeth had several of his plays acted before her, and without doubt gave him many precious marks of her favour: it is that maiden princess plainly whom he intends by

"A fair vestal, throned by the west." * * *

She was so well pleased with that admirable character of *Falstaff*, in the two parts of "Henry IV.," that she commanded him to continue it for one play more, and to show him in love. This is said to be the occasion of his writing "The Merry Wives of Windsor." How well she was obeyed the play itself is an admirable proof. Upon this occasion, it may not be improper to observe, that this part of *Falstaff*, said to have been written originally under the name of *Oldcastle*, some of that family being then remaining, the queen was pleased to command him to alter it, upon which he made use of *Falstaff*. The present offence was indeed avoided, but I do not know whether the author may not have been somewhat to blame in his second choice, since it is certain that Sir John Falstaff, who was a Knight of the Garter and a Lieutenant-General, was a name of distinguished merit in the wars in France in Henry the Fifth and Henry the Sixth's times. What grace soever the queen conferred upon him, it was not to her only he owed the fortune which the reputation of his wit made. He had the honour to meet with many great and uncommon marks of favour and friendship from the Earl of Southampton, famous in the histories of that time for his

c

friendship to the unfortunate Earl of Essex.   It was to that
noble Lord he dedicated his poem of "Venus and Adonis."
There is one instance, so singular in the magnificence of
this patron of Shakespeare, that, if I had not been assured
that the story was handed down by Sir William Davenant,
who was probably very well acquainted with his affairs, I
should not have ventured to have asserted that my Lord
Southampton at one time gave him a thousand pounds to
enable him to go through with a purchase which he had
heard he had a mind to—a bounty very great and very
rare at any time, and almost equal to that profuse generosity
the present age hath shown to French dancers and Italian
singers.

The lines containing the compliment to the queen, one
of which is quoted above, are in themselves so beautiful,
and evince such courtly tact and refined delicacy on the
part of the author, that I shall take leave to transcribe the
passage in extenso from "A Midsummer Night's Dream,"
act ii. scene 2.

> *Oberon.*   My gentle Puck, come hither : thou remember'st
> Since once I sat upon a promontory,
> And heard a mermaid, on a dolphin's back,
> Uttering such dulcet and harmonious breath,
> That the rude sea grew civil at her song ;
> And certain stars shot madly from their spheres,
> To hear the sea-maid's music ?
>
> *Puck.*   I remember.
>
> *Oberon.*   That very time I saw (but thou could'st not),
> Flying between the cold moon and the earth,
> Cupid all arm'd : a certain aim he took
> At a fair vestal, throned by the west ;
> And loos'd his love-shaft smartly from his bow,
> As it should pierce a hundred thousand hearts :
> But I might see young Cupid's fiery shaft
> Quench'd in the chaste beams of the watery moon ;
> And the imperial votaress passed on,
> In maiden meditation, fancy-free.

We will not call the ghosts of Raleigh, Leicester, or
Essex into the witness-box on the point of " fancy-free ; "
but no compliment could be conceived likely to make a
more favourable impression.   No poet laureate ever paid a

tribute to royalty with a nicer perception of character or in diction more beautifully figurative. The royal favour extended by Elizabeth was continued by James, with whom Shakespeare is said to have been on certain terms of intimacy. The king had been a warm patron of the drama in Scotland, and some biographers believe there is sufficient proof that Shakespeare was one of his "servants" at Aberdeen; and it is certain, on the 17th of May, 1603, only a few days after the king arrived in London, there was issued a patent authorising "these our servants, Lawrence Fletcher, William Shakespeare, Richard Burbage, Augustine Phillippes, John Hemmings, Henrie Condell, William Sly, Robert Armyn, Richard Cowlye, and the rest of their associates, freely to use and exercise the arte and faculty of playing tragedies, histories, interludes, &c., within theire now usuall house called the 'Globe,' within our county of Surrey, as also within anie towne halls, or mouthalls, or other convenient places within the liberties and freedome of any other citie, university, towne, or borough whatsoever within our said realmes and dominions," &c.

Thus favoured by royal patronage, and commanding the universal suffrages of the people to whom the stage was the grand source of instruction and recreation, he rapidly acquired that competency on which depended the time of his retirement to Stratford-on-Avon. We have seen how the first fruits of his industry were devoted to the purchase of New Place, and as some believe to the repairing of his father's broken fortunes, for in the same year John Shakespeare tendered the redemption money, £40, to recover the estate of the Ashbies, a portion of his wife's dowry, which had been mortgaged.

This circumstance suggests a retrospective glance at the condition of his father's affairs, which are supposed to have been declining for a number of years before his son removed from Stratford. Mr. Knight, who differed from Malone on this point, states the case as follows :—" The corporation books have shown that on particular occasions, such as the visitation of the plague, in 1564, John Shakespeare contributed like others to the relief of the poor ; but now, in

January, 1577-8, he is taxed for the necessities of the
borough only to pay half what other aldermen pay, and in
November of the same year, whilst other aldermen are
assessed to pay 4d. weekly to the relief of the poor, John
Shakespeare 'shall not be taxed to pay anything.' In 1579
the sum levied upon for providing soldiers at the charge of
the borough is returned amongst similar sums of other
persons as 'unpaid and unaccounted for.' Finally, this
unquestionable evidence of the books of the borough shows
that this merciful forbearance of his brother townsmen was
unavailing, for in an action brought against him in the
Bailiff's Court, in the year 1586, he during these seven
years having gone on from bad to worse, the return of the
sergeants at mace upon a warrant of distress is that John
Shakespeare has nothing upon which distress can be
levied.   There are other corroborative proofs of John
Shakespeare's poverty brought forward by Malone. In
the year 1578 he mortgages his wife's inheritance of
Ashbies to Edmund Lambert for £40; and in the same
year the will of Mr. Roger Sadler, of Stratford, to
which is subjoined a list of debts due to him, shows that
John Shakespeare was indebted to him £5, for which sum
Edward Lambert was a security. 'By which,' says Malone,
'it appears that John Shakespeare was then considered
insolvent, if not as one depending rather on the credit of
others than his own.'   It is of little consequence to the
present age to know whether an alderman of Stratford,
nearly three hundred years past, became unequal to main-
tain his social position; but to enable us to form a right
estimate of the education of William Shakespeare, and of
the circumstances in which he was placed at the most
influential period of his life, it may not be unprofitable to
consider how far these revelations of the private affairs of
his father support the case which Malone holds he has so
triumphantly proved. The documents which he has brought
forward certainly do not constitute the whole case, and
without lending ourselves to a spirit of advocacy, we believe
that the inferences which have been drawn from them,
and adopted by men of higher mark than their original

promulgators, are altogether gratuitous and incongruous. * * * * We hold, and we think more reasonably, that in 1578, when he mortgaged Ashbies, John Shakespeare became the purchaser, or rather occupier of lands in the parish of Stratford, but not in the borough; and that in either case the money for which Ashbies was mortgaged was the capital employed in this undertaking. The lands which were purchased by William Shakespeare of the Combe family in 1601, are described in the deed as 'lying or being within the parish fields or town of old Stratford;' but the will of William Shakespeare, he having become the heir at law of his father, devises all his lands and tenements within the towns, hamlets, villages, fields, and grounds of Stratford-upon-Avon, Old Stratford, Bishopton, and Welcombe. Old Stratford is a local denomination essentially different from Bishopton or Welcombe; and therefore whilst the lands purchased by the son in 1601 might be those recited in the will as lying in Old Stratford, he might have devised from his father the lands of Bishopton and Welcombe, of the purchase of which by himself we have no record. So in the same way the tenements referred to by the will as being in Stratford-upon-Avon, comprised not only the great house (New Place) purchased by him, but the freeholds in Henley Street, which he inherited from his father. Indeed it is expressly stated in the document 1596, a memorandum upon the grant of arms in the Heralds' College to John Shakespeare, 'he hath lands and tenements of good wealth and substance £500.' The lands of Bishopton and Welcombe are in the parish of Stratford, but not in the borough. Bishopton was a hamlet, having an ancient chapel of ease. We hold then that in the year 1571, John Shakespeare, ceased, though perhaps not wholly so, to reside within the Borough of Stratford. Other aldermen are rated to pay towards the furniture of pikemen, billmen, and archers, six shillings and eightpence; whilst John Shakespeare is to pay three shillings and fourpence. Why less than other aldermen? The next entry but one, which relates to a brother alderman, answers the question: 'Robert Pratt, *nothing* IN THIS PLACE.' Again, ten months after, 'it is ordained that every alderman shall pay weekly towards the relief of the poor, fourpence, save John Shakespeare and Robert Pratt, who shall not be taxed to pay anything.' Here John Shakespeare is associated with Robert Pratt, who, according to the previous entry, was to pay nothing in this place; that is in the Borough of Stratford, to which the orders of the Council alone apply. The return in 1579, of Mr. Shakespeare as leaving unpaid the sum of three shillings and three pence, was the return upon a Company for the Borough, in which, although the possessor of property, he might have ceased to reside. Seven years after this comes the celebrated return to the warrant of distress, that John Shakespeare has nothing to distrain upon. The jurisdiction of the bailiff's court of Stratford is wholly confined to the Borough; and out of the Borough the officers could not go. We have traced the course of this action in the bailiff's books of Stratford, beyond the entries which Malone gives us. It continued before the court for nearly five months; proceeding after proceeding being taken upon it, with a pertinacity upon the part of the defendant which appears more like the dogged resistance of a wealthy man to a demand which he thought unjust, than that of a man in the depths of poverty, seeking to evade payment which must be ultimately enforced by the seizure of his goods, or by a prison.   *   *

But at the Hall on the 6th of September, in the 28th of Elizabeth, is this entry : 'At this Hall William Smythe, and Richard Courte are chosen to be Aldermen in the place of John Wheler and John Shaxpere; for that Mr. Wheler doth desyer to be put out of the Company, and Mr. Shaxpere doth not come to the Hall when they be warned, nor hath not done of long tyme.' Is it not more credible that from the year 1579 till the year 1586, when he was removed from the Corporation, in all probability by his own consent, John Shakespeare was not dwelling in the Borough of Stratford; that he had ceased to take an interest in its affairs, although he was unwilling to forego its dignities, than that during these seven years he was struggling with hopeless poverty ; that he allowed his brother aldermen and burgesses to sit in judgment on his means of paying the assessments of the Borough ; that they consented to reduce and altogether to discharge his assessments, although he was the undoubted possessor of property within the Borough ; that he proclaimed his poverty in the most abject manner, and proclaimed it untruly whilst he held any property at all, and his lands were mortgaged for a very inadequate sum, when the first object of an embarrassed man would have been to have upheld his credit by making an effort to meet every public demand ? "

Whether the reader rejects Mr. Malone's conclusion, or, taking the number of facts that seem to point in the same direction, regards Mr. Knight's argument as a piece of clever special pleading to save the father of his hero from being classed amongst paupers, the question is interesting and important, as bearing not only on Shakespeare's education but his motive for leaving Stratford, and the position he is likely to have taken up on arriving in London.

John Shakespeare's was not like ours, a fast age ; fortunes were not lost and won, nor are they now, rapidly in country villages, and the proceedings which he undoubtedly took in relation to the grant of arms, are certainly favourable to the view Mr. Knight adopts.

It has not been established to universal satisfaction that John Shakespeare obtained a "grant of arms" while he was bailiff of Stratford, but he certainly applied for this heraldic honour in 1596, and is at that period described as a man having lands and tenements—of good wealth and substance of the value of £500 ; and in the following year, that in which Shakespeare purchased New Place, this grant was conceded, and in 1599, on application, another grant was made, authorising the arms of Shakespeare to be impaled with those of Arden. This latter application is believed to have been made at the instigation of the successful dramatic author and theatrical manager, whose profession of an actor would have operated fatally against any petition he might have presented to " Garter."

Shakespeare's father was evidently in comfortable circumstances at this period, but did not long survive such
comfort as "grants of arms" could give to his declining
years, for he died in September, 1601.   Mary Arden, his
wife, lived seven years after him, dying also in September,
1608.   Their famous son was then an independent man.
He had purchased and repaired the great house—New
Place, a title not given to it by him, as generally
believed.   It is so called in the survey made in 1590.   To
this possession he added in 1602, four yard lands (107
acres), in the Stratford fields, which he purchased for £320.
All this property was sold to Sir Edward Walker, Knight,
"Principall Garter, King at Armes," for £1060.   Shakespeare
also purchased a house in Blackfriars for £140, and he was
the owner at the time of his death of three other houses
(two of them freehold and one copyhold) in Stratford.
The lease of the moiety of the great and small tithes he
purchased in 1605 for £440.   To the incomes arising from
these properties may be added at least £150 per annum
from the theatre, and it has been calculated that his personal
property was worth £500.   The favourite of the Muses,
and the darling of fortune, he ought to have been a happy
man, and he doubtless was as much so as the majority of
mortals.   But as we hear throughout all his married life
nothing whatever of his wife—as the commencement of that
relationship was inauspicious, and as it is clear he could
not have forgotten his own case when he wrote in " Twelfth
Night "—

> " Let still the woman take
> An elder than herself; so wears she to him—
> So sways she level to her husband's heart,"

it is feared there was an incompatibility between the gentle
Anne and sweet Will not conducive to domestic felicity.
There is no positive proof, however, of this misfortune, and
if it existed he was a man " whose blood and judgment
were so well commingled " that he was not likely to have
permitted it to weigh unduly on the heart.
That his mind's eye was turned steadily towards Stratford from the time he acquired possession of New Place there

can be no question, and that he visited it frequently afterwards seems equally certain. Of his way of life in London we know little. It is stated that in 1598 he resided in St. Helen's, off Bishopsgate Street. He appears in that year at the top of the cast of Ben Jonson's comedy, "Every Man in his Humour." He was a member of the Mermaid Club—an eminent resort of the day, founded by Walter Raleigh. Brilliant, no doubt, were the dialectical encounters amongst the gifted *habitués* of the place. Of the relative powers and merits of the two dramatists of the day, the following description is given by Thomas Fuller in the succeeding generation :—"Many were the wit combats between him (Shakespeare) and Ben Jonson, which two I behold like a Spanish great galleon and an English man-of-war. Master Jonson, like the former, was built far higher in learning, solid but slow in his performances ; Shakespeare, with the English man-of-war, lesser in bulk but lighter in sailing, could turn with all tides, tack about and take advantage of all winds by the quickness of his wit and invention."

But neither the profits nor pleasures of the theatre, "the feast of reason," nor "the flow of soul" could wean him from the richly-clad hills and flowery vales of Warwickshire, where, "exempt from public haunt," *he*, if ever man did, "found tongues in trees, books in the running brooks, sermons in stones, and good in everything." In June, 1607, Susanna, his eldest daughter was married, at the age of twenty-five, to Mr. John Hall, physician, of great reputation and extensive practice at Stratford. Dr. Hall, we are also told, was a scholar of more than ordinary attainments; "he had been a traveller" too, and being at the time of his marriage only thirty-two years of age, the union with Susanna Shakespeare, "witty above her sex," was a suitable and auspicious one.

His permanent residence at Stratford was certainly taken up in 1613, if not much sooner. That he had business transactions there for many years previously is proved by his suing, as recorded, Philip Rogers, to recover the sum of £1 15s. 10d., due for malt sold and delivered at several

times ; and in 1609, John Addenbroke, for a debt of £6 and
costs, in which case he obtained a verdict. It would
appear that he had long previously ceased to be " a motley
to the view," for we have no record of his acting after 1603,
when he played in Ben Jonson's tragedy of " Sejanus."
In the month of March, 1612-13, he is in London, but
apparently only for a short time on business. At that date
he purchased a house with ground attached near the
Blackfriars Theatre. In the indenture of the conveyance
of this property he is described as William Shakespeare,
of Stratford-upon-Avon.

In 1613, how long soever he may have been previously
settled in Stratford, he certainly terminated his connection
with London Theatres. The year is memorable as that in
which the Globe Theatre, founded in 1593, and built for
the most part of wood, was destroyed by fire. The loss
Shakespeare sustained by the accident (if any) has not
been ascertained. Most probably he had a portion of his
wardrobe and precious MSS. stored in the building. If
so, it was indeed a calamitous burning.

On the 9th July, 1614, a similar but much more extensive disaster took place in Stratford. On that day a
dreadful fire broke out, and " within the space of less than
two houres consumed and burnt fifty and foure Dwelling
Houses, many of them being very faire houses besides
Barnes, Stables and other Houses of office, together with
great store of Corne, Hay, Straw, Wood and Timber therein,
amounting to the value of Eight Thousand pounds and
upwards." A few months following this catastrophe an
attempt was made to enclose some of the Common lands in
the neighbourhood of Welcombe. The project was opposed
by the Corporation, on the ground that the inhabitants of
Stratford had recently suffered from a disastrous fire and
would be still further endamaged by the carrying out of
this measure. It seems to have been one of those conflicts
between the interests and opinions of the town and the
country, which occur occasionally in most places, not
excepting Stratford, until this day. Shakespeare, who
had a deep interest in opposing the scheme, took very

prudential means to preserve his property from injury by it. The Corporation sent their clerk, Thomas Greene, to London, with a petition to the Privy Council, the prayer of which was granted four years afterwards, and the work of the enclosure, which had been in the meantime accomplished, was ordered to be undone. It was in connection with this business that Shakespeare is believed to have paid his last visit to London. Greene, who claimed relationship with the great poet, has left a memorandum, under date 17th November, 1614, recording that his cousin Shakespeare coming to town the previous day he went to see him.

The events of his life during the last seven or eight years are principally marked by lawsuits, and births, marriages, and deaths in connection with his family. His brother Edmund died in London, December, 1607, and was buried at St. Saviour's, Southwark. On the 21st of February, 1607-8, Elizabeth, the only daughter of John Hall and Susanna Shakespeare, was baptized at Stratford; and a few months afterwards, as mentioned above, the poet lost his mother. These events, and a chancery suit in which he became involved connected with the tithes he had purchased, but of which little is known, except that he was one of three plaintiffs in the proceedings, may have disturbed occasionally the serenity of his temper and tranquillity of life; but, on the whole, we have reason to believe that, blessed with means sufficient for his condition, he spent the evening of life in the quiet pursuits of the field, in literary recreation, and social enjoyment.

On the 10th February, 1616, his youngest daughter, Judith, was married to Thomas Quiney, vintner and wine merchant, at Stratford. On the 25th of the next month Shakespeare executed his will. It appears, however, to have been drawn prior to the marriage, as the original date was *Vicesimo quinto die Januarii*, altered afterwards to *Vicesimo quinto die Martii*. He declares himself to be in perfect health and memory, and within one month of this declaration " angels had winged him to his rest." He died on the 23rd of April (his birth-day), 1616.

However uninformed of many things concerning him, an account of his fatal illness might have been expected to be on record, faithfully and in full, for his son-in-law, the principal physician of the town, kept memoranda of the cases he attended; but from the beginning to the end of this wonderful man's life, where we desire particularity of information and trustworthy authority, we are obliged to be contented with generality and hearsay. The earliest case in the only forthcoming note book of Dr. Hall is date 1617, a year after Shakespeare's death.

Deprived of that which would have been satisfactory evidence, the Rev. John Ward, who was a vicar of Stratford in the seventeenth century, kept a diary, now in the library of the Medical Society in London, which contains the following passage:—"I have heard that Mr. Shakespeare was a natural wit, without any art at all; he frequented the plays all his younger time, but in his elder days lived in Stratford, and supplied the stage with two plays every year, and for itt had an allowance so large that he spent att the rate of £1,000 a year, as I have heard. Shakespeare, Drayton, and Ben Jonson had a merrie meeting, and it seems drank too hard, for Shakespeare died of a feavour there contracted." A visit to Shakespeare from two such "cronies" is likely enough; and that one of them was a "drouthie" one is well known; but the reader who may be aware of the curse of villages—idle tattle, tale bearing, and petty scandals—will receive the story *cum grano salis*.

On the 25th April, 1616, the mortal coil which the mighty soul of Shakespeare had shuffled off was borne to its last resting place, on the north side of the chancel of the Church of the Holy Trinity, Stratford-upon-Avon. There, under a flat stone, which ought to be better protected, it mingles with its kindred dust. The epitaph is as follows:—

> "GOOD FREND FOR Jesus SAKE FORBEARE
> To DIGG THE DUST ENCLOASED heare
> BLESTE be ye man yt spares THES stones
> AND CURST be he yt MOVES my bones."

Shakespeare's Tomb—The Chancel,

STRATFORD ON AVON CHURCH.

The celebrated monument or bust is erected against the wall, immediately above the grave. It is believed to have been executed by Gerard Johnson, very shortly after the poet's death. Leonard Digges refers to it clearly in the following lines of his verses, prefixed to the folio edition of the poet's works, published in 1623 :—

> " Shake-speare, at length thy pious fellowes giue
> The world thy Workes : thy Workes, by which out-liue
> Thy Tombe, thy name must : when that stone is rent,
> And Time dissolues thy *Stratford* Moniment."

The bust is considered the most authentic likeness extant; beneath is the following inscription :—

> " Judicio Pylium, genio Socratem, arte Maronem,
> Terra tegit, populus maeret (mœret) Olympus habet." *
> " Stay, Passenger, why goest thou so fast ?
> Read, if thou canst, whom envious Death hath plast
> Within this monument. SHAKESPEARE with whome
> Quick nature dide : whose name doth deck ye tombe
> Far more than cost ; sith all yt he hath writt
> Leaves living Art but page to serve his Witt
>
>   " Obiit Ano Do¹ 1616
>   " Ætatis 53, die 23 Ap."

On Shakespeare's character as a man I have no intention of expatiating, but may be permitted to remind the reader that all we positively know of him, with the exception of the circumstance in connection with his marriage, is in his favour. That error he did all that an honourable man could do to correct, and when extreme youth is taken into due consideration, the offence will not be regarded as one excluding him from absolution. Of the deer stealing accusation we have no proof. That nothing of the kind ever occurred with him I will not take upon me to assert. There may have been some foundation for the story, but it is scarcely to be placed above the category of " the three black crows." I am satisfied that he must have been intensely industrious in his youth. When

---

* The earth covers, mankind mourns, Olympus holds, a Nestor in clearness of intellect, a Socrates in intuitive talent, a Virgil in elegance of style.

as an actor and manager he wrote plays in London he had no time for reading or study. The vast stores of his mind's common place book were ample for his requirements, and in laying up the mass of information he possessed, I feel assured that, " like the spirit of a youth that meant to be of note, he began betimes," and if the whole truth were known, instead of our knowledge of his early manhood being confined to an improbable, unauthenticated, and discreditable story, we would be informed that even then his name was " great in mouths of wisest censure." Chettle says of him in London, " Myselfe have seene his demeanor no lesse civill than he excelent in the qualitie he professes ; Besides divers of worship have reported his uprightness of dealing, which argues his honesty and his facetious grace in writting, that approoves his art." And not only was he an industrious man of business-like habits, of "civill demeanor," and " uprightness," but appears to have been a generous man, as the following letter (the only one of all he received which we possess: now to be seen at the Birthplace) would seem to prove :—

" Loveinge Contreyman, I am bold of yow, as of a ffrende, craveinge yowr helpe with xxxli uppon Mr. Bushells and my securytee or Mr. Myttons with me. Mr. Rosswell is nott come to London as yeate, and I have speciall cawse. You shall ffrende me muche in helpeinge me out of all the debettes I owe in London, I thanck God, and muche quiete my mynde, which wolde not be indebeted. I am nowe towardes the Cowrte in hope of answer for the dispatche of my buysenes. You shall nether loose creddytt nor monney by me, the Lorde wyllinge ; and nowe but perswade yowrselfe soe as I hope, and yow shall nott need to feare, but with all heartie thanckefullnes I wyll holde my tyme and content yowr ffreende and yf we bargaine farther yow shal be the paiemaster yowrself. My tyme biddes me hasten to an ende ande soe I committ thys (to) your care and hope of yowr helpe. I fear I shall nott be backe thys night ffrom the Cowrte. Haste. The Lorde be with yow and with us all, Amen ! ffrom the Bell in Carter Lane, the 25th Oct., 1598.
" Yours in all kyndenes,
" RYC. QUYNEY.
" To my loveinge good ffrende and contreyman Mr. Wm. Shakespere deliver thees."

That he was a loving good friend may be readily believed, and those who judge from positive fact, rejecting baseless rumour, must be satisfied with his character.

Seven years after Shakespeare's death, in 1623, the players, Heminge and Condell, mentioned in his will as "my fellows," published the first complete edition of his plays, and the same year Mrs. Shakespeare died, aged 67. The eldest daughter, Susanna, married, as above-mentioned, Dr. Hall. Their only child, Elizabeth, was married to Thomas Nash, son of Anthony Nash, Esq., of Welcombe, and afterwards to Sir John Barnard, Knight, of Abington, in Northamptonshire; but she died 1669-70 without issue by either husband. Judith, who married Mr. Thomas Quiney, had three sons, who all died unmarried. Thus in the direct line Shakespeare's family became extinct in the second generation.

Respecting his works, the following is the order in which Mr. Malone, who gave much attention to the subject, believed they had been produced :—

1.	Titus Andronicus	1589
2.	Love's Labour Lost	1591
3.	First Part of King Henry VI.	1591
4.	Second Part of King Henry VI.	1592
5.	Third Part of King Henry VI. ... , ...	1592
6.	The Two Gentlemen of Verona	1593
7.	The Winter's Tale	1594
8.	A Midsummer Night's Dream	1595
9.	Romeo and Juliet	1595
10.	The Comedy of Errors	1596
11.	Hamlet	1596
12.	King John	1596
13.	King Richard II.	1597
14.	King Richard III.	1597
15.	First Part of King Henry IV.	1597
16.	The Merchant of Venice	1598
17.	All's Well that Ends Well	1598
18.	Second Part of King Henry IV.	1598
19.	King Henry V.	1599
20.	Much Ado about Nothing	1600
21.	As You Like It	1600
22.	Merry Wives of Windsor	1601
23.	King Henry VIII.	1601

Augustus William Schlegel, who, at the end of the last century, gave his countrymen a splendid translation of Shakespeare, and thereby naturalised the works of the English dramatist in Germany, took so just a view and gave so clear an exposition of his fame, genius, and marvellous creations, and the beauties of his style, that I shall be excused for quoting from it here at some length, as the most appropriate conclusion to this memoir :—

" Shakespeare," says Schlegel, " is the pride of his nation. A late poet has with propriety called him the genius of the British isles. He was the idol of his contemporaries; and after the interval of puritanical fanaticism which commenced in a succeeding age and put an end to everything like liberal knowledge; after the reign of Charles the Second, during which his works were either not acted or very much disfigured, his fame began to revive with more than its original brightness; towards the beginning of the last century and since that period it has increased with the progress of time and for centuries to come— I speak with the greatest confidence—it will continue to gather strength like an Alpine avalance, at every period of its descent. As an important earnest of the future extension of his fame, we may allude to the enthusiasm with which he was naturalised in Germany the moment that he was known. The language, and the impossibility of translating him with fidelity, will be ever, perhaps, an invincible obstacle to his general diffusion in the south of Europe. In England the greatest actors vie with each other in the characters of Shakespeare; the printers in splendid editions of his works; and the painters in transferring his scenes to the canvas. Like Dante, Shakespeare has received the indispensable but cumbersome honour of being treated like a classical author of antiquity.   *   *   *

"To me Shakespeare appears a profound artist, and not a blind and wildly luxuriant genius. In such poets as are usually considered careless pupils of nature I have always found, on a closer examination, when they have produced works of real excellence, a distinguished cultivation of the mental powers, practice in art, and views worthy in themselves, and maturely considered. That idea of poetic inspiration which many lyric poets have brought into vogue, as if they were not in their senses, and like Pythia, when possessed by the divinity, delivered oracles unintelligible to themselves, is least of all applicable to dramatic composition—one of the productions of the human mind which requires the greatest exercise of thought. It is admitted that Shakespeare reflected and deeply reflected on character and passion, on the progress of events and human destinies, on the human constitution, on all things and relations of this world; so that it was only respecting the structure of his own pieces that he had no thought to spare. Shakespeare's knowledge of mankind has become proverbial; in this his superiority is so great that he has justly been called the master of the human heart. His characters appear neither to do nor say anything on account of the spectator; and yet the poet by means of the exhibition itself, without any subsidiary explanation, enables us to look into the inmost recesses of their minds. How each man is constituted Shakespeare reveals to us in the most immediate manner. He demands and obtains our belief even for what is singular and deviates from the ordinary course of nature. Never, perhaps, was so comprehensive a talent for characterisation possessed by any other man. It not only grasps the diversities of rank, sex, and age, down to the dawnings of infancy; not only do his kings and beggars, heroes and pickpockets, sages and fools, speak and act with equal truth; not only have his human characters such depth and comprehension that they cannot be ranged under classes and are inexhaustible, even in conception; but he opens the gates of the magic world of spirits, calls up the midnight ghost, exhibits witches amidst their unhallowed mysteries, peoples the air with sportive fairies and sylphs; and these beings existing only in imagination, possess such truth and consistency that even in the case of deformed monsters like Caliban he extorts the conviction that if there should be such beings they would so conduct themselves. If the delineation of all his characters separately taken is inimitably correct he surpasses even himself in so combining and contrasting them, that they serve to bring out each other. No one ever painted as he has done the facility of self-deception, the half self-conscious hypocrisy towards ourselves, with which even noble minds attempt to disguise the almost inevitable influence of selfish 'motives on human nature. Shakespeare's comic talent is equally wonderful with his pathetic and tragic. He is highly inventive in comic situations and motives; it will be hardly possible to show whence he has taken any of them. His comic characterisation is equally true, various, and profound with his serious. The language is here and there somewhat

D

obsolete, but much less so than that of most of the writers of his day—a sufficient proof of the goodness of his choice. He drew his language immediately from life, and possessed a masterly skill in blending the element of dialogue with the highest poetical elevation. Certain critics say that Shakespeare is frequently ungrammatical. To prove this assertion they must show that similar constructions do not occur in his contemporaries; but the direct contrary can be established. In no language is everything determined upon principle; much is always left to the caprice of custom, and because this has changed is the poet answerable for it? In general, Shakespeare's style yet remains the very best model, both in the vigorous and the sublime, the pleasing and the tender. The verse of all his plays is generally the rhymeless iambic of ten or eleven syllables, occasionally intermixed with rhymes, but more frequently alternating with prose. No one piece is wholly written in prose, for even in those which approach the most to the pure comedy there is always something added which elevates them to a higher rank than belongs to this class. In the use of verse and prose Shakespeare observes very nice distinctions, according to the rank of the speakers, but still more according to their characters and dispositions. His iambics are sometimes highly harmonious and full sounding, always varied and suitable to the subject; they are at one time distinguished for ease and rapidity; at another they move along with mighty energy. All Shakespeare's productions bear the stamp of his original genius; but no writer was ever farther removed from a manner acquired from habit and personal peculiarities."

SHAKESPEARE'S WILL.

Whilst confessing a full appreciation of the value of the entries in the register, Shakespeare's will must be admitted to be the most interesting, trustworthy, important, and altogether the most valuable document we possess relating to the illustrious poet. It consists of three sheets of brief paper. By the direction of the present Judge of the Court of Probate, it has been very carefully cleaned and each sheet placed in an elaborately-polished oak frame, between sheets of plate glass. The frames are made air-tight, and on the top of each is a brass plate, engraved "Shakespeare's Will, 25th March, 1616," and each one is fastened with one of Chubb's patent locks. This excellent plan prevents its being handled when shown to the public, and will very much add to its preservation. It is drawn in the following terms :—

" Vicesimo quinto die Martii, Anno Regni Domini nostri Jacobi nunc Regis Angliæ, &c., decimo quarto, et Scotiæ xlix o. Annoque Domini 1616.

" In the name of God. Amen. I, William Shakespeare, of Stratford-upon-Avon, in the county of Warwick, gent., in perfect health and memory (God be praised), do make and ordain this my last will and testament in manner and form following ; that is to say :

" First. I commend my soul into the hands of God my Creator, hoping and assuredly believing through the only merits of Jesus Christ my Saviour to be made partaker of life everlasting ; and my body to the earth whereof that is made.

" *Item*. I give and bequeath unto my daughter Judith one hundred and fifty pounds of lawful English money, to be paid unto her in manner and form following ; that is to say, one hundred pounds in discharge of her marriage portion, within one year after my decease, with considerations after the rate of two shillings in the pound for so long a time as the same shall be unpaid unto her after my decease; and the fifty pounds residue thereof, upon her surrendering of or giving of such sufficient security as the overseers of this my will shall like of, to surrender or grant all her estate and right that shall descend or come unto her after my decease, or that she now hath of, in or to one copyhold tenement, with the appurtenances, lying and being in Stratford-upon-Avon aforesaid, in the said county of Warwick, being parcel or holden of the Manor of Rowington, unto my daughter Susanna Hall and her heirs for ever.

" *Item*. I give and bequeath unto my said daughter Judith, one hundred and fifty pounds more if she or any issue of her body be living at the end of three years next ensuing the day of the date of this my will, during which time my executors to pay her consideration, from my decease, according to the rate aforesaid ; and if she die within the said term without issue of her body, then my will is and I do give and bequeath one hundred pounds thereof to my niece Elizabeth Hall, and the fifty pounds to be set forth by my executors during the life of my sister Joan Harte, and the use and profit thereof coming shall be paid to my said sister Joan, and after her decease the said fifty pounds shall remain among the children of my said sister, equally to be divided amongst them ; but if my said daughter Judith be living at the end of the said three years, or any issue of her body, then my will is and so I devise and bequeath the said hundred and fifty pounds to be set out by my executors and overseers for the best benefit of her and her issue, and the stock not to be paid unto her so long as she shall be married and covert baron ; but my will is that she shall have the consideration yearly paid unto her during her life, and after her decease the said stock and consideration to be paid to her children, if she have any, and if not, to her executors and assigns, she living the said term after my decease ; provided that if such hus-

band as she shall at the end of the said three years be married unto,
or at and after do sufficiently assure unto her and the issue of her
body, land answerable to the portion by this my will given unto her,
and to be adjudged so by my executors and overseers, then my will
is that the said hundred and fifty pounds shall be paid to such husband
as shall make such assurance, to his own use.

"*Item.* I give and bequeath unto my said sister Joan twenty
pounds and all my wearing apparel, to be paid and delivered within
one year after my decease; and I do will and devise unto her the
house with the appurtenances, in Stratford, wherein she dwelleth, for
her natural life, under the yearly value of twelve pence.

"*Item.* I give and bequeath unto her three sons, William Hart,
Thomas Hart (christian name omitted ,in the original will), and
Michael Hart, five pounds a piece, to be paid within one year after
my decease.

"*Item.* I give and bequeath unto the said Elizabeth Hall, all my
plate that I now have, except my broad silver and gilt boxes, at the
date of this my will.

"*Item.* I give and bequeath unto the poor of Stratford aforesaid
ten pounds; to Mr. Thomas Combe my sword; to Thomas Russel, Esq.,
five pounds; and to Francis Collins, of the Borough of Warwick, in
the County of Warwick, gent., thirteen pounds six shillings and eight
pence, to be paid within one year after my decease.

"*Item.* I give and bequeath to Hamlet (Hamnet) Sadler
twenty-six shillings eight pence to buy him a ring; to William
Reynolds, gent., twenty-six shillings eight pence to buy him a ring;
to my god-son, William Walker, twenty shillings in gold; to Anthony
Nash, gent., twenty-six shillings eight pence; to Mr. John Nash
twenty-six shillings eight pence; and to my fellows, John Heminge,
Richard Burbage, and Henry Condell, twenty-six shillings eight
pence a piece to buy them rings.

"*Item.* I give, will, bequeath, and devise unto my daughter
Susanna Hall, for the better enabling of her to perform this my
will, and towards the performance thereof, all that capital messuage
or tenement, with the appurtenances, in Stratford aforesaid, called
The New Place, wherein I now dwell, and two messuages or tenements,
with the appurtenances, situate, lying, and being in Henley Street,
within the borough of Stratford aforesaid; and all my barns, stables,
orchards, gardens, lands, tenements, and hereditaments whatsoever,
situate, lying, and being, or to be had, reserved, preserved, or taken,
within towns, hamlets, villages, fields, and grounds of Stratford-upon-
Avon, Old Stratford, Bushaxton, and Welcombe, or in any of them, in the
said county of Warwick; and also all that messuage or tenement,
with the appurtenances, wherein one John Robinson dwelleth, situate,
lying, and being in the Blackfriars, in London, near the Wardrobe;
and all other my lands, tenements, and hereditaments whatsoever, to
have and to hold all and singular the said premises, with their ap-

purtenances, unto the said Susanna Hall, for and during the term of her natural life; and after her decease to the first son of her body lawfully issuing, and to the heirs males of the body of the said first son lawfully issuing; and for default of such issue to the second son of her body lawfully issuing, and to the heirs males of the body of the said second son lawfully issuing; and for default of such heirs to the third son of the body of the said Susanna lawfully issuing, and of the heirs males of the body of the said third son lawfully issuing; and for default of such issue the same to be and to remain to the fourth, fifth, sixth, and seventh sons of her body lawfully issuing, one after another, and to the heirs males of the bodies of the said fourth, fifth, sixth, and seventh sons lawfully issuing, in such manner as it is before limited to be, and remain to the first, second, and third sons of her body, and to their heirs males; and for default of such issue, the said premises to be and to remain to my said niece Hall, and the heirs males of her body lawfully issuing; and for default of such issue, to my daughter Judith, and the heirs males of her body lawfully issuing; and for default of such issue, to the right heirs of me, the said William Shakespeare, for ever.

"*Item.* I give unto my wife my second best bed, with the furniture.

"*Item.* I give and bequeath to my said daughter Judith my brown silver gilt bowl. All the rest of my goods, chattels, leases, plate, jewels, and household stuff whatsoever, after my debts and legacies paid and my funeral expenses discharged, I give, devise, and bequeath to my son-in-law, John Hall, gent., and my daughter, Susanna, his wife, who I ordain and make executors of this my last will and testament. And I do entreat and appoint the said Thomas Russel, Esq., and Francis Collins, gent., to be overseers hereof; and do revoke all my former wills and publish this to be my last will and testament. In witness whereof I have hereunto put my hand, the day and year first above written.

"By me,
"WILLIAM SHAKESPEARE.

"Witness to the publishing hereof,

"Fra. Collyns,
"Julius Shaw,
"John Robinson,
"Hamlet (Hamnet) Sadler,
"Robert Whattcott.

"Probatum coram Magistro Willielmo Byrde, Legum Doctore Comiss, &c., xxjj^do die mensis Junii, Anno Domini 1616; juramento Johannis Hall, unius executorum, &c., cui, &c., de bene, &c., jurat, reservat potestate, &c., Susannae Hall, alteri executorum, &c., cum venerit petitur (Inv^t ex^t)."

Painters and poets have, to some extent, counterbalanced the seeming inattention of biographers to Shakespeare. The following is the summing up of the latest writer (Mr. Friswell) with respect to his portraits :—

"After having closely examined the great number of portraits asserted to be those of William Shakespeare, the mind is somewhat embarrassed. This embarrassment is considerably increased by the fact that for many years the eye has been familiar with a half-dozen of incongruous portraits, the claims of which it has lazily allowed, without taking the trouble of weighing them. The patrons of some of these portraits have evidently considered it sufficient that the picture should be the face of a man, and not of an animal, to give it sufficient chance for the admittance of its claim. A mouth, a moustache, a fair amount of forehead, and two eyes, have been, for a long time, all the sanguine inhabitants of Wardour Street demand, when they wish to christen the most villanous daub of an incompetent and in-conscientious painter with the name of the greatest genius that the world has ever produced. It is in vain that Shakespeare complained, prophetically, that he had 'made himself a motley to the view,' his outward seeming, as well as his inward soul, has become motley. The claimants to the possession of original portraits have indeed been good enough to concede that the poet must have had two eyes and a nose; but, if we believe them equally those eyes must have been at the same time black, hazel, blue, and deep brown; the nose must have been Roman, aquiline, somewhat snub, and 'cogitative;' the upper lip must have been extremely short and extremely long; the hair and beard straight and curling, black, brown, dark brown, reddish brown, and flaxen ; the complexion of all shades, varying from very dark to very light.

"Now it needs no consideration to prove that no human individual could, under any circumstances of change of age, or stupidity or want of skill in the painter, have ever presented such extreme variations. We must, there-fore, by finding out the characteristics in which the most authentic portraits agree, endeavour to reconstruct a

Shakespeare, and from such a reconstruction judge the portraits brought before us. From what we have, therefore, we may presume that Shakespeare was of the middle height, fairly built and proportioned, broad-chested and upright. His hair was a warm brown, his beard lighter than the hair of his head; his chin round and full (bust, Droeshout print, and print by Marshall); the jaw strong and powerful (Droeshout print, and bust); the forehead ample, broad, and high, the supra-orbital ridges oval, and well marked (Felton head, bust, and Droeshout); the hair, at an early period, thin, and well off the forehead—at the close of his life he was bald, and the forehead seemed very much higher; his complexion was fair, and the tint of a warm healthy hue, with probably a full colour in the cheeks; the mouth not very small, the lips full and red, the eyes hazel, and, we may presume, instinct with life and intelligence. This is as near an approach to a correct description of Shakespeare as we can well form. There can be no reason why he should not have had many portraits painted, but we must remember that we have no direct proof that he ever sat to any artist of the highest excellence."

Selecting from a large number, I think right to give a place here to the following commendatory verses :—

"To the Memory of my beloved, the Author,
MR. WILLIAM SHAKSPERE,
AND WHAT HE HATH LEFT US.

" To draw no envy, Shakspere, on thy name,
Am I thus ample to thy book, and fame;
While I confess thy writings to be such,
As neither man, nor muse, can praise too much;
'Tis true, and all men's suffrage: but these ways
Were not the paths I meant unto thy praise;
For seeliest ignorance on these may light,
Which, when it sounds at best, but echoes right;
Or blind affection, which doth ne'er advance
The truth, but gropes, and urgeth all by chance;
Or crafty malice might pretend this praise,
And think to ruin, where it seem'd to raise:
These are as some'infamous bawd, or whore,
Should praise a matron; what could hurt her more?

But thou art proof against them; and, indeed,
Above the ill-fortune of them, or the need:
I, therefore, will begin:—Soul of the age,
The applause, delight, the wonder of our stage,
My Shakspere, rise! I will not lodge thee by
Chaucer, or Spenser; or bid Beaumont lie
A little further, to make thee a room:
Thou art a monument, without a tomb;
And art alive still, while thy book doth live,
And we have wits to read, and praise to give.
That I not mix thee so, my brain excuses;
I mean, with great, but disproportion'd Muses:
For, if I thought my judgment were of years,
I should commit thee surely with thy peers;
And tell—how far thou didst our Lily outshine,
Or sporting Kyd, or Marlow's mighty line.
And, though thou hadst small Latin, and less Greek—
From thence to honour thee, I would not seek
For names; but call forth thund'ring Æschylus,
Euripides, and Sophocles, to us,
Pacuvius, Accius, him of Cordova dead;
To live again, to hear thy buskin tread
And shake a stage: or, when thy socks were on,
Leave thee alone—for the comparison
Of all, that insolent Greece, or haughty Rome,
Sent forth, or since did from their ashes come.
Triumph, my Britain! thou hast one to show,
To whom all scenes of Europe homage owe.
He was not of an age, but for all time,
And all the Muses still were in their prime,
When, like Apollo, he came forth to warm
Our ears, or, like a Mercury, to charm.
Nature herself was proud of his designs,
And joy'd to wear the dressing of his lines;
Which were so richly spun, and woven so fit,
As, since, she will vouchsafe no other wit:
The merry Greek, tart Aristophanes,
Neat Terence, witty Plautus, now not please;
But antiquated and deserted lie,
As they were not of Nature's family.
Yet must I not give nature all; thy art,
My gentle Shakspere, must enjoy a part:—
For though·the poet's matter nature be,
His art doth give the fashion: and that he,
Who casts to write a living line, must sweat
(Such as thine are), and strike a second heat
Upon the Muses' anvil; turn the same

(And himself with it), that he thinks to frame;
Or, for the laurel, he may gain a scorn—
For a good poet's made, as well as born:
And such wert thou: Look, how the father's face
Lives in his issue; even so the race
Of Shakspere's mind, and manners, brightly shines
In his well-toned and true-filed lines;
In each of which he seems to shake a lance,
As brandish'd at the eyes of ignorance.
Sweet swan of Avon! what a sight it were,
To seé thee in our waters yet appear;
And make those flights upon the banks of Thames,
That so did take Eliza, and our James!
But stay; I see thee in the hemisphere
Advanc'd, and made a constellation there:—
Shine forth, thou star of poets! and with rage,
Or influence, chide, or cheer, the drooping stage;
Which, since thy flight from hence, hath mourn'd like night,
And despairs day, but by thy volume's light!"

BEN JONSON.

―――

"AN EPITAPH ON THE ADMIRABLE DRAMATIC POET,
WILLIAM SHAKSPERE.

" What needs my Shakspere for his honour'd bones,
The labour of an age in piled stones;
Or that his hallow'd reliques should be hid
Under a star-ypointing pyramid?
Dear son of memory, great heir of fame,
What need'st thou such weak witness of thy name?
Thou, in our wonder and astonishment,
Hast built thyself a live-long monument:
For whilst, to the shame of slow-endeavouring art,
Thy easy numbers flow; and that each heart
Hath, from the leaves of thy unvalued book,
Those Delphic lines with deep impression took;
Then thou, our fancy of itself bereaving,
Dost make us marble with too much conceiving;
And, so sepulcher'd, in such pomp dost lie,
That kings, for such a tomb, would wish to die."

JOHN MILTON.

STRATFORD:

A WALK THROUGH THE TOWN.

OF the many places in our own country from which the
ordinary tourist's attention is withdrawn by scenes to
which distance lends enchantment, and that very arbitrary
deity, " Fashion," their main attraction, no region can, in
ordinary times, prefer a stronger complaint of ingratitude
than the picturesque town of Stratford-upon-Avon.   True,
during the last London Exhibition year some seven thousand names were enrolled in the visitors' book of the
church containing Shakespeare's tomb, but many of these
were Germans and Americans ; and in the course of the
past fortnight at least one hundred thousand persons came
to Stratford.   But, generally speaking, tourists have not
taken that interest in the locality which it is to be hoped
the late celebration may create.

Yet Stratford-upon-Avon is the true " British Mecca "
—to which every thoughtful pilgrim, every man of poetic
feeling, every traveller with the slightest tincture of
philosophy or philanthropy, must ever delight to wend his
way.   Here he will find food for meditation—a town
scarcely surpassed in the beauty of its situation on the
lovely

" Winding Avon's willowed banks,"

and unapproachable in the universal interest of its associations.   For here, it can never be forgotten, in Stratford-
upon-Avon, William Shakespeare was born ; here the man
for whose fame " Kings might wish to die," and which
has been for generations " as broad and general as the
casing air," first saw the light; here he received such

education as he possessed ; and from this picturesque spot his young muse, destined to ascend "invention's highest heaven," first began her upward flight. Here his wondrous mind expanded and received glowing impressions of external nature and that marvellous insight into the mysteries of humanity which enabled him to produce those creations "not for an age, but for all time." In this greatly-favoured place occurred all the important events of his life; and in this spot, so far as a being "born for the universe" could be limited by locality, he may be said, in his own words, to have "garner'd up his heart with his life's dearest treasures." Here his honoured dust lies entombed, and his "sacred relics" are with all due rever-ence preserved ; and, furthermore, in Stratford-upon-Avon has been gleaned all that is known of the personal history of the "genius of our isle."

Stratford-upon-Avon is a very ancient, very clean, very quiet, and, at the same time, very cosy market town, located nearly in the centre of England, about a hundred miles from London, and to general tourists be it known, not more than twenty or thirty off the direct route from the North to South. It is scarcely possible to proceed with its history without at once touching on Shakespeare, for all the public institutions are more or less mixed up with his name, and some notion may be thereby formed of their antiquity. As the stranger steps out of the train, he may discover that the "iron horse" which has brought him along is called "Will Shakspere." His attention will be next attracted to the portrait of Shakespeare, sur-rounded by certain mystic emblems, appropriately on "the counterfeit presentment" of the man who said, "One touch of nature makes the whole world kin," whether "Will" was "a brother" or not. This tablet informs those whom it concerns that Mr. Fred. Bolton, grandson of an alder-man who officiated at Garrick's Stratford Jubilee in 1769, now keeps the "Shakespeare Hotel." On emerging from the station, half a minute's walk will bring our travelling companion to the Shakespearian Foundry (!) A few steps beyond that point is Garrick Court. Then a hundred yards nearer the town is the "White Swan," reminding the stranger of Garrick's ode—

> " Flow on, silver Avon, in song ever flow ;
> Be the swan on thy bosom still whiter than snow."

Whether the enthusiastic actor's aspiration has been realised or not, the swans on the Avon are sufficiently white and stately, and numerous too. But this is by the way. Our tourist will at this point pass the Rother (Cattle) Market, a fine spacious street in which the principal building is Mr. Knight's Shakespearian Needle Works (!) Leaving Henley Street, where Shakespeare's birthplace stands, on the left hand *pro temp.*, and proceeding in the usual course along Wood Street, Bridge Street comes in sight. This is an admirable thoroughfare—one of the broadest to be found in any town of similar size and population. The top of it, where five streets converge, has been chosen for the Shakespeare Monument—an excellent situation. The principal hotel of the town—" The Red Horse "—is kept by Mr. Lowry, in this street. It is a large and well-managed establishment, favourably known to many travellers and tourists, particularly Americans, from the complimentary references made to it in the charming " Sketch Book " of Washington Irving. Having glanced towards the bridge which spans the Avon, erected by Sir Hugh Clopton, in the reign of Henry VII., the visitor may turn to the right into the principal business thoroughfare—High Street. Here he will notice on the left "the Shakespearian bookbinding and printing establishment," opposite to Mr. Adams's Shakespearian book and print warehouse and the *Stratford Herald* office, where he may also inspect nearly every article to which the name of Shakespeare has been attached by the most ingenious contrivers of *bijouterie*. A few yards further on he must be attracted by a splendid specimen of Elizabethan street architecture, bearing date 1597. This house, with its fine old carved oaken front, was certainly a familiar object to Shakespeare. It is now in the possession of Mr. Williams, who is engaged in the occupation of a

Banks & Co Edinr

HIGH STREET & TOWN HALL,
STRATFORD ON AVON

glover. A number of relics of Shakespeare, and auto-graphs of distinguished visitors to the birthplace, are to be seen at Mrs. James's, corner of Ely Street. Proceeding a few yards, towards the left side of the way, the eye will catch the life-size statue of the great poet in a niche of the Town Hall gable. This is the statue presented by Garrick to the Corporation, when the building was reconstructed, and dedicated to Shakespeare nearly a hundred years ago.

The poet is represented in the same attitude as on the cenotaph in Westminster Abbey, resting on some volumes placed on a pedestal, where appear the busts of Henry V., Richard III., and Queen Elizabeth. He points to a scroll on which are the following lines taken from the " Midsummer Night's Dream."

> " The Poet's eye, in a fine frenzy rolling,
> Doth glance from heaven to earth, from earth to heaven,
> And, as imagination bodies forth
> The forms of things unknown, the poet's pen
> Turns them to shapes, and gives to airy nothing
> A local habitation and a name."

On the upper border of the plinth are these words:—

> " Take him for all in all,
> We shall not look upon his like again."

On the plinth is the following inscription :—

> "THE CORPORATION AND INHABITANTS OF STRATFORD, ASSISTED BY THE MUNIFICENT CONTRIBUTIONS OF THE NOBILITY AND GENTLEMEN OF THE NEIGHBOURHOOD, REBUILT THIS EDIFICE IN 1768. THE STATUE OF SHAKESPEARE WAS GIVEN BY DAVID GARRICK, ESQ."

The substantial stone building, which is of the Tuscan order, underwent extensive alterations and improvements prior to the Tercentenary Festival, according to the plans of Messrs. Hawkes, Architect, Birmingham. The doorway is now under the Shakespeare statue, in the gable instead of being as formerly in the front street. A spacious apartment has been formed on the ground floor, which will be used for public meetings and in transacting the business of the Corporation.   Another smaller apartment has been constructed parallel with the principal room in the upper story, which is approached by three flights of solid oaken stairs.   The visitor passes from the smaller hall through a very handsome archway, supported by Corinthian pillars, into the main assembly room or the Shakespeare Hall.   The floors are of oak, and, like the majority of the ancient buildings in Stratford, oak enters largely into the structure.   The size of the hall is 60 ft. by 30 ft. in breadth and height.   The stucco decorations and cut glass gasaliers give it a handsome appearance, but its chief decorations are the life-size portraits of Shakespeare, by Wilson; the "British Roscius," by Gainsborough (a splendid picture) ; The Duke of Dorset, who was Lord of the Manor, and High Steward of the Borough in 1769 (the year of the jubilee) ; and, on the same side of the room, a full-length painting of Queen Anne, which formerly belonged to Stratford College, and was purchased and placed here a short time before that building was taken down.   The view of the hall in the *Illustrated London News* will convey a very correct idea of its splendid appearance during the late exhibition of paintings which formed so attractive a feature in the celebration.

The Shakespeare Hotel, above referred to, adjoining the Town Hall, is an ancient hostelry, with oaken stairs and floors and many marks of antiquity.   The rooms are entitled and known by names derived from Shakespeare's plays, which are placed above each door.   On the left of the spacious hall is the commercial room, not inappropriately named "The Tempest;" opposite it is a private coffee room, called "As You Like It."   "Romeo and Juliet," "Taming of the Shrew," "Midsummer Night's Dream," and "Love's Labour's Lost," are sleeping apartments.   In the hall stands an antique clock, which is stated to have belonged to Shakespeare, enclosed in an extra glass case to preserve it from "decay's effacing fingers."

Leaving "The Shakespeare," the next Shakespearian object of attraction is the site of New Place, where stood the poet's dwelling.   It is situated at quite an interesting corner.

Guild Chapel & Vestiges of New Place,

STRATFORD ON AVON.

The Guild Chapel—the school to which Shakespeare went, not, let us hope, unwillingly;—the Falcon Inn, where 'tis said "he took his ease," and all that serves for a Theatre in the town being clustered in the immediate neighbourhood. No authentic drawing of Shakespeare's house is known to be in existence. It was built, we know, by Sir Hugh Clopton in the reign of Henry VII., not later than 1490. Another Sir Hugh Clopton utterly demolished this fabric. "An entirely new house," says Mr. Bellew, "was erected about 1720 ; and it was this structure (of the Dutch William or Queen Anne's style of building) which the ruthless Gastrell rased to the ground." The "Vandalic priest" is thus far exonerated from the more serious charge of destroying the actual house in which Shakespeare lived ; but his organ of destructiveness is nevertheless accountable for the pulling down of the house erected on the site of Shakespeare's, and the uprooting of the mulberry tree which Shakespeare had planted. The boundaries of Shakespeare's garden have been ascertained, and the whole of New Place estate, with the exception of the plot occupied by the Theatre, has been purchased by general subscription, and secured to the public mainly by the instrumentality of Mr. Halliwell. The foundation stones of the poet's house—"the very stones that prate of his whereabouts"—are now laid bare. Shakespeare's well, still in good order, was discovered in the grounds. Portions of rooms, believed to have been his offices, kitchen, &c., have been found out. It is proposed to preserve these interesting excavations and to put the garden in appropriate order in accordance with the deep importance that must ever be attached to the spot where Shakespeare lived, laboured, and died.

A few hundred yards from the geographical point at which we have now arrived, at the extreme end of the town, stands the venerable edifice in which the precious dust of Shakespeare lies entombed. And thus from end to end of Stratford-upon-Avon, by objects insignificant and titles not very significant as well as by institutions of the highest dignity and importance, the visitor is reminded at every step that this is the town rendered all classic and in some places sacred by the memory and associations of Shakespeare. And now let us take a view of the places with which his name is specially connected, commencing with that which is nearest to us in this imaginary tour, and at the same time the most important.

THE CHURCH.

The heart must be divested of all feelings of things at once sacred and beautiful that can approach the church of the Holy Trinity, at Stratford-upon-Avon, unmoved by thoughts too deep and too high for expression. Here indeed is a rare combination of objects and associations to charm, elevate, and solemnize the soul. The eye is first delighted by the picturesque. The avenue, under whose broad flagway lie that which no following spring revives—"the ashes of the urn,"—whilst over head interlace in the Gothic arch of beauty the entwining branches and lovely green leaves of the graceful lime trees ; on either side " the forefathers of the hamlet sleep ; " towards the river the sable-suited crows build in the tall old trees, and sweep croaking about on heavy wing, fit tenants of the scene ; the nightingale's delightful note at eve is heard ; the little small birds have made in " the jutty frieze and coigne of vantage their pendant bed and procreant cradle." But not the music of the grove, the beauty of the flowers, all the features of the landscape, or the solemn temple that stands in grey majesty before the visitor, can impress him with that sentiment of awe and reverence which must arise as he contemplates the fact that here verily lies the awful dust of the man whose genius outstripped time and " exhausted worlds."

The cruciform building of " perpendicular Gothic " containing the poet's precious ashes is almost of cathedral dimensions. The windows rise above the trees, and the square Norman tower supports a tall and graceful spire, which may be observed—an object of beauty and solemn interest—for miles all around the country. Having arrived

North Porch and Avenue,

STRATFORD ON AVON CHURCH.

at the porch, I must borrow the beautiful description of the interior from Mr. Lee's "Stratford in connection with Shakespeare." "As we progress," he says, "up the nave, we perceive that the hand of discriminating taste has been at work, for its whole interior, and the chancel also, has been recently carefully restored, and the carved timber roofs renewed. The nave is divided from the aisles by hexagonal pillars supporting six early English pointed arches, and above this is the clerestory, forming a continual range of windows, two above each arch, admitting almost an excess of light. The windows of the aisles belong to the fourteenth century, the south aisles being erected by John de Stratford at that period. The north aisle is probably of earlier date. The chancel and choir is the most remarkable part of the fabric, and from its height and simplicity has a beautiful effect. Five elegantly-shaped windows rise to the roof on either side, while above the altar is a lofty east window, once brilliant with stained glass, of which, until recently, a few imperfect and jumbled relics only could be seen. The pristine glory of this noble window is now, however, through the exertions of the estimable vicar, being gradually restored. Against the northern wall of this splendid chancel is the monumental bust of Shakespeare, and beneath it his undisturbed ashes rest in peace. We silently approached the hallowed spot, and, forgetting for a moment aught else—encaustic pavement, glittering altars, emblazoned arms, sedilia, stalls, and modern tombs,—contemplated that placid countenance and lofty brow. Immediately beneath the stone receding from the wall are the gravestones of Shakespeare, his wife, and some members of his family." The recumbent figures of the Cloptons in white marble, and that of John Combe, and other monuments, impart quite a Westminster Abbey sort of effect to the striking beauty of the general interior; and since Mr. Lee's description was written additional improvements and adornments have been made, and others are projected, which I fervently hope the Rev. Mr. Granville, the revered vicar, and his universally esteemed curate, the Rev. Mr. Morton, will live to see carried out to their

E

complete satisfaction.   Five thousand six hundred persons
visited the church during the late celebration.

ANNE HATHAWAY'S COTTAGE.

Passing from the church to " Old Town," the tourist
may proceed into Bree Street, and thence strike into the foot
road which crosses the Great Western Railway and leads to
the village of Shottery, where stands Anne Hathaway's
picturesque cottage.   Like the birth-place, it is a residence
of much interest in itself, apart from its associations.   How
still, and quiet, and retired the scene is ! a place for lovers
and lovers only.   The antiquated cottage is situated in a
beautifully secluded nook, surrounded by every object
suggestive of Arcadian times.   The gable is towards the
road.   A vine, which bore grapes until three years ago,
and appears to have become exhausted through age, still
decorates the front of the house.   Sundry flowering plants
are also trained up the walls; the thatch is very thick, and
the little dormer windows manifest great antiquity.   An old
well, moss-grown, is also an object of much interest in the
garden.   The interior is in many respects like the poet's
birth-place.   The kitchen, and, no doubt, principal sitting
apartment, has a stone floor, a low ceiling, and a very large
fire-place.   Oaken wainscotting surrounds it; and the whole
place indicates the fact that the Hathaways were a well-
to-do family in their time.   On the left of the capacious
fire-place is the old cupboard, with grated door, where many
a good flitch of bacon was smoke-dried.   On this venerable
adjunct of the *cuisine* the initials of two Hathaways,
I.H. E.H., are carved.   The family long continued to
reside here.   Passing up the narrow stairs to the bed-
chambers, a remarkably old bedstead is shown.   It is of
carved oak, four-post, and said to be as old as Anne's
time.   Some linen, appearing to correspond with the bedstead in age, is also exhibited.   Of Anne Hathaway herself
we know nothing, except that she was a yeoman's daughter,
five and twenty years of age when she entered into a
relationship which imparted an abiding interest to herself

ANN HATHAWAY'S COTTAGE
Shottery Stratford-upon-Avon

Published by E Adams

and her cottage. Passing through green lanes, where the peasant lives undangered and at ease, the pedestrian will return to Stratford by Alcester road, proceeding through Greenhill and Meer Street, and arriving at the spot, which, but that a general view of the town was taken before examining particular places, should have been visited first.

SHAKESPEARE'S BIRTH-PLACE.

It is a very old house in very good condition, stands alone, and cannot be mistaken, not because the country has been lately flooded with admirable photographs of it, but that its antiquity and style of building claim for it in unmistakable terms the honour it possesses. Some fifty years ago it was purchased by a far-sighted though very humble man for £140, and some ten years ago was "knocked down"—the Fates forbid!—I mean sold, by George Robins to the "nation" for £3,820! Since then it has undergone general repairs and a thorough cleaning—the whole renovation being carried out in proper spirit, and with a view to preserve its original appearance as much as possible. The houses formerly adjoining on both sides have been pulled down to preserve it from fire. The solidity of the structure is, fortunately, sufficiently guaranteed by the massive beams of oak that gird it and strengthen it in all directions. No fire is allowed on the premises ; damp and consequent dilapidation are kept away by steam pipes. The kitchen floor is of stone, the fire-place being ample, and with the large cosy corners reserved for the head of the family and distinguished guests to sit and smoke and drink in. "If," says a late writer, "the fire is out now, our feelings, sparkling back upon the past, must re-kindle 'it. That Shakespeare himself has stood here before the cheerful blaze no one can doubt. Perhaps as a boy he may have sat in the corner feasting his galloping imagination from a spark in the ashes. His father, at any rate, lived and died here, and he must have often walked in when in Stratford to see the old man." The chief apartment is the room in which Shakespeare was born, approached by a flight of ten solid oaken stairs, which having been ascended, the most thoughtless or the boldest may "hold his breath for a time." The walls are whitewashed, but there is "not an inch of nameless plaster." The window contains sixty small square panes, every bit covered with autographs— indeed, that of the great Walter Scott, who resembled Shakespeare in more than the initials of his name, has been scribbled over by the impudent diamond of some snobbish nobody. No more signatures are permitted to be written, for many reasons, *one* of which may be mentioned—there is no room. Many interesting autographs are effaced or cannot be traced from amongst others of less importance. But amongst those still to be discovered, in addition to Walter Scott, above-mentioned, are Alfred Tennyson and Sam. Rogers to the immediate right of the entrance. On the same side of the room, lower down, may be seen Chas. Dickens, Mark Lemon, Augustus Egg; and W. M. Thackeray is on the ceiling. Amongst actors, whose autographs are principally to be observed about the fire-place, are Edmund Kean, Helen Faucit, Madame Vestris, Chas. Kean, J. B. Buckstone, Mrs. Fitzwilliam, Robert Elliston (whose much respected son died in Leamington a few days ago), Albert Smith, Gustavus V. Brooke, Chas. Mathews, &c.

Behind this interesting room is another curious old apartment crossed by heavy oaken beams. Old portraits of Shakespeare decorate the walls. The principal of these is a life-size bust in oil. It is kept in an iron safe, which is thrown open during the day and closed at night. This portrait was in the family of W. O. Hunt, Esq., for upwards of a century. On the frame of the safe a brass plate bears the following inscription :—

"This portrait of Shakespeare, after having been in the possession of Mr. William Oakes Hunt, Town Clerk of Stratford-upon-Avon, and his family, for upwards of a century, was restored to its original condition by Mr. Simon Collins, of London, and being considered a portrait of much interest and value, was given by Mr. Hunt to the town of Stratford-upon-Avon, to be placed and preserved in Shakespeare's house.—April 23, 1860."

Banks & Co Edin.ᴿ

SHAKESPEARE'S HOUSE.

FROM THE GARDEN

In an autograph book now prepared for visitors one thousand six hundred and sixty names and addresses were entered during the ten days over which the late festival extended. Amongst the first names signed in this volume are the Rev. Henry Ward Beecher (Brooklyn), and "ton Seyers" (Pugilist!). The total number of visitors during the period referred to was two thousand eight hundred. The gardens at the rear of the house are laid out very neatly and planted with flowers mentioned in Shakespeare's plays. And in the Museum may be seen :—

Deed made in 1596, proving that John Shakespeare, father of the poet, resided in the house called the birth-place.

MS. document. The original fine levied on the purchase of New Place by Shakespeare—Easter Term, 1597.

The celebrated letter from Mr. Richard Quyney to Shakespeare, 1598, asking for a loan of £30; *the only letter addressed to Shakespeare known to exist:* quoted in the above biography.

Original grant of four yard lands in Stratford fields— William and John Combe to Shakespeare, 1602.

Copy of court roll, 1602. Surrender by Walter Getley to William Shakespeare of premises in Chapel Lane, Stratford (copyhold of the Manor of Rowington), which the poet specifically devised by his will.

Declaration in an action in the Borough Court— William Shakespeare *v.* Philip Rogers, to recover the price of malt sold by Shakespeare, 1604.

Assignment of lease of a moiety of the tithes of Stratford-upon-Avon—Ralph Huband to William Shakespeare, 1605.

Deed with the autograph of Gilbert Shakespeare, brother of the poet, 1609.

Original precepts in the Borough Court in Shakespeare's suit against John Addenbrooke, 1609.

Settlement of Shakespeare's estates in 1639 by his daughter, Susanna Hall; his grand-daughter, Elizabeth Nash; and her husband, Thomas Nash.

Declaration of uses relating to New Place and other Shakespearian property, 1647. Susanna Hall, daughter, and Elizabeth Nash, grand-daughter of the poet, are parties to this deed.

Disposition of New Place and other estates of Shakespeare, made by his grand-daughter, Elizabeth Barnard, in 1653.

Probate of Lady Barnard's will, 1669.

Shakespeare's gold signet ring, with the initials 𝖂.𝖘. and a true-lover's knot between.

Charter of foundation, 22 Edwd. IV., 1482, by Thomas Jolyffe, of the Free Grammar School at Stratford, at which Shakespeare was educated.

Ancient desk, said to have been Shakespeare's, removed from the Grammar School.

Cast, considered to be the best, from the bust in the Chancel, by G. Bullock—*two only were taken.*

The old sign of the Falcon at "Drunken Bidford," where Shakespeare is said to have drunk too deep.

Model, in plaster, of Shakespeare asleep under the crabtree, by *E. Grubb.*

Shakespeare's jug, from which Garrick sipped wine at the jubilee in 1769.

A phial, hermetically sealed, containing juice from mulberries gathered from Shakespeare's mulberry tree. The tree was cut down in 1758.

Specimen from an original copy of "The Merry Wives of Windsor."

Portrait of Garrick, in the character of *Kiteley.—Sir J. Reynolds.*

Portrait of Mrs. Garrick—supposed to be by *Gainsborough.*

A variety of interesting articles discovered in making the excavations at New Place, the last residence of Shakespeare.

Having now hastily disposed of the principal places associated with the immortal name of Shakespeare, I will take a hurried

RETROSPECTIVE GLANCE AT THE TOWN.

Stratford-upon-Avon is, I need hardly say, a thoroughly English town in its appearance, manners, and customs.

There is a sort of Gradgrind description of it in the "Post Office Directory," which, for those who delight to "condescend upon particulars," I had better quote. That charming little official *brochure* says:—

"Stratford-on-Avon is a municipal borough, market and union town and railway station, on the junction line of the West Midland and Great Western Railways in old Stratford parish, division and union of its own name, Barlichway, diocese and archdeaconry of Worcester, and deanery of Kineton, South Warwickshire. It is the centre of several turnpike roads, and on the old road from London to Holyhead, eight miles south-west of Warwick, eight south-east from Henley-in-Arden, ten north-east from Kineton, ten and a half north-east from Shipston-on-Stour, and ninety-four from London by the road, and one hundred and two by rail."

Its antiquity is discovered by the visitor at a glance. Variety of gables form the façade of some important buildings. Few houses have been constructed in accordance with fashionable principles of street architecture. Oaken floors are to be found in many of them, and massive beams of oak strengthen the walls. They are placed in horizontal and vertical positions, whilst diagonal stays of oak tie up these beams substantially in all directions. The windows are bay —not a few the genuine bow, many dormer. In the very old houses, the "sashes" are of lead, very small panes, diamond and square. The customs of old English towns still prevail. Here are to be found the stocks which raised the ready ire of *Lear*—not the identical pair, let me observe, but looking sufficiently antiquated to suggest the idea of their having done active service on the ankles of knaves at the somewhat misty period when that choleric worthy reigned in Britain—"every inch a King." Here is that terror of very small farmers and cottagers who keep goats, pigs, and horned cattle of a vagrant character—the pound. In Stratford, the matin bell is rung, and "the curfew tolls the knell of parting day." Here may be seen the beadle resplendent in scarlet and gold. And last, but not least, in our dear love, as the aforesaid *Lear* remarks, here, calling away at his lawful calling, is the town crier—a direct descendant of, and true heir-at-law, for aught I know, of

the gentleman whom the poet had as lief hear speak his
lines as a "mouthing player."

The manufactures and trade of Stratford are not extensive, although the inhabitants are naturally business-like
and formal in their habits—anything but ideal, poetical, or
artistic.   Staid, regular, and temperate; squalid poverty,
theft, and drunkenness are almost unknown amongst them ;
and if cleanliness be next to godliness, as has been well be-
thought, no people can be more adjacent to that which
"is profitable unto all things."   Public worship—church
going, at least—is nearly universally observed.   I hope it
does not "fulfil the law" with some ; but certainly John
Milton would have been suspected of something worse than
Unitarianism or polygamy by not a few Stratfordians.

THE FORMER JUBILEES.

GARRICK'S: 1769.

THE first jubilee in honour of Shakespeare, which took place at Stratford-upon-Avon, in 1769, is generally called " Garrick's." He originated and carried out that much ridiculed—somewhat unfortunate—but, on the whole, successful and praiseworthy celebration. Garrick had been at that time no less than twenty-eight years on the stage, unprecedentedly successful as actor and manager. He was not a profound student of Shakespeare, nor had he unqualified reverence for his genius. In compliment to the greatest if not only detractor of Shakespeare in the literary world —Voltaire—he maimed " Hamlet " by cutting out the grave scene and "burking" *Osric*. The rapidity and intensity of his style enabled him to give a novel and spirited picture of *Richard* and his wonderful mimetic faculties account to me largely for the effects he created in *Lear;* but as a tragedian, in the strict sense of the term, he was almost as mentally dwarfed as he was physically stunted, however otherwise his biographers, the Irish dramatist and barrister, Murphy, or " the author," as Johnson said, " engendered from the corruption of a bookseller," Davies, may describe him. He had not the dignity of Quin, the power of Mossop, or the physical endowments of Barry. Certainly he was nowhere with Barry in *Othello*, and came up to him in only the banishment scene of *Romeo*. His *Hamlet*, I feel persuaded, was not equal to that of Betterton or Charles Mayne Young, or his *Macbeth* to that of William Charles Macready.

This, I am aware, is not the traditional opinion of
Garrick in tragedy, and acting will, it is true, ever be a
matter of opinion, even amongst those who judge from personal knowledge, whilst it is almost impossible from descriptions in books to form a positive notion of what an actor was
on the stage; but the authority which fortifies me in the
foregoing opinions happily warrants me in believing that
Garrick was, nevertheless, beyond all question, the greatest
histrionic artist of his time, or perhaps of any time, because
the most original and most comprehensive. He was the
author of excellent farces and prologues, and acquainted not
only with books but men as they are or were in his time.
Full of tact and the peculiar cleverness of a showman, he
was a thorough man of the world, so that "as deep·as
Garrick" was a phrase of the times. Although Dr.
Johnson affected occasionally to despise both the actor and
his art, he lamented Garrick's death as "that stroke which
had eclipsed the gaiety of nations and robbed the public
stock of harmless pleasure;" and Goldsmith describes him
as "a medley of all that is pleasant in man." Take him for
all in all, therefore, no one could have been more thoroughly
qualified to manage a national jubilee than he who undertook it in Stratford-upon-Avon in 1769.

I have thought it well to occupy thus much of the
reader's attention with some account of the man whose
name is to be seen on the walls of Stratford, whose picture
is the handsomest ornament of the principal building in
the town, and whose name will ever be remembered in
Warwickshire. Happy would it have been for the Stratford
Committee, during the late celebration, if an actor so
accomplished and generous had been forthcoming and
permitted to take full charge of the dramatic portion of the
business. They would have been spared vast-labour, no
end of anxiety, and enormous pecuniary expenditure. The
celebration which made him famous in this county
(Warwick) is stated to have originated under the following
circumstances :—

Towards the latter end of the year 1768, a jollification
took place amongst congenial spirits at the White Lion

Hotel, then the principal hostelry in Stratford-upon-Avon. Naturally mixing up the ever recurring Stratfordian topic of Shakespeare with the local events of the day, the conversation turned on the newly erected Town Hall, the then vacant niche in the northern gable, and the desirability of having it filled up by a statue of the immortal dramatist—Ben Jonson and Jack Milton to the contrary notwithstanding. One of the party, the celebrated George Steevens, who happened to be the chief guest of the evening, suggested an application to the great actor and successful manager, David Garrick, for assistance in giving practical effect to this happy idea. Now nothing could have been more natural than to seek the aid of the English Roscius in carrying out the notion.

Accordingly Mr. Steevens was deputed to communicate with him upon the subject, and he did so with more hope of working effectively upon Garrick's love of money and fame, than of Shakespeare's memory. That Roscius did go in for glory there is no doubt, but in such a man a degree of self was natural and pardonable under the circumstances: he was an artist and an author; he had some knowledge and "feeling of his business." Besides, there appears to have been no one ready and willing to share with him the honours and responsibilities of the undertaking. But however mingled the motives that stimulated Garrick, Steevens received in the course of a few days a favourable answer from him. A correspondence subsequently arose between Garrick and the Stratford Corporation, in which the "wit—if not first, in the very first line" succeeded in raising himself to the highest position in the esteem and admiration of the "potent, grave, and reverend seigniors." They voted him a triumph. In other words presented him with the freedom of the borough in a box made of Shakespeare's mulberry tree. Garrick was delighted, and in turn voted them himself and Shakespeare a national jubilee. He submitted his programme to the Corporation, it was approved of, and he mentally at once commenced operations; and when winding up his season the following summer, announced to his audience the grand work in hand in the following terms :—

> " My eyes till then *(his next season)* no sights like this will see,
> Unless we meet at Shakespeare's jubilee
> On Avon's banks, where flowers eternal blow ;
> Like its full stream our gratitude shall flow.
> There let us revel, show our fond regard ;
> On that loved spot first breathed our matchless bard.
> To him all honour, gratitude is due,
> To him we owe our all—to him and you."

This of course was but another way of saying "be in time, and take your places" in the amphitheatre, subsequently erected on the banks of the Avon. This magnificent octagonal building was erected upon the Bancroft, close to the river Avon, at the expense of the Corporation, assisted by the neighbouring gentry. It was constructed on the model of the Ranelagh Rotunda, and measured 70 feet diameter, and was calculated to hold one thousand persons ; the orchestra giving accommodation to one hundred performers. It was supported by a circular colonnade of Corinthian columns, the capitals and bases of which were richly gilt. From the centre of the dome, which was beautifully painted, was suspended a splendid chandelier, containing eight hundred wax lights; in various compartments of the wainscotting were tasteful and appropriate devices richly executed.

The jubilee began at five o'clock on Wednesday morning, the 6th September, 1769, not in a "mighty genteel" tepid indecisive way, but vigorously and heartily amid the roaring of cannon, relieved by the concord of sweet sounds. The leading lady visitors were serenaded by a company of comedians in full professional costume. They sung an appropriate song with full band accompaniment. The Corporation assembled at eight o'clock, and having appointed Mr. Garrick master of the revels or of ceremonies, or to stick to the text of our authority (Mr. Wheler) "steward," invested him with the insignia of his office, namely, a medal (on which was carved a bust of Shakespeare, richly set in gold) and a wand, both formed of the celebrated mulberry tree. At nine o'clock a public breakfast was held at Shakespeare's Hall, during which a band played martial and popular music. At half-past ten o'clock the company proceeded in regular order to the church, where the oratorio of "Judith," composed by Dr. Arne, was performed under his direction, in a temporary orchestra erected under the organ. The choruses were full, and the band, which comprised the whole of Drury Lane orchestra, was excellent. A sumptuous dinner, to which upwards of seven hundred ladies and gentlemen sat down, in the amphitheatre, formed the next item of the ample programme. At night there was a brilliant ball, the town was illuminated, and there was a grand display of fireworks, under the management, we are told, of "M. (not Michael, surely) Angelo." Thus the curtain was rung down, amid enthusiastic applause, on the first act of this national three-act melo-drama.

On the second day the festive proceedings commenced as before, with the firing of cannon, the ringing of bells, and the serenading of ladies. After another public breakfast the company repaired to the amphitheatre, where an ode on the dedication of the newly-erected Town Hall to the memory of Shakespeare, and the erection of the statue presented by Garrick, was performed. The music was by Dr. Arne. The recitative portions were very effectively delivered by Garrick, so that music it is said was forced to yield the palm to elocution on this occasion. Garrick also delivered a very impressive and eloquent oration. At three o'clock a public dinner was given, which was numerously attended, and in the evening the town was again very brilliantly illuminated. Transparencies were invented for the five front windows in Shakespeare's Hall. In the centre window was a whole-length figure of Shakespeare, turning with animation to a person holding Pegasus, and exclaiming, "O for a muse of fire!" *Falstaff* and *Pistol* decorated the windows on his left hand, and in those on his right were *Lear* in the execration passage, and *Caliban* drinking from *Trinculo's* keg. The birth-place of the bard was covered with a curious emblematical transparency, depicting the sun struggling through the clouds to enlighten the world, and underneath was this motto : "Thus dying clouds contend with growing light,"—a figurative representation of the fate and fortunes of the much-admired bard. In front of the amphitheatre were three well-executed allegorical paintings, after designs by the celebrated Sir Joshua Reynolds. In the centre, Time was leading Shakespeare to immortality ; a figure of Tragedy graced him on one side, and Comedy on the other. His bust in the chancel had not been neglected, being adorned with festoons of laurel, bays, &c., and at the head of his gravestone some pious hand had placed a garland of flowers and evergreens.

At night the masquerade at the amphitheatre was attended by nearly one thousand persons, of whom many were well-dressed, and sustained their parts with great propriety ; but some who could not hire dresses, or did not choose to pay extravagantly for their use, were admitted with masks only ; and there were many present even without masks, and some with their faces blackened or otherwise coloured. Amongst the company was James Boswell, in a Corsican "make up," armed with a gun and pistols and having " Paoli and Liberty " as a motto for his cap.

On the 8th (Friday) the festival was continued with unabated spirit after the fashion of the preceding days ; but as the weather continued unpropitious the pageant, which was expected to be one of the most effective out-door features of the jubilee, was abandoned. The race, however, upon Shottery Meadow, for the jubilee cup, value fifty guineas, was largely attended. Five colts ran. " Pratt the groom," who rode his own horse, won. Pratt declared he never would part with the prize, though, as he honestly avowed, "he knew very little about plays or Master Shakespeare."

There was a grand ball in the evening, at which Mrs. Garrick distinguished herself by her inimitably graceful dancing, as may be readily believed, the lady having been a professor of the art prior to her marriage. The night of this third day was fine, and the fireworks went off with great success.

Thus terminated the first of Shakespearian jubilees—a great undertaking—the design of which was creditable to the manager, who was in no way responsible for any disappointments which arose from a cause over which he had no control.

In the following year an effort was made to get up a jubilee on a smaller scale, but it failed. In 1794 Mr. Malone contemplated a celebration of the poet's memory, but the unsettled state of our national affairs at that period frustrated his intentions, and it was not till 1827 that any imitation of Garrick's great jubilee took place.

THE SECOND CELEBRATION, 1827.

Of the history of this jubilee the *Times* lately published the following admirable abridgment:—

In April, 1824, a Shakespearian Club was established, the members of which, nearly two hundred in number, comprised the most respectable inhabitants of the borough. These determined to hold a Triennial Commemoration Festival on St. George's Day, which is likewise the birthday of Shakespeare, and this intention was first carried into effect in April, 1827.

The festival of 1827 lasted three days, on the first of which (the 23rd) a pageant such as Garrick had projected nearly sixty years before, but which weather did *not* permit, moved from the Guildhall to the poet's birth-place in Henley Street. The committee of the club, with Mr. John Mills, the Mayor, at their head, and carrying their banner, marched in front, and was followed by a procession in this order :— The Royal Standard of England; a Military Band; St. George, on horseback, bearing a sword of the time of Edward III.; St. George's Banner, carried by his Esquire; the Banner of the Borough; Melpomene, the Tragic Muse, in a car drawn by four fiends; *Lear* and *Edgar; Richard III.* and the *Prince of Wales; Macbeth, Banquo,* and the *Three Witches; King John,* the *Cardinal,* and *Faulconbridge; Othello* and *Iago ; Hamlet,* the *King,* the *Ghost,* and the *Gravediggers; Romeo, Juliet,* and *Friar Laurence.* Thus was completed the tragic series, which was followed by the Banner of Shakespeare's Arms. Now comes the turn of comedy. Thalia, the Comic Muse, in a car drawn by four satyrs, led the way, and was followed by *Caliban, Trinculo, Ariel,* and *Prospero ; Autolycus* and the *Shepherd ; Touchstone* and *Audrey ; Oberon, Titania* (in a car drawn by *Puck* and fairies), and

Bottom, with the ass's head; *Shylock* and *Portia* (as Doctor of Laws); *Sir John Falstaff* and the *Two Merry Wives; Henry V., Bardolph,* and *Pistol;* the Union Flag concluding the whole.

On reaching the house in Henley Street the procession halted, and Melpomene and Thalia, descending from their cars, crowned with laurel a bust of Shakespeare that had been placed on a pedestal. An address in blank verse, written by Mr. Serle, then of Covent Garden, was delivered by Mr. Bond, one of the theatrical company engaged by Mr. Raymond, who hoped that a day was approaching in which Stratford would become an arena for the development of histrionic talent. Indeed, one of the objects of the festival was to lay the foundation-stone of a new theatre. To the site of this projected edifice the pageant now proceeded, and the stone was duly laid, a plate with the following inscription being inserted in the cavity :—

" Genio loci
Hoc Theatrum,
D. D. D.
Consocintis Shakspeareana,
Die Aprilis XXIII,
A.D. MDCCCXXVII.
Natali Poetæ,
Stratfordia idcirco jubilante."

A vocal performance, the music from " Macbeth," followed the ceremony on the spot.

At four o'clock a dinner, at which two hundred gentlemen sat down, was held in the large room of the Town Hall, a scroll, inscribed " We ne'er shall look upon his like again," being suspended over the painting of Shakespeare, and another, " He suited the action to the word," over the portrait of Garrick. Over the entrance was a transparency representing the head of Shakespeare surrounded with a radiant glory dissipating the previous darkness. The speeches on the occasion were numerous and long, the chief orator apparently being the Rev. Dr. Wade, vicar of St. Nicholas's, Warwick. A public breakfast at the White Lion Hotel, a large house in Henley Street, adjacent to the birth-place, and a masquerade held in a temporary amphitheatre, erected in Rother Market, were the chief amusements of the second day, which terminated with a display of fireworks. Garrick's amphi-theatre, it seems, had been erected close to the Avon, but the Rother Market, which looks like a large village green, long since destitute of verdure, was again selected for the pavilion of 1830. The wooden edifice of the present festival is in quite a different part of the town, the chief entrance being in a narrow street called Southern's Lane, situated near the church and river. A concert at the White Lion contributed the principal entertainment of the third day, the musicians being amateurs and members of Mr. Raymond's company.

The festival of 1827 is still recollected with pleasure by the older inhabitants of the town, and the pageant seems to have been exceedingly well contrived. Mr. Raymond had already taken a lease of the projected theatre, and its opening was eagerly anticipated as likely to prove a lasting source of amusement. Those sanguine expectations were never realised, and, though the theatre was indeed completed, and now stands an unsightly edifice in Chapel Lane, not far from the Grammar School where Shakespeare is supposed to have learnt Latin, it is rarely used at present for dramatic purposes.

THE THIRD CELEBRATION, 1830.

At the termination of the jubilee of 1827, it was publicly announced that a triennial celebration of the poet's birthday would take place at Stratford-upon-Avon. In pursuance of this determination the Shakespearian Club began in the autumn of 1829 to make preparations for the celebration to take place in 1830. The applications from the Committee to many distinguished individuals having been favourably received, it was determined that Royalty itself should be solicited to patronise the celebration. A petition was accordingly drawn out and presented by the then Right Honourable Robert Peel to George IV., praying for the countenance and support of His Majesty in the undertaking. An immediate assent was conveyed in the most gracious terms to the anxious expectants. Thus honoured, the gala was invested with regal importance. The co-operation and contributions of the nobility and gentry throughout the country followed as a matter of course, and the preparations being at last completed the jubilee commenced on Friday, the 23rd of April—the day sacred to Shakespeare and St. George.

A dull and unpropitious morning was ushered in by the customary firing of cannon from the Bancroft and the heights of Welcombe, the hoisting of flags and the ringing of bells. Rain fell copiously, but, despite that misfortune, by nine o'clock all the roads leading to the town were thronged with all sorts of people—pedestrians, equestrians, and carriage folk. The fine old English gentleman, " who

F

entertained the rich, and ne'er forgot the poor," was alive
in the land.   In Rother Street a pavilion had been erected,
in which the business of the day commenced with a public
breakfast.   The characters for the Shakespearian procession (which formed a portion of the programme) were all
ready about mid-day, but the weather continued so unpropitious that the Committee issued orders for a postponement until the following day, when the clouds suddenly
dispersed, the sun shone forth, and the day continued fair
for several hours.

Exactly at two o'clock a royal salute from the cannon,
the ringing of bells, and the shouts of the multitude
announced to eager expectants that the procession had left
the pavilion, from which it issued in the following order :—
Mr. Ashfield, on horseback, attired as a Chief Constable
of the Elizabethan period ; Mr. Palmer, Tavistock Street,
Covent Garden, Costumier, on horseback.   The Royal
Standard of England, borne by Messrs. Tomkins and
William Morris ; the Band of the Second Warwickshire
Local Militia ; a Banner, on which the arms of Shakespeare
and the borough of Stratford were embroidered ; the Committee of the Shakespearian Club, on horseback, headed
by the Mayor (T. Ashwin, Esq.), each wearing the jubilee
scarf and a medal suspended from the neck by the jubilee
or rainbow tinted ribbon ; St. George (the tutelar saint of
England), seated on a grey horse, richly caparisoned : the
hero was personated by Mr. Charles Kean (then about
twenty years of age) ; St. George's Esquire (Mr. Goodwin,
of Stratford), with his Banner ; the Banner of the Borough,
borne by F. Findon and J. Paine; Melpomene (Miss Harvey
of Mr. Raymond's company), with dagger and chalice,
seated on a dark-coloured car, surrounded by fiends ; *Lear*
and *Cordelia*, by Mr. W. Williams and Miss Churchill, of
Stratford ; *Edgar* (as mad Tom), by Mr. Timberley, of
Warwick ; Heralds bearing Eagles ; *Coriolanus*, by Mr.
Gardner, of Kingsthorpe, Northamptonshire ; *Cominus*, by
John Warner, of Charlecote ; *Titus Lartius*, by Mr.
Pittaway ; twelve Lictors ; a Banner ; a Herald, carrying
the Roman Eagle ; *Julius Cæsar*, by Mr. Chas. Wright, of

London ; *Brutus* and *Cassius*, by (respectively) Mr. Winchester, of London, and Mr. James Keeley, of Warwick ; Herald, with Black Eagle ; *Anthony* and *Cleopatra*, by George Heritage, of Stratford, and Miss Turnbull, of Warwick ; *Macbeth* and *Lady Macbeth*, by Mr. Morris, of Leamington, and Mrs. Granby, of Mr. Raymond's company ; *Banquo*, by Mr. Samuel Hodgkinson, of Stratford ; the *Three Witches*, by John Penn, Joseph West, and J. Drury ; *King John*, by Mr. Granby, of Mr. Raymond's company ; *Prince Arthur*, by Master Grossmith ("the Young Roscius") ; *Faulconbridge*, by Mr. John Keeley, of Stratford ; *Henry the Fourth*, by Mr. Rogers, of Leamington ; *Prince of Wales*, by Mr. T. Arkell, jun., of Stratford ; *Hotspur*, on horseback, by Mr. Raymond ; *Douglas*, on horseback, by Mr. Jos. Sheldon, of Stratford ; *Romeo* and *Juliet*, by Mr. Harris and Miss Newman, of Mr. Raymond's company ; *Peter* and *Nurse*, by Mr. and Mrs. Watson, of Mr. Raymond's company ; the *Apothecary*, by Mr. Geo. Mann, of Stratford ; *Richard the Third* and *Lady Anne*, by Mr. Harrison and Mrs. Gifford, of Mr. Raymond's company ; *Hamlet*, by Mr. Biddle, of Mr. Raymond's company ; the *Ghost*, by J. Norton, of Stratford ; *Polonius*, by Mr. Mantle; *Ophelia*, by Mrs. Booth ; *Henry the Eighth*, by Mr. Thomas Mansell, of Preston ; *Queen Katharine*, by Mrs. Goodwin, of Stratford ; *Page*, by J. Bishop, of Warwick ; *Earl of Surrey*, by Mr. Street, of London ; *Ladies in Waiting*, Miss Plumb and Miss Robbins, of Stratford ; *Cardinal Wolsey*, by Mr. Cherry, of Stratford ; *Cromwell*, by Mr. W. Rose, of Warwick ; *Othello*, by Chas. Bolette (a man of colour), of Warwick ; *Desdemona*, by Miss E. Box, of Stratford ; *Iago*, by Mr. Allan, of Leamington ; *Cassio*, by Mr. S. J. King, of Stratford ; *Roderigo*, Mr. Obbard, of London; Banner of Shakespeare's Arms ; Thalia, by Miss Bailey ; *Satyrs ;* the Banner of the Kensington Shakespearian Club; *Prospero*, by Mr. Simpson ; *Ariel*, by Miss Wright, of Stratford ; *Caliban*, by Mr. W. Buckingham, of Stratford ; *Trinculo*, by Mr. Turner, of Warwick ; *Sir John Falstaff*, by Mr. Rowland Green, of Birmingham ; *Mrs. Ford*, by Mrs. Mantle ; *Mrs. Page*, by

Miss Robbins, of Stratford; *Antipholi of Ephesus and Syracuse*, by Mr. Thomas Hyde, of Stratford, and Mr. Joseph Hyde, of Ryon Hill, twin brothers; the two *Dromios*, by twin brothers, the Messrs. Smith, of Bidford; *Petruchio* and *Katharine*, by Mr. Edward Ashwin and Mr. Isaac Cory, of Stratford; *Grumio*, by Mr. Charles Gill, of Mr. Raymond's company; *Orlando*, by Mr. James Bearley, of Stratford; *Adam*, by Mr. Morris; *Touchstone* and *Audrey*, by Mr. and Mrs. Reynolds, of the Stratford Theatre; *Shylock* and *Portia*, by Mr. Gifford (actor) and Miss Bierley, of Stratford; *Oberon* and *Titania*, by Master Mills and Miss White, of Stratford; *Bottom the Weaver*, by Thomas Lay, of Stratford.

The dresses and appointments are described as of great splendour. Banners were carried in the procession, announcing the plays to which each pair or group of characters belonged. Minor characters, not mentioned above, were introduced to give a completeness to the representation, and the whole pageant appears to have been managed in a most praiseworthy manner. "However brilliant," says the author from whom I have made the foregoing condensed description, "the success which attended the first jubilee of the Shakespearian Club, it fell far short of the triumph they achieved on this occasion; upwards of seventy-five of the more prominent characters of Shakespeare burst upon the sight at one view, with a vividness and splendour really astonishing." Certainly it made a lasting impression on the minds of the people of Stratford. Many inhabitants, not forty years of age, can give a graphic description of it, and it was not to be wondered at if under such circumstances they felt disappointed to find the pageant formed no part of the programme of the Tercentenary Celebration Committee, by whom it was pooh poohed as tomfoolery calculated to bring them into public ridicule, forgetful that Garrick, who was no fool, introduced it, and that the same spirit of criticism scouted a fancy ball—nay, that Diogenes, raising his lamp and extending his ken, joined with *Mawworm* and *Cantwell* in denouncing the whole celebration as an absurd turmoil of profane and idly busy craziness!

The pageant, however, arranged as above stated, having quitted the pavilion, proceeded through Wood Street to Henley Street, and halted in front of the birth-place, where a temporary stage had been erected. The ceremony of crowning a bust of Shakespeare was then gone solemnly through, amid the acclamations of the thousands who blocked up the thoroughfare. An appropriate address was then recited by Mr. Booth (comedian), which had been written for the occasion by A. Wright, Esq. The procession then passed through the town by the Post Office, along the Guild Pits, John Street, Payton Street, Warwick Road, Back Bridge Street, High Street, Chapel Street, Church Street, Old Town, to the Church Gates. Shakespeare's epitaph, set to solemn music, was here, we are told, very impressively sung! The procession then moved through Southern's Lane, along Lower Water Side, Sheep Street, High Street, Front Bridge Street, Upper Water Side, Sheep Street, Ely Street, and Rother Street to the pavilion.

In the afternoon a dinner took place at Shakespeare's Hall, at which about three hundred attended. The loyal and patriotic toasts having been proposed and drunk with enthusiasm the memory of Shakespeare was duly honoured, and the health of the Mayor was drunk and that of the Secretary, Mr. S. Gwinnett. Some of the speeches were very good, especially that of the Rev. Dr. Wade (above mentioned). A loyal and dutiful address to the King, who was prevented by indisposition from being present, was read and adopted. A dramatic performance at the theatre, in which Mr. Kean appeared, and a *bal masque* in the pavilion terminated the first day of the jubilee of 1830.

The second day, Saturday, April 24th, was ushered in with firing of cannon and joy bell-ringing. There was a public breakfast at the White Lion. To the breakfast succeeded recitations and songs. Between two and three there was a miscellaneous concert, which was opened with an ode written expressly for the occasion by Isaac Cowen, Esq., and set to music by the author's nephew, Mr. Charles Salaman, whose name appears on the Committee of the tercentenary celebration. In the evening the theatre proved again attractive, and there was another masquerade and fancy ball.

Sunday appears to have been both legally and so far as the jubilee was concerned a *dies non* in 1830: not so in 1864, we are thankful to say.

The third day, Monday, April 26th, was favoured with delightful weather, and it was calculated that from twenty-five to thirty-five thousand persons assembled in Stratford. The pageant took place under the most favourable circumstances. There was a public dinner, attended principally by the Shakespearian Club and their friends, at which the health of Dr. Conolly was drunk. Theatrical performances and dancing in masks wound up the third day; and the fourth day was like its predecessors, the beauty of the weather contributing to the brilliancy of the concluding festivities.

The anonymous analyst to whom I am indebted for the foregoing particulars of this jubilee winds up his narrative in the following terms:—"We close with observing that a small band of men have raised up a spirit in their native town which will perhaps never be destroyed, and long after they are slumbering under the turf which surrounds the sacred edifice where lie interred the hallowed ashes of the great dramatist himself, their children's children may justly exclaim in his own inspired language—

'How many ages hence
Shall this our lofty scene be acted o'er
By men unborn, and accent yet unknown.'"

THE

TERCENTENARY FESTIVAL.

No people can appreciate more highly the possession of an honourable distinction than the inhabitants of Stratford-upon-Avon. Not encumbered with the questionable blessing of poetic propensities in themselves, they, nevertheless, view with keen perception and enlarged comprehension the genius of Shakespeare. Proud of their town, to which his great name has bequeathed a world-wide celebrity, they have invariably felt that as inhabitants thereof they had special duties to discharge towards his memory. His remarkable attachment to Stratford contributes not a little to their estimate of the honour he conferred upon the town, and largely accounts for their abiding anxiety to prove to the empire and the world that they understand the responsibilities as well as the honours of their position. Such seems to me to have been the feeling of Stratfordians time out of mind, although it is not many years since active steps began to be taken for securing to the nation and preserving from decay the place of his birth and residence. The feeling of respect for his memory has ever been deep, broad, and general. It only required Garrick to unfurl the flag of Shakespeare in order to arouse the town and attract around him the county a hundred years ago. The jubilee of 1827 formally transferred from the adherents of Garrick to their children that Shakespearian enthusiasm they had witnessed amongst their relatives, and which blended with their earliest recollections; and the celebration of 1830, with its royal, although nominal patronage, and its splendid pageantry, is treasured with pleasurable remembrance by every inhabitant of Stratford whose memory extends to the event.

It would, therefore, have been singular indeed if the great epoch of the poet's three hundredth natal day had been allowed to pass away in his birth and burial place, where his memory is so revered, without a demonstration in some degree corresponding with the occasion. That many looked for years forward to 1864, and beheld in their mind's eye an unprecedented demonstration in Stratford, I feel quite assured. The Burns' centenary suggested a national celebration of a similar description to Shakespeare. It was, however, the good fortune of the late excellent actor and estimable man, Mr. Harries Tilbury, to give the first expression to the feeling upon the subject. He happened to take the chair at the Shakespeare Club dinner, in Stratford, on the 23rd of April, 1859, and in proposing the toast of the evening made the following observations on the approaching event:—" 'Time,' " he said, " 'with his stealing steps' will quickly bear to you the year 1864. In that year prove that Scotia's educated sons are not alone enough clannish to honour native genius, as they so creditably did by the Burns' centenary, but show an English, a British spirit of clanship, and such, if possible, with triple energy and impressiveness, upon the tercentenary of great Shakespeare's nativity. [Loud cheers.] Time changes most things; but it has not affected the appreciation of Shakespeare, unless indeed, it be to multiply and extend it. Invite then all the lands to display their fervour, and send their deputations at the tercentenary, and who can doubt the sublimity of the response? That would be another thrilling stamp of honour to your town, and to the memory of the 'sweet swan of Avon.' And I will not hesitate to suggest another and a lofty mode to perpetuate honour to him, which I cannot but think is practicable, and would confer upon your town of Stratford an additional, a gravely significant, record to the bard, and which would establish a dignified advantage. At this tercentenary festival, nay, before it, solicit contributions; extend your askings to the county —Shakespeare's county—nay, to the kingdom; even petition our deservedly-beloved Sovereign, who is so frequently an enjoyer of the representations of your great bard's plays, and her illustrious Consort, the elegant and liberal patron of art and pen; add to these any balance which may be available from the munificent bequests of that glorious, generous deviser, the noble John, who boasted privilege of fellowship in the poet's name, and, with the gathered proceeds of these and any other means which may be enlisted to advance the noble purpose, found at one of the Universities an exhibition to be periodically competed for by the scholars of your Grammar School; that school which, established by the sixth Edward, the beneficent to education, did under the wise and mighty Elizabeth contain as pupil beneath its roof, as student at its desk, that very youth whose after successes and celebrity have invested the fabric with a halo which will assuredly survive in history, even when its perishable materials have succumbed to the slow but certain inroads of all-powerful time. [Applause.] With such an exhibition established you would not only boast the birth house, now renovated by public and individual liberality, and his hallowed sepulchre, but possess an educational memorial, such as similar to, and dear with, and of frequent institution in our age, as they earlier marked the enlightened liberality of good and considerate men in centuries which have preceded us, and which may serve to enhance the acquirements attained by successful labourers in your local school, and by their passage through more severe and elevated classes, fit future men of Stratford to be, when drafted into the world, not only honours to him whose name their exhibition should wear, but to be shining lights and true advantages in their particular periods."

These admirable sentiments, and the no less admirable practical suggestion by which they were accompanied, obtained general approval. The matter was taken up by the Committee of the Shakespeare Club, and at the next meeting, in April, 1860, Dr. Kingsley, the President, stated that "at the request of the Committee, the Rev. Mr. Granville and himself had an interview with the Lord-Lieutenant of the county, in order to obtain his co-operation in the due

celebration of the tercentenary which was to take place there
in 1864. No person could have evinced more interest in
the project than did Lord Leigh on that occasion. His
Lordship assured them both that he was quite willing to
take any part in the proceedings for doing honour to the
day. [Applause]. He now wished to remark that although
some persons in the neighbourhood might consider that the
members of the Committee were somewhat lukewarm in the
matter, yet they were nevertheless working silently but
steadily, and he hoped successfully, in the matter. There
were many circumstances to be taken into consideration.
Their primary object was to obtain the sanction of royalty,
and secure the patronage of the leading celebrities of the
day to their proceedings in Stratford. They would make it
known that the object intended was not alone a grand
celebration in honour of the master-spirit of a former age.
They desired to accomplish what Mr. Tilbury suggested the
previous year, by devoting funds obtained from subscriptions,
donations, &c., to the foundation of Shakespeare scholarships at the Universities. A direct benefit would thus accrue
to the town of Stratford-upon-Avon; for the fact that
scholarships were free to the children of resident parents
would induce many to take up their abode on that account."
Subsequently, in the same year, Dr. Kingsley succeeded in
obtaining the consent of the amiable and accomplished Earl
of Carlisle, K.G., Lord-Lieutenant of Ireland, to accept the
office of President of the Committee, to be formed for the
celebration of the Shakespeare tercentenary. A list of
Vice-presidents was afterwards opened, to which names of
eligible parties were added from time to time up till the end
of February, 1864. [See programme.] And at the dinner,
which took place in the afternoon of the birthday this
year (1860), the Rev. Julian Young, who was chairman,
referred to the contemplated celebration in the following
terms :—" Nearly three hundred years have gone by since
the birth of him whose memory and reputation are cherished
by the civilised world; and what has hitherto been done
by his own countrymen to mark their obligation to the man
who has elevated their tastes, enriched their literature, and

shed more unperishable renown on his land than any who have gone before or followed after him ? I need not say, because I am sure you feel that the glory which the literary immortality of this great sun in the intellectual hemisphere has reflected on the country at large shines with especial effulgence on this, the town of his birth, his education, his earliest and latest memories, and his death. Now this day four years hence, those of us who may be spared so long shall hope to witness the celebration of his tercentenary ;— [applause]—and, that it may be fittingly observed, I would suggest that we should not regard it as an event merely of local, or provincial, or metropolitan, or national, or European but of world-wide significance ; and I believe that in such a cause every enlightened foreigner—Italians by their tens, Frenchmen by their hundreds, Germans by their thousands, and Americans by their hundreds of thousands—would gladly and proudly identify themselves with it. I would therefore suggest that, by circulars transmitted abroad as well as at home, the formation of committees in different large towns—abroad as well as at home, by every person of literary, aristocratic, and artistic distinction, especially by those professing love for Shakespeare—who should show their sincerity by exerting themselves in behalf of the cause we have at heart—by the powerful agency of the press ; by the theatres, provincial and metropolitan, which should be induced to devote certain nights to the purpose—by all these means I say we should work, and then I cannot help thinking that a celebration, which shall far eclipse in splendour the jubilee of Garrick, will be obtained."

It was in this enlarged and comprehensive spirit the late celebration was conceived and projected. If it has failed to realise all the early anticipations indulged with regard to it, no blame can attach to the Stratford Committee, who could not have done more than they accomplished in the eight or nine months they were really at work in the matter. The agitation was to comprehend the civilised globe ; and pity 'tis that those who took a view of the matter so properly extensive did not think of the time necessary for the purpose. It was a mistake not to com-

mence the great work on the very night when Mr. Young
fore-shadowed its magnitude.   Rome was not built in a day;
neither was the world to be stirred in any cause, substantial
sympathy obtained, a great project developed, and all the
details perfected in the little time at the Committee's disposal; for it is but now some nine moons wasted since
the object to be aimed at, and a plan of operations, were
settled with any degree of unanimity and certainty.

In 1860, several of the leading men in the business were
solicited to take immediate action in it, but they did not see
the necessity of despatch.   They had the whole four years
before them, little thinking how soon "Time with his
stealing steps" would claw that slice of our brief existence
in his clutch.   Procrastination prevailed and nothing was
done or said publicly on the subject till 14th September, five
months after Mr. Young's speech, when a letter on the
subject appeared in the *Herald*, from a member of the old
Shakespearian Club.   The writer said he had heard that
a gentleman had gone to London to enquire how far proba-
bilities were in favour of obtaining royal patronage to the
tercentenary celebration, and that having had interviews
with the noblest of the land, one and all were of his opinion,
that it was too early to moot the question.   "What, in the
name of common sense," asks the old Shakespearian, "do
these people imagine the festival is to consist of? one act
from an Italian opera? a masquerade? a Shakespearian
procession? If that be the extent of the programme, a very
short period will suffice for the preparations."   Having
deprecated that view of the matter, the correspondent says,
"Let a town meeting be called immediately, that the feeling
of the inhabitants upon the subject may be ascertained, and
if favourable, let an active and energetic Committee be
formed at once."

The suggestion was not acted upon.   With the restoration of the bust and the birth-place, and the opening of
the railway, the public mind was so occupied that the
projected tercentenary celebration was allowed to fall into
abeyance.   Singular to say, it seems to have been forgotten
even by the members of the Shakespearian Club, as the

report of the Committee for 1861 makes no reference to the subject. The establishing of the Shakespeare Fund in the October of this year, disclosed a scheme so comprehensive as to make ample demands on the public purse for some time to come, involving as it did—1. The purchase of the garden at New Place.—2. The purchase of the remainder of the birth-place estate.—3. The purchase of Anne Hathaway's cottage.—4. The purchase of Getby's copyhold, Stratford-upon-Avon.—5. The purchase of any other properties at or near Stratford-upon-Avon, &c. The matter was not however entirely lost sight of. A beginning was made in this year by the Shakespearian Club, who held a meeting on the 22nd July, at the Town Hall, under the presidency of Dr. Kingsley, "for the purpose of considering the propriety of taking preliminary steps for the celebration of the tercentenary of Shakespeare in 1864." The question was decided in the affirmative, and a Committee was formed consisting of Sir Robert Hamilton, Bart., C. H. Bracebridge, Esq., Rev. G. Granville, Rev. Julian C. Young, Dr. Thomson, William O. Hunt, R. H. Hobbes, E. F. Flower, Mark Philips, F. Kendal, and J. S. Craig, Esq., with Dr. Kingsley as Hon. Sec. The Committee may have worked from this period forward, as Dr. Kingsley said the Shakespearian Club had done previously, "silently but steadily" in the business, but it was then full time to commence the public agitation. France and Germany, America and Australia, ought to have been made thus early acquainted with the intentions of Stratford-upon-Avon, so as to give time for their co-operation. Prompt and decided action at this time might moreover have completely forestalled London in public attention, and prevented that confusion of ideas and rivalry of interests so injurious to both parties. But the apparent inertness of Stratford gave an opening to the town, and hence we heard in June of this year (1861), of a national monument, to which subscriptions were invited, Mr. Macready's name being mentioned in connection with the project, but certainly without his authority, for the great tragedian does not approve of the monumental idea, as I clearly perceive by

his directing the ten guineas he sent through me, as Secretary to the tercentenary Committee, to be appropriated
to the scholarship.

Little progress was however made at Stratford beyond
the appointment of the Committee in 1861. The opening
of 1862 was rendered sadly memorable by the dreadful
calamity of the Hartley Colliery, and the distress in Lancashire. These melancholy events rendered any general
collection for a national festival utterly impossible, whilst
the people of Stratford and the county were being strongly
urged to contribute to the Shakespeare fund for the purposes above-mentioned. The Shakespeare Club met on the
23rd April, when a report was submitted from the birthplace Committee, but no mention made of the tercentenary celebration. It was referred to at the dinner by
Mr. James Bennett, who occupied the chair, and by other
speakers, but beyond the obtaining consent from a small
number of gentlemen to enrol themselves as Vice-presidents, no "tercentenary work" appears to have been done
in 1862. Hence the day and night work of the Committee
during the past six months, and the limits to which the
movement was ultimately confined, no action having been
taken on behalf of Stratford by three-fourths of the towns
of England.

Early in 1863 the Amateur Dramatic, Literary, and
Debating Society, recalled the attention of the people of
Stratford to the subject by debates held in relation to it,
and the Shakespearian Committee, in their annual report
on the 23rd April, submitted a sketch of the programme
which comprised—(1) Dramatic Reading; (2) a Shakespearian Fancy Ball; (3) an Inaugural Address by the
President, the Earl of Carlisle (this was a mistake, as his
Lordship had not consented to deliver any special address);
(4) the Ceremony of opening New Place Gardens; and
(5) a Banquet. The Oratorio, Concert, and Dramatic
Performances, which subsequently caused so much trouble
and expense, were not, it appears, contemplated at that
period. "This scheme," said the *Stratford Herald* in an
article on the subject, published 22nd May, "has been

pronounced rather meagre, but in justice to the Committee it must be admitted that the difficulties which presented themselves in every direction during the past twelve months, particularly upon the primary question of raising funds while distress pervaded the manufacturing districts to such an alarming extent, were sufficient to damp the ardour of the most enthusiastic, and at one time were considered all but insurmountable." The condition of the people of Lancashire had however become reconciled, and a "county meeting" was convened in the Town Hall, on the 28th May. To that meeting the *Herald* solicited the attention of the town in the following terms :—" We earnestly entreat every inhabitant of the borough and neighbourhood to attend that meeting. Let us not subject ourselves to the reproach of having settled in this locality with a view of sharing the advantages with which the prestige of Shakespeare's name and fame has endowed it, while we shirk the responsibility connected with the becoming celebration of the three hundredth anniversary of his birth."

This appeal was not made in vain, for the attendance at the meeting was very large and highly influential. The chair was taken by Lord Leigh ; and amongst others present on the occasion and taking part in the proceedings, were Sir Robert N. C. Hamilton, Bart., the Rev. the Vicar, C. H. Bracebridge, Esq., E. F. Flower, Esq. (Mayor), J. J. Nason, Esq., Rev. J. C. Young, Dr. Kingsley, J. Jaffray, Esq., Samuel Timmins, Esq., Birmingham, R. H. Hobbes, Esq., James Bennett, Esq. (Tragedian), Mark Phillips, Esq., Mr. R. M. Bird, Mr. James Cox, &c. Sir Robert Hamilton, Bart., submitted for the consideration of the meeting the recommendations of the Committee. An Oratorio, a Concert, and Theatrical Performance were now suggested for the first time, and met with the approval of the meeting.

With respect to the permanent results of the celebration the following propositions were submitted :—

"That the names of persons subscribing one shilling and upwards to a National Memorial of Shakespeare should have their names inscribed on rolls of parchment, to be collected, deposited, and carefully preserved, bound in volumes, and placed in the Museum at the birth-place. That the money thus obtained should be applied as follows :—Firstly, towards extending the educational advantages of the Free Grammar School of King Edward VI., in which Shakespeare received instruction. Secondly, in founding and establishing one or more scholarships or exhibitions at the English Universities in connection with the above school. Thirdly, in giving a triennial prize for the best poem or essay on Shakespeare, open to public competition. And, fourthly, in laying out the gardens at New Place ; opening them to the public, and otherwise celebrating the tercentenary."

After a somewhat desultory discussion on these topics, Lord Leigh put the first resolution to the meeting as follows :—" That the roll of subscribers inserting their names and contributions of one shilling and upwards towards raising a fund for a National Memorial to Shakespeare in the town of his birth shall be carefully bound in volumes and deposited and preserved in the Museum at the birth-place."—Mr. James Bennett then rose, and after some preliminary remarks said : " The scheme laid before them by Sir Robert Hamilton embraced objects that were highly worthy of adoption. Still, the scheme was headed ' National Memorial,' though it was not such. To submit it to the country in its present narrow and local shape, without any addition, and to ask the nation to support it, would ensure nothing but a cold and chilling reception. There was nothing national in it. [Hear, hear.] To be national it must be general. It must be something the nation could participate in and enjoy—[applause]—something of a substantial nature in return for the nation's money. [Applause.] No tribute, in his opinion, could be offered to Shakespeare more appropriate than a statue in his native town, as magnificent as could be a work of art, which should be admired by the succeeding generations—a lasting memorial to the transcendent genius of Shakespeare. [Cheers.] Mr. Bennett concluded by moving that the words, " And that a memorial statue be erected on an appropriate spot in Shakespeare's native town of Stratford-upon-Avon," be added to the foregoing resolution. This proposal having been seconded by Mr. William Harding, and supported in an admirable speech by Mr. James Cox, the Mayor of Stratford (Mr. E. F. Flower) said " he thought that they were now only called upon to decide upon a certain scheme, and it would depend upon the funds at their disposal whether the Committee were able to carry out all the suggestions. With respect to a statue, he knew the liberality of the Corporation of Stratford was such that they would give the ground for its erection, but he could not himself give preference to a statue before the school. As Mayor of the town, he should be happy to assist in carrying out any scheme that might be decided upon." To these views the Mayor has rigidly adhered, and acted upon them steadily throughout the business. Mr. Bennett's proposal, after some discussion, was submitted to the meeting as a substantive motion, when thirty-two voted for, and thirty-two against it. The noble Chairman supported the latter division, and the motion was lost by his casting vote. The propositions of the Committee having been confirmed, it was announced that Lord Leigh's subscription would be a hundred guineas, and Sir Robert Hamilton's twenty guineas, towards the scholarship. The proceedings of this important meeting then terminated; but the people of Stratford were by no means satisfied with the result of the motion in relation to the monument. Determined not to let matters rest where they were, or the important question of monument or no monument to be decided by a single vote, a number of influential promoters of the celebration went vigorously to work, got up a numerously signed requisition to the Mayor requesting him to convene a town's meeting "to discuss the propriety of appealing to the tercentenary Committee, asking them to re-consider their decision " with respect to the monument. Public feeling at this time ran very high on the subject. The Mayor convened the meeting but declined to take the chair, and regarded the movement as a mistake in point of order. " He was," he said, " Mayor of the town, and wanted to serve the towns-people, but he was also one of the tercentenary Committee, and he must obey the order of the public meeting. He felt himself bound by what that

meeting (of the 28th May) did.   It would be painful to
himself and to many others to disregard the expressions of
the public meeting of the town, but it would be impossible
for them to disregard the instructions received from a
public meeting which had been already held, and in which
the town took part." Finding it impossible to change the
Mayor's view of the case, or bring him to see that the town
meeting had a right to ask a re-consideration of a decision
come to by the narrowest possible majority, it was moved,
seconded, and carried, that Mr. Councillor Stephenson take
the chair.   Mr. Stephenson at once acceded to the wishes
of the meeting, and, having taken the chair, Mr. James
Cox, jun., in an eloquent speech which elicited loud cheers,
moved, " That this meeting being of opinion that no scheme
for the commemoration of the three hundredth anniversary
of our great national poet can be considered complete that
does not embrace as a prominent feature a statue or
monumental memorial, to be erected in this his native town,
strongly recommends the tercentenary festival Committee
to take this matter into its most serious consideration with a
view, if possible, to add to the scheme already adopted, and
suggests that separate subscription lists should be opened
to receive such donations as may be offered by the public
for this object."   Mr. John Lane seconded the motion in the
absence of Mr. Robert Walker, who was to have done so.
Messrs. Hobbes and Kendall dissented from the proceedings
and expressed their concurrence in the course taken by the
Mayor.   Mr. E. T. Craig, phrenologist, Warwick (who had
previously promulgated the idea of the exhibition of
portraits, which was ultimately carried out and formed a
handsome feature in the late celebration), ably supported the
motion, which was carried unanimously, and addressed to
Dr. Kingsley, Honorary Secretary of the Committee.
    To show that they meant all they said, the promoters
of the monument proceeded to collect funds for the purpose, and succeeded so well (having obtained in a very short
time subscriptions amounting to nearly £1,000), that the
Committee felt constrained to accept as part of their scheme
the erection of a monumental memorial at Stratford-upon-

Avon. It proved far and away the most popular item of the programme, shoved the prize poem idea aside, and obtained five times as much support as any project of the Committee ; and it may be here remarked that, as the money then and subsequently subscribed cannot be applied to any other object without the permission of the subscribers, the monument is not yet by any means "past praying for."

The next move of the promoters of the monumental memorial was made in the Corporation, on the 4th of August, when, after some discussion, the following resolution was carried :—" That the Corporation, highly concurring in the objects of the tercentenary Committee, offer a subscription of £50 for each of the three objects announced, on the same conditions as the other subscribers." On the 26th of the same month, a general meeting of the Committee was held at the Town Hall, presided over by Sir R. N. C. Hamilton, Bart., K.C.B. The minutes of the meeting held in June having been read, the report of the finance Committee was submitted by Mr. R. H. Hobbes, by which it appeared that £253 for the school, £931 for the monumental memorial, and £231 for the general expenses had been promised to be subscribed. Of these sums £61 14s. had only been paid, and £31 14s. 4d. expended. The report then suggested several matters for the consideration of the meeting, among others, that of a paid Secretary, the appointment of a working Committee, &c. This report was adopted, and it was agreed that a paid Secretary should be appointed. A letter to the Chairman from Dr. Kingsley, tendering his resignation as Honorary Secretary was read. The resignation was accepted, and a vote of thanks passed to Dr. Kingsley for his services. Mr. J. S. Leaver, who had been acting Secretary with Dr. Kingsley, remained in office for a fortnight longer. The business terminated after the adoption of the following resolutions :—Moved by the Rev. G. Granville, seconded by Mr. F. Kendall, and resolved :— " That the Secretary be authorised to call meetings of the tercentenary Committee at the request of any of the

Sub-committees, and that the Mayor be appointed a Vice-chairman of the tercentenary Committee, and that meetings of the Committee be held every alternate Monday, at the Town Hall, at eleven o'clock." Proposed by Mr. R. H. Hobbes, seconded by the Rev. G. Granville, and resolved :—
" That all subscribers be requested to pay the amount of their subscriptions into the banks, upon the assurance that if the separate objects cannot be carried out the amount of subscriptions, after a *pro rata* deduction for the expenses, shall be repaid to the respective subscribers." Proposed by Mr. W. O. Hunt, seconded by Mr. Hobbes, and resolved :—
" That no resolution passed at any meeting shall be re-scinded but at a special meeting called for the purpose, of which notice shall be given to each member. That Mr. R. H. Hobbes, as Chairman of the finance Committee, be requested to write to Mr. R. E. Hunter, and ascertain his terms for his services as Secretary to the Committee."

The Sub-committees referred to in the first resolution comprised, as originally named, the Finance, Building, Déjeuner, Miscellaneous Concert, Dramatic Representations, Dramatic Readings, Excursion, Fancy Ball, General Amusement, Oratorio, Prize Poem, Scholarships, Railway, Address and Advertisement, and New Place Gardens Committees. Subsequently a Site and Memorial Committee was appointed, and all the small Committees having charge of any of the amusements were broken up and a General Entertainment Committee formed to carry out the programme. On the 7th of September I received the appointment of Secretary, an office which I held until the 23rd of March following, when I resigned, and subsequently rapidly recovered my health and spirit, both impaired by domestic calamities and the toils and anxieties of my situation. Enough of self.

On the Committee at the date of my advent, I found the following gentlemen :—

Sir ROBERT N. C. HAMILTON, Bart., K.C.B., *Chairman.*
The Rev. G. GRANVILLE, Vicar of Stratford, *Vice-chairman.*
E. F. FLOWER, Esq., the Mayor (ex-officio), *Vice-chairman.*

Mr. W. J. Harding, *Baraset* (Gentleman). | Mr. C. H. Bracebridge (Gentleman).

Dr. Thomson, *Leamington*.
Mr. M. Philips (Gentleman).
The Rev. W. Morton (Curate of Stratford).
Mr. Robert H. Hobbes (Solicitor).
Mr. J. S. Craig (Surgeon).
Mr. W. O. Hunt (Solicitor).
Dr. Kingsley, *Stratford*.
The Rev. Julian C. Young (Rector of Ilmington).
Mr. C. E. Flower (Brewer).
Mr. F. Kendal (Dispensing Chemist).
Mr. E. Adams (Bookseller, &c.).
Mr. W. Stephenson (Watchmaker).
Mr. Edgar Flower (Brewer).
Mr. Bird (Wine and Spirit Merchant).
Mr. Edward Gibbs (Architect).
Mr. W. G. Colbourne (Architect).
Mr. W. Thompson (Architect).
Mr. William Gibbs, *Alveston* (Farmer).

Mr. H. Mathews (Professor of Music).
Mr. J. Archer (Maltster).
Mr. W. G. F. Bolton (Shakespeare Hotel).
Mr. W. Lowry (Red Horse Hotel).
Mr. James Cox (Timber Merchant).
Mr. Atkinson (Second Master of the Grammar School).
Mr. J. J. Nason (Surgeon).
Mr. H. Samman (Draper, &c.).
Mr. M. Lucy, *Malvern*.
Mr. J. Morgan (Bookseller, &c.).
Mr. E. Nason, *Leamington*.
Mr. E. R. Hartley (Commercial Traveller).
Mr. James Bennett (Tragedian).
Mr. J. C. Warden (Attorney).
Mr. H. Lane (Surgeon).
Mr. C. F. Loggin (Chemist).
Mr. W. L. Norris (Family Grocer).

Sir Robert Hamilton, Bart., although not in the habit of attending the committee meetings, was ever ready when called upon to give his advice and co-operation; to which, it is needless for me to say, his character and distinguished position imparted no ordinary value. The Vicar occupied the chair occasionally, and always to the advantage and general gratification of the members present, by whom his dignity and courtesy were fully appreciated. His spare time was always at the command of the Committee. Mr. E. F. Flower (the Mayor), on his return from a tour in Germany, became, in theatrical language, the "stock" Chairman. He almost invariably conducted the proceedings; and his labours in travelling on deputations, in the writing of public and private letters, the making of speeches, and in the consultations and negotiations connected with the arduous undertaking, are matters of general notoriety. Whether a division of labour, by which deputations from the general Committee, selected weekly, would have made the movement known throughout the provinces, and delegated authority, being thus more generally shared, would have conduced to a more lively festival or a more fortunate *dénouement* than I shall have it in my power to record, I will not take upon myself in this place to affirm, inasmuch as the prodigious activity of the Mayor received not only the *fiat*, but the high commendation of the Committee.

Touching the general body, I may remark that although warmly interested in the cause, Messrs. W. J. Harding, C. H. Bracebridge, and M. Philips, were but occasionally in attendance. Messrs. W. O. Hunt, Edward Gibbs, E. Nason, and Mr. .H. Lane I never saw in the committee room. The Rev. Mr. Young's attendance was interrupted by indisposition. When present he took every occasion to impress the members with his own lively apprehension of unwarrantable pecuniary liabilities. The Rev. Mr. Morton was always ready to discharge his share of the duties of membership, and rendered good service in getting up the musical department of the entertainments. Messrs. C. and E. Flower were energetic lieutenants, as well as sons of the Mayor. Dr. Kingsley acted as Hon. Secretary at first and last, and had his full share of the troubles and fatigues of office. Mr. F. Kendall was a useful member, whose opinions, being those of a magistrate of the borough, and ex-mayor, always commanded the attention of the Committee. Mr. Edward Adams officiated prior to my advent as Secretary to the finance Committee, and as the proprietor of the *Stratford Herald* extended to the movement those advantages which the newspaper press alone can confer. Mr. Stephenson and Mr. Cox had clear and lofty views of the rights and duties of Stratford-upon-Avon on the tercentenary of Shakespeare's birthday. They never feared an agitation in London, or the prestige of any name as against Stratford, and worked earnestly, particularly the latter mentioned gentleman, to secure the success of the festival. Mr. R. H. Hobbes acted as Chairman of the finance Committee, a post of sufficient trouble and difficulty. Mr. R. M. Bird and J. Archer were in constant attendance at all meetings, general and committee, and indefatigable in their exertions, especially in the business connected with the erection of the pavilion. Mr. Atkinson was a clear headed and sound counsellor. Mr. Nason, a member of the finance Committee, and very regular in his attendance, as became a medical practitioner. Mr. James Bennett must be always a useful coadjutor in every matter involving dramatic performances, and *when* authorised by the Committee, discharged the duties allotted to him conscientiously. Mr. Morgan, as correspondent of the *Birmingham Post*, and proprietor of the *Stratford Chronicle*, gave full and regular publicity to the proceedings, and as assistant Hon. Secretary worked for a period night and day in forwarding the business. Messrs. Thompson and Colbourne were generally present at the weekly meetings, but as architects of the building their time and attention were fully occupied. The other members either resided at a distance, or were so engaged in their own affairs, as to have little time to devote to the public service. To the above list several valuable members were subsequently added. Amongst these the first place must be assigned to Mr. William Greener, gunmaker, whose constant attendance and active services made it a matter of regret that the Committee had not had the benefit of his co-operation from the commencement. Messrs. Langford and Chance, of the *Birmingham Gazette*, came also rather late into the field, but made up for that in some measure by the regularity of their attendance, and the interest they took in the proceedings.

Amongst those who, whilst not connected with the Committee, were amongst the most active and useful friends of the cause, I am bound to record the names of Mr. Robert Walker (ex-mayor), and Mr. John Lane, Solicitor, whose absence from the roll of the Committee must be regarded as a serious loss to the celebration. By their exertions the fund was first established, and by their ability as financiers, had they been on the Committee, the exchequer would have been much benefited, whilst grave mistakes might have been prevented in the important business of expenditure.

As some curiosity will probably exist hereafter to know not only the names but the occupations of the Committee, and the part enacted by each, or the degree of service rendered to the memory of Shakespeare in 1864, I have thought it not irrelevant to make this brief notice here of the respective claims of the members on the gratitude of those who, looking back to the memorable year, may regard their labours with approval ; and I now return to the narrative.

On the 7th September, the date last mentioned, the building Committee brought up their first report, in which they stated that having taken into consideration the various purposes for which a building would be required in the celebration of the Shakespeare tercentenary, they recommended the erection of a structure capable of accommodating five thousand persons, and the immediate advertising for tenders. At the next meeting, on the 21st September, a difficulty which might have become serious was removed, when Mr. R. H. Hobbes informed the meeting that an excellent site had been obtained for the erection of a spacious decagon building for the festival, Mr. T. Mason having in the kindest manner consented to place his paddock in Southern's Lane at the disposal of the Committee. It was then proposed by Mr. Hobbes, seconded by Mr. Charles Flower, and resolved :—" That the best thanks of the Committee be given to Mr. T. Mason for his liberality in granting the use of the field in Southern's Lane for the tercentenary festival, and the Committee engage to make compensation, and to repair all damage that may be done, and to give up possession as soon as possible after the 31st April next."

That matter of somewhat important detail having been disposed of, it was moved by Mr. Bennett, seconded by Mr. Kendall, and resolved :—" That steps be immediately taken to form branch Committees at Birmingham and other towns, to co-operate with the general Committee in Stratford, in making arrangements for the tercentenary celebration." Messrs. Cox, Bennett, and the Secretary, were authorised to act in the matter, and to proceed to the neighbouring towns for the purpose mentioned in the resolution.

This was the first step taken towards obtaining the co-operation of the country. As authorised, we proceeded to Birmingham a few days afterwards. At this period the London Committee were "making the running;" every copy of the *Athenæum* contained the names of magnates of all descriptions added to their lists. The hopes of Stratford were, comparatively speaking, anything but brilliant. I never, however, despaired of the attractions of the birth and burial place of Shakespeare, and, in an article I published at this period, prophesied that wherever a statue might be founded the festival would be in Stratford-upon-Avon.

It so happened, however, that on the evening prior to the visit of the Stratford deputation to Birmingham a public meeting had been held there, on behalf of London—the Rev. Dr. Miller in the chair. We thought the field pre-occupied, but determined nevertheless to call upon Dr. Miller. He received us with courtesy, admitted the claims of Stratford upon Birmingham under all the circumstances, and suggested that a conference, to which he kindly offered accommodation in his own house, should be held by the friends of the celebration, with a view of coming to a common understanding respecting the somewhat conflicting interests of London and Stratford, to see what amount of support could be extended to both by the people of Birmingham, keeping at the same time in view their own project of a Shakespearian library.

We at once adopted the Doctor's suggestions, and waited upon a number of influential gentlemen, who all consented to attend the conference on receiving timely notice to that effect. The holding of this conference was, however, postponed from time to time, for one reason and another, and ultimately Dr. Miller, not approving of some portions of the Stratford Committee's programme, declined to have anything to do with the conference. It was not therefore till the 18th December that any action was really taken in Birmingham on behalf of Stratford, when Mr. Holliday, the Mayor, convened a town's meeting, which was attended by Mr. E. F. Flower, Mr. Cox, and Mr. W. Greener. Speeches having been made by the Mayors of Birmingham and Stratford, it was moved by Alderman Hawkes, seconded by Mr. S. Timmins, and resolved:—"That this meeting fully recognises

the strong claims which the local Committee of Stratford-
upon-Avon have upon the public generally throughout the
kingdom, and especially upon Birmingham, for co-operation
and assistance in their determination to celebrate the
tercentenary of Shakespeare's birth." Stratford has now
celebrated with some splendour, and at considerable expense,
the tercentenary of Shakespeare's birth; and, as Birmingham has sanctioned all the proceedings of the local
Committee, it is to be hoped the metropolis of Warwickshire will really give that "co-operation and assistance"
necessary to not only balance the ledger, as matters now
stand, but carry out the programme in its entirety.

A commencement having been thus made in the agitation
of the country, other modes were adopted for obtaining
support and patronage to the undertaking. Early in October
a circular letter was published by the Committee. I was
amongst a few who thought the address from Stratford to
the public, even if a little florid in style, ought to be drawn
up with a view to excite a degree of enthusiasm on the
subject in the general mind, but a brief and bald statement
of facts was preferred, and the Committee issued the following epistle :—

" Tercentenary of the Birth of Shakespeare.

" Committee Room,
" Sir,   " Town Hall, Stratford-upon-Avon, 1863.

"As the town in which Shakespeare was born, bred, and educated;
which he chose for his home in the decline of life, and in which he
died and was buried, Stratford-upon-Avon is assuredly the most
appropriate spot for a tercentenary celebration in his honour. The
better to secure this object in 1864, the following noblemen and
gentlemen have agreed to act as President and Vice-presidents, and
a local Committee has been appointed with power to add to its
numbers. [Here the list of the Vice-presidents and local Committee,
which appears in full hereafter, was given, as it stood at this early
stage of the business.]

" The festival will be extended over four or five days.

" On Saturday, the 23rd of April, there will be a banquet for ladies
and gentlemen, at which the Earl of Carlisle will preside, and deliver
an address. He will be supported on the occasion by many Members
of both Houses of Parliament, and others eminent in the walks of art,
literature, and science.

" On other days there will be Excursions to various places in the vicinity of Stratford-upon-Avon, illustrative of incidents in Shakespeare's life, under the guidance of gentlemen well qualified for the task ; Critical Analyses of Shakespeare's Plays ; a Grand Oratorio (to which many of our leading vocalists have already consented to contribute their services), and a Miscellaneous Concert. The comedy of 'As You Like It,' and one of Shakespeare's tragedies will be represented by a combination of metropolitan and provincial talent. There will also be a Shakespearian Fancy Ball.

" One day will be devoted exclusively to popular amusements.

" Each day's proceedings will be fully specified in a subsequent prospectus.

" The substantial objects to which the pecuniary results of the festival will be devoted, are—

"1st—The Endowment of one or more Scholarships to one of the Universities, open to the competition of those who have received their education at the same school at which Shakespeare received his, viz., The Free Grammar School founded by King Edward VI.

" 2nd—The Erection of a Monumental Memorial at Stratford-upon-Avon.

" The Committee respectfully solicit your favourable consideration of their enterprise, and trust that with your countenance and co-operation the issue may be worthy of the cause.

" While they reserve to themselves the privilege of expanding or modifying their programme according to circumstances, they beg to assure you that the larger the funds with which they may be entrusted the more energetic will be their efforts to render the occasion august and memorable.

" Signed on behalf of the Committee,
" ROBERT E. HUNTER,
" Secretary.

" Donations and subscriptions will be received by Messrs. Glyn and Co., Messrs. Smith, Payne, and Smith, and Messrs. Hanbury and Co., Bankers, London ; Messrs. Greenway, Smith, and Greenway, Bankers, Warwick ; the Stourbridge and Kidderminster Banking Company, and the Warwick and Leamington Banking Company, Stratford-upon-Avon.

" Subscribers are requested to specify the object for which they desire their subscriptions to be appropriated, viz., M for the Monumental Memorial ; S for the Scholarship ; and F for the Festival Fund."

Of this document no less than twenty thousand were circulated, the greater number through the post office.

It was also deemed advisable and desirable that the co-operation of the great societies and organisations of the country, as the Masons, Odd-Fellows, Foresters, Trade Societies, &c., should be enlisted, but the time for all this mass of work was extremely limited. A beginning was however made with the Odd-Fellows, from whom one penny each would have realised upwards of £1,300. The following circular letter was addressed to nearly four thousand lodges:—

" Tercentenary of the Birth of Shakespeare.

" Committee Room,

" Sir,   " Town Hall, Stratford-upon-Avon, December, 1863.

" As instructed, I have the pleasure of addressing to you a copy of the following resolution, unanimously adopted by the Shakespeare and Bank of Avon Lodges of Odd-Fellows :—

' That having had a full official statement of the intentions and plans of the Stratford Committee, organised for the celebration of the Shakespeare tercentenary, laid before us, we fully approve of the same, and subscribe *each one penny* towards the fund for the erection of a monument to the memory of Shakespeare in this town, and respectfully but earnestly recommend the brethren of the Unity to do likewise ; and that application be made to the next District Committee, and to the Board of Directors for leave to circulate the address throughout the Unity.'

" I have also to acquaint you that the above-named lodges conferred an additional favour on the tercentenary Committee by sending a deputation to the Quarterly Meeting of the Birmingham District Committee, held on the 5th Oct., and their representations to that important body resulted, I am happy to say, in the following resolution :—

' That the memorial from the Shakespeare and Bank of Avon Lodges, on behalf of the Shakespearian tercentenary Committee, be received and adopted, and that they be allowed to circulate it throughout the district ; and that this meeting recommend it to the next A.M.C. for general adoption.'

" Thus accredited I take leave to request that you would have the great kindness to lay these resolutions before the next meeting of your lodge, and trust that they will have the goodness to give their patronage and pecuniary support in a similar manner to this national effort to do honour to the memory of Shakespeare. I enclose a copy of the Committee's programmes for the festival, and

" I am, Sir, very faithfully yours,

" ROBERT E. HUNTER,

" Secretary.

" N.B.—The names of the lodges with the amounts respectively contributed will be recorded on parchment, and deposited at Shakespeare's birth-place.

" P.S.—Since the lodges were first addressed as above, several generous responses have been received."

The responses to this appeal came in very slowly indeed; and as I knew the Odd-Fellows to be a highly intelligent body of men, who must have perceived that with very little exertion on their part they had it in their power to contribute largely to the funds of a laudably national demonstration, I could not account for their apathy. At last it was discovered there was an informality in the mode of procedure. The Odd-Fellows who stimulated the Committee to address the body at large misunderstood the extent of authority requisite for the purpose. A counter circular was issued by, I believe, the "A.M.C.," and a very few pounds came in towards the defraying of the expenses incurred by an appeal to the Odd-Fellows. Surely they must know that the informality of the procedure was a mere error of judgment on the part of one of their own Order, and I trust it is not yet too late to induce them to do themselves the honour of contributing to the tercentenary celebration at Stratford-upon-Avon.

Reverting to the labours of the Committee in the forming of branch Committees in the neighbouring towns, I find that, after Birmingham, their efforts were next directed to Worcester, whither Mr. Charles Flower, the Rev. Mr. Morton, and I, proceeded about the middle of October. We were very well received by the Mayor, Mr. F. Parker, and a number of other gentlemen, who all consented to act on a Committee to collect funds, and co-operate with Stratford in the celebration. A public meeting was afterwards held, which was attended by the Mayor of Stratford, at which this Committee was regularly constituted, and subsequently a considerable number of parchment documents (provided for the enrolment and preservation of the names of subscribers, as mentioned in the first proposition of the Committee to the public meeting) were sent to Mr. Parker (local Secretary) at his request; but the amount realised in Worcester towards the object has not yet been ascertained.

Having thus enlisted Worcester in the service, a deputation consisting of Mr. Nason, Mr. Bird, and myself, as requested by the Committee, visited Warwick on the 4th of

November.   We were received by the Mayor (Mr. Smith),
Mr. C. D. Greenway, Mr. C. Redfern, and some other gentlemen at the Court House.   Having explained our mission, the
Mayor and other gentlemen present expressed their hearty
sympathy with the movement.   Mr. Smith said that in
consequence of his term of office having nearly expired,
his retirement from the position of Chief Magistrate would
prevent him giving that official prestige and support to the
undertaking which it was desirable it should receive, and
to which it was fairly entitled.   However, he hoped his
successor would extend his patronage to the laudable movement, and take an interest in the labours of any Committee
which might be formed in the town, and he (Mr. Smith)
would certainly give in his own name as a member of such
Committee.   The cause, so far as the co-operation of Warwick was concerned, was committed to these gentlemen; but
the full fruits of their labours have not yet been ascertained.

Having made a move in Birmingham and Warwick, the
Committee lengthened their cords, and the Mayor, duly
accredited, visited Manchester as an ambassador from
Stratford.   A meeting of the Committee, previously formed
" for the purpose of promoting some worthy commemoration
of our great poet," took place in the Mayor's parlour on
the 14th of December.   This Committee had no special
purpose in their mind's eye, or any plan of action drawn up.
They were in communication with the London Committee,
then very popular—the Thackeray *fiasco* had not come to
light—and they contemplated a Shakespeare scholarship at
Owen's College and the Grammar School.   Mr. Flower having
made a lucid statement of the case of Stratford-upon-Avon,
several gentlemen (I quote from the *Examiner* and *Times*
of the following day) said the Manchester Committee was
agreed about not sending money to the London Committee.
It was also stated that the Manchester scholarships would
cost about £2,500, and the bust £120 ; and to render the
desired assistance to the Stratford Committee, it would be
necessary to collect a sum of £4,000.   The raising of this
sum was agreed to.   Mr. Ashton then proposed the
following resolution :—

" That this Committee fully recognises the strong claims which the local Committee of Stratford-upon-Avon has upon the public generally throughout the kingdom for co-operation and assistance in their determination to secure at Stratford a national monument; and that this Committee undertakes, in such a manner as may be hereafter determined, to give their cordial assistance to such local Committee."

The motion was seconded by Mr. Oliver Heywood. Mr. Walker and Dr. Watts were added to the list of Honorary Secretaries, and Mr. Crossley was appointed Treasurer. The Committee then adjourned. The "cordial assistance " undertaken to be given has not yet appeared, but there is no doubt it will come in good time. The people of Manchester would be the last in the world to waive any legitimate responsibility or forget any public engagement.

Proceeding on his mission in the north the Mayor visited Liverpool on the 21st of this month (Dec.), where he found the minds of the influential inhabitants preoccupied with the London scheme and the splendour of its list of Vice-presidents. The Mayor, however, and a number of the leading men of the great commercial *entrepôt* were present at the meeting, and subsequently enrolled their names amongst the Vice-presidents of the Stratford-upon-Avon Committee. Early in January a public meeting was held in Leamington, pursuant to arrangement for some time in formation. The chair was taken by J. Haddon, Esq., and the following resolution, proposed by Mr. Alexander Campbell, and seconded by Mr. Muddeman, was carried unanimously :—

" That this meeting recognises the propriety of celebrating the tercentenary of the birth of Shakespeare in the town of Stratford-upon-Avon, where he was born, where he passed a great part of his early and late life, where he died, and where his remains have been interred, and which has become the resort of pilgrims of all the civilised nations of the earth."

The next resolution was moved by the Rev. G. F. Clark, seconded by Dr. Thomson, and also carried unanimously:—

" That this meeting, acknowledging the strong claims Stratford-upon-Avon has upon the public generally for co-operation and support, and recognising the peculiar obligations of this county to take part in properly celebrating the tercentenary of the birth of the Warwickshire poet, readily accepts the call now made upon the town of Leamington and the neighbourhood for its sympathy and cordial support."

A Committee to carry out these resolutions was next formed, to consist of J. Haddon, Esq., Chairman, the Revds. Dr. Bickmore and T. B. Whitehurst, Drs. Thomson and Jeaffreson, Signor Brezzi, Messrs. P. W. Martin, M.P., A. Campbell, F. Dinsdale, F. Manning, J. Hitchman, J. Glover, J. Biddle, — Bushby, T. Muddeman, W. Cookes, T. Wilson, L. Bishop, — Gascoyne, — Watkin, H. Uppleby, and J. Leech. A considerable sum was subscribed in the room, and it was resolved to open lists at the various banks, to receive further subscriptions. The pecuniary result of this canvas of Leamington was two hundred odd pounds, some time afterwards lodged to the credit of the tercentenary Committee, and although the sum did not quite realise the expectations of Stratford, it is, I regret to say, about the only instance of prompt and business-like action as yet worked out to completion by any of the branch Committees.

The next important step taken towards securing the co-operation of the country was in Newcastle-on-Tyne, where the *Press* had prepared the way for a deputation from Stratford. On Monday, the 1st February, an influential meeting was convened by the Mayor (Thomas Hedley, Esq.), at which Mr. Flower attended. A Committee had been previously formed to arrange a local demonstration, but after hearing a statement from the Mayor of Stratford, and subsequent explanation of matters of detail connected with the festival, it was moved by Mr. Bainbridge, seconded by Mr. John Clayton, and resolved:—" That in the opinion of this meeting, Stratford-upon-Avon is the proper place for the erection of a monumental memorial to Shakespeare," and with the view of extending substantial sympathy to their undertaking, it was moved by Mr. Cowen, jun., seconded by Mr. William Lockey Harle, and resolved :—" That a subscription list be opened for contributions in aid of the

Stratford Committee, with liberty for any subscriber to allot his subscription to any one or more of the proposed objects—the Stratford Festival—the Scholarship, or the Memorial." Arrangements were then made for the carrying out of this resolution in a business like manner, and the proceedings terminated.

The Mayor subsequently visited Edinburgh, Glasgow, and other towns, and addressed public meetings. He elicited expressions of individual sympathy and promises of support, but not those positive pledges of co-operation which the occasion might have called forth, and which would have been more encouraging to the Stratford Committee. Efforts were made in London too, at sundry times and in various ways, on behalf of Stratford, but to little purpose.

In further pursuance of the plan of organisation adopted, Mr. James Bennett, who was proceeding to the south of England on professional business, was authorised to promote the ventilation of the subject in Southampton, Portsmouth, Brighton, and other towns which he purposed visiting. He did so and obtained the cordial support of the gentlemen of the press, by whom the agitation was made familiar to the wide circle of their readers.

That no other city or town disposed to assist Stratford in the effort being made to do honour to Shakespeare's memory should have any reason to hold back from so doing, the following circular letter was addressed to mayors and chief magistrates throughout England and Scotland :—

" *Tercentenary of the Birth of Shakespeare.*

" Committee Room, Town Hall,
" Stratford-upon-Avon, December, 1863.

" Sir (or My Lord),
" At the request of the Committee I have the honour to apprise you that the movement having for its object the celebration of the tercentenary of Shakespeare's birth, and which has existed at Stratford-upon-Avon with more or less activity for two years, has so far realised the expectations of the Committee as to assume a truly national character.

" The Committee are in communication with London, Edinburgh, Dublin, Manchester, Liverpool, Birmingham, Worcester, Gloucester,

H

Leicester, Warwick, Leamington, Rugby, Southampton, Portsmouth, Brighton, Newcastle-on-Tyne, Banbury, Redditch, West Bromwich, Stroud, &c., &c., at many of which places auxiliary Committees have already been formed.

"The erection of a grand national monumental memorial in the town where Shakespeare was born, lived, and died, will necessarily involve considerable outlay. Several thousand pounds have already been subscribed, and it is fully expected that adequate funds will be realised for the purpose.

"The Committee meet weekly, and Sub-committees daily, to carry out the necessary arrangements for the celebration. A pavilion to accommodate between five and six thousand persons is now in course of construction.

"The dramatic performances will be supported by the most eminent metropolitan and provincial actors. The oratorio and concert by the first *artistes* of the musical world, a number of whom have already promised their gratuitous services.

"All the arrangements are being rapidly perfected, so as to make the celebration one of truly national grandeur, and worthy of the transcendent genius whose memory it is designed to honour.

"As it is important to enlist the active sympathies of all the principal towns in the United Kingdom, permit me to request that you will kindly acquaint me with your views as to the best means of securing the co-operation of the town over which you preside.

"I remain, Sir,
"Your obedient Servant,
"R. E. HUNTER, Secretary."

Whilst thus struggling to bring about the joint operation of all England in discharging the national duty of doing homage to the memory of the "genius of the isle," anxious eyes were cast daily to the *press* to see what amount of support was likely to come from that quarter. The Mayor sent the following letter to the *Times*:—

"*To the Editor of the* TIMES.
"Sir,
"The small borough of Stratford-upon-Avon, of which I am Mayor, appeals to you in a difficulty. As the town where Shakespeare was born and bred, where he lived his last days, and where he lies buried, it is a sort of Mecca, which many pilgrims visit, and which, without any choice in the matter, is forced to undertake a great work in view of the next anniversary of the poet's birthday. Months ago we believed that if there would be any national celebration of that day it would, in these railway times, be held at Stratford, and with the help of our Lord-Lieutenant we formed a Committee, under the presidency of Lord Carlisle, to make preparations accordingly. No sooner

was this done than a Committee was formed in London, not to assist us, but to get up a national celebration in the metropolis. This cut to pieces the nationality of our undertaking. We accepted our altered circumstances with the greatest humility, and set to work upon a smaller scale, content if we could but make a good local celebration of our great townsman's birthday. A few weeks elapsed and we found the provincial towns generally looking to Stratford-upon-Avon as their centre, applying to us to know what we were doing, and offering to aid us if we would undertake what might be regarded as a national celebration. In fear and trembling we again accepted the altered circumstances, and have put forth a scheme much too comprehensive to be met alone by local labour and money. Now, therefore, we want a metropolitan organisation to help us in carrying out this vast undertaking—the arrangement of a festival worthy of a nation, the erection of a monument to the world's greatest poet, and the application of a fund to some useful educational purpose.

"I have nothing to say against the London Committee; on the contrary, I wish them God-speed; but I find that a number of eminent men have joined that Committee in ignorance that we at Stratford are engaged in a similar work; and we appeal to you as the leader of the press to give that publicity to our design which the London Committee enjoy through many channels.

"I know that London is willing to help us. In one day's canvas there I obtained more names as Vice-presidents of our Committee and more money than I expected to find in many days, and already we have had more than £2,000 subscribed.

"And now, Sir, we appeal to you to favour us by publishing this letter. Circumstances have forced the little town of Stratford to undertake duties and responsibilities which, without assistance, it cannot fulfil. Provincial assistance we obtain without stint, but we desire also the sympathy of the metropolis.

"We are plain men of business, engaged in a simple duty which we have not sought. As such, however, we have claims which are entitled to respect. It was only the other day that *Punch* accused various persons who propose to build monuments to Shakespeare of only wishing to raise pedestals to their own glory. I do not know whether this sarcasm is merited, but at all events it cannot apply to us. We have no selfish object to serve; we have no literary reputation to buoy up by pushing ourselves needlessly forward.

"We are in a peculiar position from which we cannot escape, and we now desire the co-operation and advice of all men—men of rank, men of wealth, men of letters, men of influence, in any class who think that Stratford-upon-Avon, as the birth-place, the chosen residence, and the burial place of Shakespeare, is the most appropriate spot for a national celebration of the tercentenary of his birth.

"I remain, Sir, your obedient servant,

"E. F. FLOWER,

"The Hill, Dec. 8."   "Mayor of Stratford-upon-Avon.

As a matter of course this letter attracted the general attention of the country to the movement for the celebration of Shakespeare's three hundredth birthday, and procured adherents to Stratford from various quarters.

The local newspapers, the press of Birmingham, and several provincial journals had given steady support to Stratford. The London press apparently, and naturally too, expecting something overwhelming and all-absorbing from the labours of the London Committee and their formidable list of Vice-presidents, for several months ignored the exertions of the Committee here to celebrate the memory of Shakespeare; but on the 29th of October, the *Morning Post* (the early and steady friend of the Stratford celebration) declared, in an article on the subject, " it was impossible that Stratford could be left out in any adequate commemoration of the great bard." One might say that was a very safe platitude at any time, but at the period in question it was a very startling deliverance to many a metropolitan lover of "the poet of all circles," who had never thought of a rival celebration.

Expectation was on tip-toe respecting the performance of the London or "National Committee," and I know that their own anticipations were in the zenith of hope touching the achievement of the 23rd of April; but throughout November they did nothing save add names to their list of Vice-presidents, and the public became impatient to see something practical projected. Stratford was then some months in the field with a well-digested programme. Early in December occurred the wretched blunder by which that marvellous compound of genius and literary acquirements—the author of "Vanity Fair"—was excluded from the office of Vice-president. On the morning of the 24th of the same month the country heard with sad consternation that William Makepeace Thackeray was no more. The fatal event was also fatal to the National Committee. Previously complained of for slowness and mismanagement, they were now universally denounced for something worse. I have frequently thought they were a body of literary gentlemen " more sinned against than sinning ; " but be that as it may, they were most unfortunate in the management of their undertaking.

As the London Committee declined in public confidence and esteem, the Stratford Committee rose in popularity. The London press discovered their existence, and directed attention to their labours. Articles more or less favourable appeared in the *Daily News*, the *Telegraph*, and *Star*, and on the 20th of January the *Times* declared for Stratford in the following terms :—

" In honour of Shakespeare there are two Committees at work— the one in Stratford, the other in London. Both claim to be regarded as national—both declare that they are powerfully supported—and yet both cannot succeed. There may be in the public mind enough of sympathy for one : there is not enough for two. One of the two must either be extinguished altogether or become auxiliary to the other. See what is wanted. Each of the Committees proposes as the principal object of its scheme to build a monument. We do not like the idea of a monument at all. There are monuments enough. Above all, we stare at the suggestion that the foundation of the monument is to be laid on the 23rd of April. In three months the money is to be collected, the site chosen, the artist appointed, the design drawn, and the first stone laid. It must be a wonderful Committee that will do all this. And we are to have two magnificent monuments, worthy of the nation, worthy of Shakespeare. Where are they to come from ? It would be a task of no ordinary difficulty to get one ; two are impossible. We warn our literary friends not to be over sanguine. They may deem themselves lucky if they get money enough for one good monument, and the question is, shall this monument be at Stratford or in London. Our sympathy, in so far as we have any sympathy with the movement, goes to Stratford, both as a matter of necessity and from a sense of justice.

The necessity lies herein that London stands for itself almost alone. The provincial towns are supporting Stratford, and will continue to support it. Against the metropolis the cry of centralisation has been raised. Manchester, Birmingham, and, if we mistake not, Liverpool, have all declared for Stratford ; and this is but a sign of what the provinces intend. They, and not only they, but all Europe and all America, when they give to Shakespeare a local habitation, think of him not in connection with London, but in connection with Stratford, where he was born, where he was educated, where he married and had children, where his family seem always to have lived even when he himself was in London, where he visited them from year to year, where as he grew in wealth he bought house and lands, where he retired in the fulness of his strength to enjoy his days, where he died, and where he now lies buried.   He came to London to push his fortune and to make his reputation; but he left it soon, there was a prospect of long days before him in his native town, and he died there in his prime, one year younger than Mr. Thackeray.   Stratford, then, is the locality with which Shakespeare's name is chiefly associated.   We of the metropolis are bound to remember this, and must not be selfish.   The country towns have often assisted London, and it would be a graceful thing for London now to assist a small country town—Shakespeare's town.   All things conspire to this end.   For not only, if London acted differently, would it fail to obtain in any important degree the support of the provinces; it is divided against itself.   We cannot take part in the feuds which distract what is elegantly called the National Shakespeare Committee of London; but there is no doubt that this Committee has been badly managed, that its executive has not been wisely chosen, and that it has lost, if it ever possessed, the public confidence.   To this day the Committee of Management is unknown to the public.   It is true that in various circulars which we have all seen the Committee is described as made up of four hundred persons, some of high station and repute.   But these are mere names.   Who are the working Committee?   At a meeting of the large Committee of four hundred held the other day to decide upon a report not a fifth part of the grand list attended; those who did attend were at daggers drawn; the acting Committee could not get their report passed; they were not allowed even to withdraw it; and they had to submit to the ignominy of its rejection by vote.   After a vote of this kind, equivalent to a vote of censure, the acting Committee, whoever they are, ought to re-consider their position and their objects.   There is nothing left for them but either to abandon their original project, or to constitute themselves into a London Committee, auxiliary to the one at Stratford.   In point of fact, a number of the names in their general Committee, such as those of Lord Carlisle, Lord Houghton, and Mr. Tennyson, have already appeared on the Stratford list, and to-day it is announced that such men as Mr. Tom Taylor, Mr. Theodore Martin, and Mr. Shirley Brooks, refuse to have anything more to do with the London Committee.   Their example is sure to be followed; the London Committee seem doomed to failure, and should be warned in time.   In whatever is done for the honour of Shakespeare unanimity is required, and our counsels are for peace and unanimity.   We speak with perfect impartiality, for we must repeat that the scheme of a monument finds no favour in our eyes, from whomsoever it comes."

It was now determined to appeal to the general press of the country, and the following letter was issued :—

" *Tercentenary of the Birth of Shakespeare.*
" Committee Room, Town Hall,
" Sir,   " Stratford-upon-Avon, January 7th, 1864.
      "I have the pleasure of enclosing several documents con-
nected with the Shakespeare tercentenary celebration in this town.

The Committee will feel much obliged by your giving space in your journal to those portions of these papers most calculated to interest your readers; and should you think well to draw public attention to this important event in your leading columns, they feel you will materially assist the efforts now being made to do honour to the memory of Shakespeare, in the place of his birth, residence, and burial.

" I am, Sir, yours faithfully,
" ROBERT E. HUNTER,
" Secretary.

" To the Editor of———"

This request was complied with by a considerable number of newspapers, and the paragraphs announcing in brief terms the doings of the Committee, which were forwarded weekly to every journal of influence throughout the empire, obtained general insertion; and that the special attention of the great and wealthy of the land might be drawn to the movement, the Mayor addressed the subjoined brief and business-like note to the Peers and Members of Parliament :—

" Stratford-upon-Avon,
" 30th December, 1863.

" Dear Sir (or my Lord),
" Since the insertion, on the 12th inst. in the *Times*, of a letter written by me on the subject of the forthcoming celebration of the tercentenary of Shakespeare's birth, in this his native town, several noblemen and gentlemen have given our Committee their aid, and permitted their names to be added to our list of Vice-presidents.

" If you will kindly allow your name to be placed on our list, and can in any way forward our undertaking, you will oblige our Committee.

" I am your obedient servant,
" E. F. FLOWER,
" Mayor and Vice-chairman.

" To———"

Whilst the Mayor, the Vicar, and other members of the Committee were labouring by personal exertions abroad, and letters were being dispatched in thousands by the Secretary (whose office at this period was no sinecure), with a view of arousing the sympathy and obtaining the support of the country at large, the general body at home were busily engaged, to the exclusion of their own business, in the collecting of subscriptions, and in perfecting the arrangement for the festival.

An address to the managers of theatres throughout the provinces had been thought of, and being strongly urged by Mr. Buckstone, and Miss Cushman, who happened to be at Stratford in October, the subjoined, together with a parchment roll, was sent to every theatre then open in the country :—

" *Tercentenary of the Birth of Shakespeare.*

" Committee Room, Town Hall,
" Stratford-upon-Avon, December, 1863.

" Sir,
      " At the request of the tercentenary Committee, I enclose a copy of their address, and am desired to express, on their behalf, a hope that you will, as soon as convenient, have the great kindness to devote a night at your theatre to a performance in aid of the funds now being raised for a truly national celebration at Stratford-upon-Avon in honour of Shakespeare's three hundredth birthday.

" A parchment document, with necessary information, is herewith forwarded, and you will confer a favour by permitting this to be so placed as to attract notice in your box-office.

" Box-keepers are allowed ten per cent. on the amount collected.

" I am, Sir, very faithfully yours,
" ROBERT E. HUNTER,
" Secretary."

Mr. Charles Gill sent a subscription, Mr. Swanborough, of Birmingham, devoted a night to the festival. Of further proceeds from the appeal to the provincial managers, deponent has nothing to testify.

But this disappointment was small indeed compared with that which arose in the negotiations with actors. The Committee probably thought this was to be a light matter of detail, but it proved from beginning to end a source of ever-recurring annoyance, and that not so much from the alleged peculiarities of this class of artistes as from the fact that those who undertook to arrange with them knew nothing at all of the business. The consequence was the loss of several of the most eminent comedians of the age, whose services might have been available, and, despite gratuitous services rendered, the entailment of an amount of pecuniary outlay which, when the balance sheet appears, will astonish the public.

The toils and troubles of stage management were certainly not anticipated when, on the 18th November, the Vicar made the agreeable announcement that, through the influence of the Rev. Mr. Bellew, the valuable and gratuitous services of Madame Tietjens, Madame Sainton-Dolby, Mr. Santley, Mr. Sims Reeves, and Mr. Alfred Mellon had been secured for the oratorio. All seemed then likely to be plain, calm, and economical sailing ; but breakers were ahead, and shipwreck at one time not impossible.

The Rev. Mr. Bellew, referred to, came down shortly afterwards to Stratford, and was elected a member of Committee, a Vice-president, member of the entertainments Committee, and Corresponding Secretary in London. He was endowed with large discretionary power in relation to all the management of the entertainments, and had, "in his effect, a voice potential, as double as the Duke's" for a time in casting the characters, and settling all the details of stage management. If this proved an unfortunate arrangement for the Committee, it was no less an unhappy one for Mr. Bellew. I shall not further expatiate on the topic, which may possibly be discussed by those more deeply interested in it hereafter.

Amongst the eminent artistes whose services were solicited for the occasion was Mrs. Fanny Kemble, who was asked to read " A Midsummer Night's Dream." The lady replied that she was going to the continent, and should not be in England in April. Miss Faucit (Mrs. Theodore Martin) was requested to act. She at once consented to assist, but before giving a definite answer desired to know the character, and whether there would be any other performance on the same evening except that in which she appeared. Mr. Webster and Mr. Phelps placed their services at the disposal of the Committee. Mr. Fechter was thought of, but it was stated that he could not close the Lyceum—the business

was so great—to come to Stratford.   However, some time
after the enlistment of Mr. Bellew, that is about the
middle of December, it was discovered that Mr. Fechter
might be obtained, and the entertainments Committee, not
without some apprehension as to the prejudice which the
step they were taking might create, invited Mr. Fechter to
play *Hamlet*.   They were led to do so by the fact that the
performance was regarded as a novelty, and had had an
unprecedented run at the Princesses' Theatre, and was
therefore likely to prove more attractive than the *Hamlet*
of any other tragedian.   There was no intention of in-
sulting Mr. Phelps, however the selection may have seemed
to imply a forgetfulness of him, or an ignorance of the
fact that since Mr. Macready's retirement he has been the
foremost man of his profession.   *Hamlet* was not supposed
to be his greatest favourite in the tragedy *rôle;* and as for
the memory of Shakespeare, it was regarded as so cosmopolitan that it mattered little what countryman was
selected to represent his hero.

These were the views of the Committee, not so a large
section of the British public ; and as for the British actors,
" indignation " is but a feeble word to express the feelings
with which they heard the news that a Frenchman, who had
only succeeded in one of Shakespeare's characters—and
although one of his greatest, yet a part so effective in the
language and telling in the situations, that amateurs and
ladies play it with success, and nobody ever signally failed in
it—had been selected to play *Hamlet* at the great celebration
of the three hundredth. natal day in Stratford-upon-Avon.
But Mr. Fechter had complied with the request of the
Committee, and reconsideration of the matter, certainly
never thought of by the Committee, was impossible.

A month elapsed before the effect of appropriating
Hamlet to Mr. Fechter was discovered in the news
that Mr. Phelps had "struck."   The history of this
unfortunate incident is so fully detailed in the correspondence which took place in relation to it that I am
induced to re-produce it here, at the risk of becoming
tedious and extending this compilation much beyond the
dimensions originally contemplated.

MR. PHELPS AND THE STRATFORD-UPON-AVON COMMITTEE.

In wishing (said Mr. Phelps, in his pamphlet), that the ensuing correspondence between myself and certain individuals acting officially on behalf of the Stratford-upon-Avon Committee for the celebration of the tercentenary of the birth of Shakespeare should be made public, I have no other desire than that I may set myself right not only with my personal friends, many of whom have already applied to me for an explanation of the causes which have induced me to refuse to take any part in the proposed performance to take place at Stratford in connection with the approaching celebration, but also that the motives which have induced me to this refusal, to vindicate my professional position in this country may not appear in a false light, either through misconception or misrepresentation, to that public whose approval has been my great encouragement and reward during the many years of study and exertion I have devoted to the cultivation of the higher drama, and more especially to the illustration of the genius of Shakespeare ; and which approval I should be unwilling to forfeit in a matter which, if it involve to a certain extent considerations which may be regarded as purely private and personal, in a much greater degree affects the estimation which I won from the public in the exercise of my profession on the one hand, and on the other the respect and deference due from me in the same capacity to the public.

Not deeming, when this correspondence opened, that its course would be otherwise than simple, natural, and satisfactory, as had been its commencement, I made no copies of my own letters, and therefore must appear most reluctantly as a narrator ; for however brief and few the sentences needed to link the sequence of letters, I should have infinitely preferred leaving the correspondence to tell its own tale.

Tercentenary of the Birth of Shakespeare.

(No. 1.)

Committee Room, Town Hall,
Stratford-upon-Avon, 7th December, 1863.

Sir,

As instructed, I take leave respectfully to address to you the annexed copy of a resolution adopted unanimously at the above date by the Committee organised here for the celebration of the Shakespeare tercentenary in Stratford-upon-Avon.

As time is now very precious to the Committee, and an accident has detained the despatch of this letter for a couple of days, would you have the great kindness to favour me with your reply by return of post.

I am, Sir,
Truly yours,
ROBT. E. HUNTER,
Samuel Phelps, Esq.   Secretary.

Moved by J. J. Nason, Esq., M.B., seconded by E. F. Flower, Esq. (the Mayor of Stratford-upon-Avon), and unanimously resolved :—
" That the Secretary be instructed to write to Samuel Phelps, Esq., requesting that gentleman to take part in the dramatic performances at the festival in Stratford-upon-Avon, in April next."

To this letter I replied, that I believed it was intended to give a Shakespearian performance at Drury Lane Theatre on the 23rd of April, and in that case that my services would be required in London, but that if it should prove otherwise, I should be happy to assist the Committee. To this came the following counter reply :—

(No. 2.)

Committee Room, Town Hall,
Stratford-upon-Avon, 12th December, 1863.

Sir,

In reply to your kind note of yesterday, consenting to take part in the Shakespeare tercentenary celebration here, " if not in requisition in Drury Lane Theatre," permit me to say that it is not intended to have any dramatic performance in Stratford on the 23rd of April. According to present arrangements " Hamlet " will be played on Tuesday, the 26th of that month.

The Rev. Mr. J. C. M. Bellew, who is a Vice-president and member of the local Committee, has, however, kindly undertaken to see you on the subject, and will probably do so on Monday next.

I take leave to inclose you a copy of our programme, a revised edition of which will be published in a few days, and I hope you will do the Committee the honour of adding your name to the list of Vice-presidents.

I am, Sir,

Your most obedient servant,

ROBT. E. HUNTER,

Samuel Phelps, Esq., &c. Secretary.

From the day on which I received this letter until the 16th of January, 1864, a space of more than one calendar month, I waited in daily and patient expectation to see the Reverend Mr. Bellew, or to hear from the Committee. At length, on that day, I wrote to Stratford-upon-Avon, asking whether the Rev. Mr. Bellew, not having appeared, as announced, in the capacity of spokesman for the Committee, I was to consider that the offer of my services, elicited by their request, had been rejected. On the evening of the same day, and before, of course, I could receive any reply to this question, the following came to hand :—

(No. 3.)

Bedford Chapel, New Oxford Street,

January 16th, 1864.

My Dear Sir,

A short time back you would receive a communication from our Secretary at Stratford, asking you to favour the tercentenary festival with your presence and support.

I have delayed writing to you until I could know definitely what play of Shakespeare's the Committee proposed to present.

It is now arranged that "Cymbeline" will be produced at Stratford-upon-Avon, on the evening of Tuesday, April 26th.

This therefore is the proper time for me to address you, and convey the invitation of the Stratford Committee to take part in their performance.

I hope it is unnecessary for me to add, that I should think the programme incomplete unless both you and Miss Faucit could be included in it.

I sincerely trust that you will feel disposed to favour the Stratford festival with your support and assistance; and I can assure you that if you will undertake the part of *Iachimo*, your consent to play that part will be received by all concerned in promoting the festival with the liveliest satisfaction.

You will greatly oblige me if you will let me hear from you at your early convenience; and I hope your engagements will not prevent you, as the foremost of English tragedians, from taking part in the performances of a festival got up to do honour to Shakespeare's memory.

Believe me,
My dear Mr. Phelps,
Yours very faithfully,

S. Phelps, Esq.   J. M. BELLEW.

Before I replied to this, I deemed it advisable to wait for an answer to my letter to the Stratford Committee. It came on the 20th, informing me simply that a gentleman would call on me. I then replied to Mr. Bellew, explaining why I had not answered immediately, and concluding with a plain statement that I declined assisting at the Stratford festival. I must here observe, in order to render the next communication from Mr. Bellew intelligible, that I had received at the same time, with the first official letter from the Secretary of the Stratford Committee, a private note from that gentleman, expressing a personal desire on his part to see me act in " Hamlet," " Othello," or " Macbeth," at the approaching Stratford performances. Unintentionally I mixed up the private note, mentioning three characters, with the official letter, mentioning only one—the first. I regret this mistake, as it has brought blame on the Secretary, but the confusion lends no strength to the case of the Committee or of Mr. Bellew, as the case may be, for the play of " Hamlet" is distinctly mentioned in the second official letter; and why is it mentioned in a letter to me, if at that time, and before Mr. Bellew's announced but never paid visit, it had been contemplated to offer the part of *Hamlet* to another person ?

(No. 4.)

Bedford Chapel, New Oxford Street,
January 20, 1864,—5 p.m.

My Dear Sir,

  Your note is just received, and I send an instant reply, because I feel assured there must be some error. The facts you state as communicated to you by Mr. Hunter are utterly unknown to me;

and the delays occasioned in my writing to you were simply because I pressed upon the Committee the folly of asking a variety of persons to play, not being able distinctly to propose to them what to play.

There cannot be any possible difference of opinion and desire among any of the Committee at Stratford upon the one point, viz.—to produce a play in which you can appear to the satisfaction of yourself and the public. I am quite certain you are labouring under some misapprehension, therefore I write again to beg you to re-consider your decision, with the perfect confidence that if you would prefer a night specially devoted to a play for you, and the parts cast as you might advise, the Committee would do all in their power to produce it with proper effect. I know it was their wish to combine you and Miss Faucit in one play, and with this view " Cymbeline" was selected. As I write in perfect ignorance regarding Mr. Hunter's letter to you, or who directed him to specify " Hamlet," " Macbeth," and " Othello," I can say nothing on that matter; but it certainly surprises me, particularly as the Committee specially requested another gentleman to appear as *Hamlet*. I can only say (feeling certain they will support my request), that if " Macbeth," or " Othello," or any other play of Shakespeare's will be more acceptable to you than joining in " Cymbeline," it shall be got up for you; and got up as far as possible according to your wishes. Whatever you may decide, *let me beg you to dismiss any misconception as to their wish,* for it would indeed be grievous if you were misled by any private letter from Stratford, and in consequence of it to form a final decision which every one concerned would regret.

I feel certain that five minutes' conversation would set the matter straight, and if agreeable to you I will call anywhere convenient.

Believe me,
Yours faithfully,

S. Phelps, Esq.   J. M. BELLEW.

Now, for the first time, I made a record of the words used by me in the letter subsequently addressed to the representatives of the Stratford Committee. Here, therefore, is what I wrote in reply to the above:—

(No. 5.)

My Dear Sir,

I claim the right, upon the following grounds to be considered the foremost man in my profession in a demonstration meant to honour Shakespeare. I have produced worthily thirty-four of his plays, which no individual manager ever did before. They were acted in my theatre four thousand times, during a period extending over eighteen years. I acted to the satisfaction of a large *English* public all his

heroes—tragic and comic—and to that public I shall appeal, and
publish this correspondence.   The Stratford Committee have insulted
me by asking any man in this country to play *Hamlet* on such an
occasion, without having first offered a choice of characters to

Yours faithfully,
S. Phelps.

(No. 6.)
Committee Room, Town Hall,
Stratford-upon-Avon, 22nd January, 1864.

Dear Sir,

Your letter to Mr. Bellew, dated January 21st, has been
handed to me, and in my capacity of Vice-chairman of the Stratford
Committee, I beg to offer the following reply.

The communications addressed to you on our behalf will, I trust,
sufficiently prove that we have most earnestly desired to present you
before the public as the foremost English tragedian, at our coming
celebration.

To you we first wrote, inviting your co-operation.

Your assertion that the Stratford Committee have insulted you,
because, in the exercise of their discretion, they have "*claimed the
right*" to "*ask any man in this country but you to play Hamlet*," while
they have freely given you the whole range of Shakespeare's plays to
choose from, and undertaken to get up any tragedy for you that you
might prefer, seems to need no further remark than for me to protest
against your attributing to a body of gentlemen an intent of which
they are innocent, and of which they find themselves accused by you
with as much amazement as I do.

If you publish the correspondence, be good enough to append this
letter.

I am, dear Sir,
Your obedient servant,
E. F. Flower,

Mayor of Stratford-upon-Avon, and Vice-chairman to the Committee.

P.S.—I do not lose sight of the fact that the Committee wish to
combine your services with Miss Faucit's in their first performance,
and after long discussion were induced to select " Cymbeline ; " but
the letters addressed to you will show that they were prepared to
consult your wishes if you preferred some other play.

(No. 7.)

Dear Sir,

When I wrote to Mr. Bellew a few days since, simply
declining to "assist at the Stratford festival," I hoped to hear no

more on the subject; but his subsequent letter, and your own of yesterday's date, which I beg to acknowledge the receipt of, have aggravated the affront already offered me. I will quote your own words :—" To you we first wrote, inviting your co-operation." I in all courtesy acceded. One would have supposed that in common decency the next step would have been to consult my inclination with regard to the character I should (at all events) wish to appear in. Instead of which, I hear no more on the subject for *weeks*, and when I do, I find that another gentleman has been solicited to act the part of *Hamlet*, which I should certainly have chosen, and that " Cymbeline " had been selected for me without one word having been addressed to me on the subject. If this is the courtesy due from the *body of gentlemen* you speak of, to another gentleman whose *assistance they had sought*, I can only say that the sooner our dictionaries find another definition of the term the better. I will comply with your request, by adding your letter to this correspondence, when the time shall have arrived for its publication.

Faithfully yours,

E. F. Flower, Esq. S. Phelps.

Mr. Hunter, the Secretary of the Committee, having been selected to bear the burthen of the miscarriage which had befallen the negotiations he had first opened with me at their request, and having written to me to vindicate him from the blame unjustly thrown on him, I wrote the last of the two following, with which happily terminates a correspondence which I content myself with leaving to the judgment of all impartial readers :—

(No. 8.)

Stratford-upon-Avon,
22nd January, 1864.

Dear Sir,
I have received to-day a letter from the Rev. Mr. Bellew, informing me that he has written to you, asking if you would like a play specially got up for you, during the festival week at Stratford-upon-Avon. As a brother actor and member of the tercentenary Committee, I beg most earnestly that you will consent to the proposition. Without you the dramatic performances would be incomplete. Mr. Fechter has been selected to play *Hamlet* (I was absent from Stratford when this arrangement was made). *You* are the acknowledged head of the English tragedians, and therefore you *have a right and ought* to appear in one of your favourite Shakespearian parts upon such an occasion.

I

I am sure that my *feeling* will be reciprocated by the profession and the English public generally.

I am, dear Sir,

Yours faithfully,

JAMES BENNETT.

(No. 9.)

8, Canonbury Square,
26th January, 1864.

My Dear Sir,

But that you seem likely to be annoyed by the blundering, or something worse, of other people, I really would not trouble myself to write another line upon this subject. I have had enough—indeed, something too much of it already. The few lines you privately addressed to me on the 12th of December have nothing to do with it. Thus stands the case:—On the 7th of December you sent me officially the copy of a resolution adopted unanimously by the Stratford Committee, requesting me to take part in the dramatic performances at the festival in April next. I wrote you acceding to that request. I concluded, as a matter of course, that no other tragedian had previously been applied to, and that I was right in my conclusion appears from the following passage contained in a letter addressed to me by Mr. Flower, on the 22nd inst. :—" *To you we first wrote*, inviting your co-operation." On the 12th of December you wrote thanking me for consenting to take part in the Shakespeare celebration in April, and saying, " according to present arrangements, ' Hamlet' will be played on the 26th of that month," and then, "The Rev. J. C. M. Bellew, who is a Vice-president, and member of the local Committee, has, however, kindly undertaken to see you on the subject, and will probably do so on Monday next." I neither *saw nor heard* from Mr. Bellew until the 16th of January. Could I suppose, from your *official* communication of the 12th of December, that Mr. Fechter had been solicited to play *Hamlet* at that time? Does not Mr. Flower's letter assert that I was the *first* whose co-operation had been invited? Is it not plain enough that I have been grossly insulted? Your private letter to me of the 12th of December contains the following passage, which, as I have said before, has nothing to do with the affair as it stands between me and Mr. Bellew or the Committee :—" I cannot resist the temptation which this correspondence holds out to me of expressing the great gratification I should experience personally in seeing you play *Hamlet, Macbeth,* or *Othello,* at the great national Shakespeare tercentenary celebration at Stratford-upon-Avon, in 1864." There is not in your letter another word which concerns the Committee in any way, and only refers to what would have taken place after the festival should be over. Will you kindly tell Mr.

James Bennett that I intended writing him by this post, but am prevented; he will know by this time how the matter stands, and I am sure will sympathise with,

Faithfully yours,

Robert E. Hunter, Esq.   SAML. PHELPS.

This correspondence having been widely circulated afforded to a number of the morning papers excellent matter for leaders. Several of them espoused Mr. Phelps's quarrel, and condemned the Committee for having cast *Hamlet* to Mr. Fechter, or solicited any foreigner to play Shakespeare's sublime *Prince of Denmark* before a great British audience and on an ever-to-be-remembered occasion. The *Morning Herald*, of the 8th of February, having given a summary of the correspondence, proceeded as follows :—

" Now, with every desire to assist the object in view, we must here record our belief that the Stratford Committee have been guilty of what must at the best be considered a very serious blunder. There are playgoers—and playgoers. Some may be more enthusiastic in their admiration of Mr. Phelps than others; but few will deny him the honour of being our best English tragedian, and all must admit that he is the first representative of the Shakespearian drama on the stage. Mr. Fechter is a great actor—nobody doubts his ability— and in one Shakespearian part he has established a certain position among us. But, except in *Hamlet*, Mr. Fechter has acquired only a comparative claim to the delineation of Shakespeare. For the rest he is a thoroughly admirable artist, but no more entitled to represent the Shakespearian drama at Stratford than Mr. Toole or Mr. Paul Bedford. Mr. Phelps, on the other hand, is an actor whose whole dramatic career has been identified with the works of the great poet. Not only has he played Shakespearian parts in preference to all others, but he has run the risk—no small risk, as managers know—of keeping Shakespeare before the public. The vanity of many men might have induced an equal amount of devotion ; but Mr. Phelps has backed up his principles in the sincerest way known to managers. He has risked his fortune in the maintenance of Shakespeare on the stage ; and if he has not lost his fortune in the attempt, the result is due to his own sterling merits, which, to the credit, be it said, of the public to whom he appealed, have been recognised as they deserved to be. Mr. Macready and others have made sacrifices to the cause of the legitimate drama—represented by the greatest of English dramatists —but although they may have made larger ventures for a time they have never offered the sustained support afforded by Mr. Phelps. That gentleman, of late years, indeed, may be considered to have kept the cause alive, and as its worthy representative he is recognised by all sections of the playgoing public. To him should have been accorded the highest honours within the gift of the Stratford Committee. Yet, through a want of judgment, or some not very creditable intrigue, we find at almost the last moment that the foremost among those who desired to honour Shakespeare upon this national occasion have managed matters so badly as to have lost the support of our greatest Shakespearian actor. As a general rule we have little sympathy with the jealousies of players, any more than the jealousies of any other class. When Flimkins throws up his part in the melo-drama at the Surrey, and Boozle declines it—positively declines it—on the ground that Flimkins had been put up in it first, and that no earthly power shall induce him to take it at second hand, we have no sympathy beyond a smile at Mr. Dickens's 'Theatrical Young Gentleman,' who rushes about with the news, thinking that it will produce a revolution in town. But upon a great national occasion like the present—and it will be a great national occasion unless it be made an absurdity—an actor of Mr. Phelps's eminence has a right to consider his position, and cannot forfeit that position if he properly respects his art. Any jesting, therefore, upon this matter will be but a sorry exhibition. For the question is not a merely personal one between Mr. Phelps and the Stratford Committee, or between Mr. Phelps and Mr. Fechter. It is a national question between the repre-sentatives of the English public and the representative of the Shakespearian drama."

These remarks were too strong to be passed over in silence. The Committee, feeling that they had offered no intentional insult to Mr. Phelps, and had acted in the entire business with a single eye to the success of the celebration, had determined to take no notice of the publication of the correspondence; but when the *Herald* talked of "a not very creditable intrigue" they felt bound to show that if intrigue existed they were innocent of it. Accordingly the follow-ing explanation of the motives and grounds on which they had proceeded was issued by the Mayor and entertainments Committee, with the full concurrence of the general body :—

"*The Shakespearian Tercentenary Celebration at Stratford-upon-Avon.*

" *To the Editor of the* ERA.

" Sir,   "Committee Room, 11th February, 1864.
          " As Chairman of the General Committee, I write to request the favour of your inserting in your paper the Report of the

entertainments Committee relating to the correspondence Mr. Phelps has seen fit to publish.

" I will only add that our Committee has undertaken a large amount of labour, and a large amount of money-risk in our efforts to achieve a great work, and if we fail, we shall have to pay for such failure out of our own pockets, and also bring upon ourselves the censure failure ever produces. Therefore, while Mr. Phelps ' claims the right to be the foremost man in his profession,' we ' claim the right,' and exercise the right also, of using every means in our power to place before the public successfully *three* of Shakespeare's plays, and I think we should have committed a great blunder if we had contracted our theatrical representations to the small dimensions we must have done had we yielded to the professional jealousy of ' the foremost man in his profession,' instead of availing ourselves of the generous support of the numerous talented ladies and gentlemen who put aside all personal considerations in rendering their valuable and valued assistance.

" I am, Sir, your obedient servant,
" E. F. FLOWER,
" Mayor of Stratford-upon-Avon."

" Report of the Entertainments Committee.

" In accordance with a resolution passed by the General Committee, we now lay before the public the facts alluded to in a correspondence recently published by Mr. Phelps.

" Upon its being decided to have three evenings devoted to dramatic entertainments at the forthcoming festival, we considered it desirable that three of Shakespeare's plays should be produced; in the cast of which every actor of note, willing to assist, might take a part.

" We accordingly put ourselves into communication with several of the leading performers, Mr. Phelps and Mr. Fechter among others, and from each of these gentlemen we received a ready response. We then considered that as *Hamlet* was the character in which Mr. Fechter had made his first and greatest impression, it would be most desirable that he should sustain that part, leaving to Mr. Phelps the whole range of Shakespeare's plays, in most of which we know that he had taken the leading characters. We accordingly wrote to Mr. Fechter, requesting that he would act *Hamlet.* He at once responded to our request, and in a most handsome manner placed the whole resources of the Lyceum Theatre at our disposal.

" Mr. Buckstone having, in the same liberal style, undertaken to produce 'Twelfth Night,' we congratulated ourselves that, with Mr. Phelps, and other distinguished performers in a play on the third night, we should be in a position to arrange a most attractive programme.

"The public are aware, through the correspondence published by Mr. Phelps, that "Cymbeline" was suggested as being one of the least known, though most beautiful of Shakespeare's plays, and one in which the talents of Miss Helen Faucit and Mr. Phelps could be combined. The public are also aware that an offer was made to produce any other play which Mr. Phelps might prefer, but that he declined to appear in any character or take any part in the proceedings because Mr. Fechter's aid had also been invited.

"We had hoped that upon such an occasion every actor would have thought only of the great name in whose honour the festival is to be held, and we deplore that a gentleman whose reputation as an actor is connected with so many of Shakespeare's works should have allowed personal feelings to interfere.

"But while we deeply regret that, amid the toil and anxiety and the many difficulties continually arising in making arrangements attendant upon the preparation of so great a festival, we should have received a check from a quarter in which we least expected it, we are happy to add that, through the generous spirit evinced by Miss Faucit and others, we shall be able to produce, on the third evening, a play in which the whole of the characters will be most worthily sustained.

"Signed on behalf of the entertainments Committee,
"R. H. HOBBES.
"Stratford-upon-Avon, February 11th, 1864."

This reply of the Committee set the matter substantially at rest. Mr. Phelps was severely criticised for putting forth his claims to recognition in the terms adopted, but ably defended, "in speaking of himself" as he did under the circumstances, by Mr. Charles Lamb Kenney and others.

In the meantime the Committee toiled on in making the best possible arrangements for the now rapidly-approaching festival; but at nearly every step in the theatrical department of their labours they were traversed by the Mr. Fechter appointment. Mr. Webster, who had consented to co-operate personally and from the resources of the New Adelphi, took such offence at the prominence given to the foreigner that he declined to have any connection with the celebration; and a delegate sent to London by the Committee to solicit the aid of a number of ladies and gentlemen of the profession found himself so encumbered and embarrassed that he wrote to the Committee requesting them, if possible, to get out of the unpopular engagement, as he could come to no speed in his mission while it existed. The proposal was received with the utmost surprise and most general disapprobation ; a strong resolution was passed requesting him to desist from further action in the business. In fact the Committee, as in honour bound, stuck to Mr. Fechter through good and evil report. Old *King Duncan* did not place in Cawdor who betrayed him a trust more absolute.

Still, despite these drawbacks, the work went on with unflagging energy and spirit. A " central ticket office " was opened in January, at No. 2, Exeter Hall, where information as to the general arrangements for the tercentenary celebration might from time to time be obtained, and contributions in aid of the memorial or the endowment of scholarships might be paid to Mr. John Carmichael, who was authorised to receive them. Considerable expense attended this metropolitan establishment, and for the *per contra* of profits I must refer the reader to the balance sheet when the finance Committee promulgate the document.

Ultimately, on the 1st of March, the Committee were enabled, by great exertions, to lay before the public, as the result of their labours in gathering around them supporters of wealth and fame, and in preparing for a celebration of befitting magnitude and splendour, the following list of patrons, parties on the Committees, and subjoined preliminary programme :—

PRESIDENT :

The Rt. Hon. The Earl of Carlisle, K.G., Lord Lieutenant of Ireland.

VICE-PRESIDENTS :

Aylesford, The Earl of
American Minister, His Excellency The
Attye, James, Esq.

Bourke, The Hon. Robert
Brewer, Professor, S. S.
Byng, The Hon. Frederick
Badham, The Rev. Dr.

Bath, The Mayor of
Battam, Thomas, Esq., F.S.A.
Buxton, Charles, Esq., M.P.
Bazley, Thomas, Esq., M.P.
Bell, Robert, Esq., F.R.S.L., &c.
Bellew, The Rev. J. C. M.
Bowyer, Lieut.-Colonel, H. A.
Bowles, Rev. J., D.D., LL.D.
Birmingham, The Mayor of

Blackburn, The Mayor of
Bracebridge, C. Holte, Esq.
Brooks, Shirley, Esq.
Bohn, Henry G., Esq.
Buckstone, J. B., Esq.

Clarendon, The Earl of, K.G.
Coventry, The Earl of
Craven, The Earl of
Campden, Viscount
Crossley, Sir Francis, Bart., M.P.
Copeland, Alderman, M.P.
Cabbell, B. Bond, Esq., F.R.S., F.S.A.
Cameron, The Rev. D.
Chambers, Robert, Esq., LL.D., F.R.S.E., &c.
Clark, The Rev. W. G., M.A.
Child, W. H., Esq.
Cobb, Timothy Rhodes, Esq.
Collier, J. Payne, Esq.
Colmore, Thomas, Esq.
Conolly, J., Esq., M.D., D.C.L.
Cox, W. Sands, Esq., F.R.S.
Creswick, T., Esq., R.A.
Creswick, W., Esq.
Crosskey, The Rev. H. W.

Dartmouth, The Earl of
Delawarr, The Earl
Dufferin, Lord, K.C.B.
Drax, John S.W.S.E., Esq., M.P.
Dickins, W., Esq.
Dinsdale, F., Esq., LL.D., F.S.A.
Dobie, Alexander, Esq.
Dugdale, James, Esq.
Dyce, The Rev. Alexander

Elton, Sir Arthur Hallam, Bart.
Ewart, W., Esq., M.P., F.R.G.S.
Ewart, Joseph, Esq., M.P.
Ellis, Joseph, Esq.
Evesham, The Mayor of
Elmore, Alfred, Esq., R.A.

Feversham, Lord
Flower, E. F., Esq.

Frith, W. P., Esq., R.A.

Graves, Sir Maxwell Steele, Bart.
Godwin, George, Esq.
Graves, The Very Rev. Charles, Dean of the Chapel Royal, Dublin
Greaves, Richard, Esq.
Greenway, Kelynge, Esq.
Gruneisen, Charles Lewis, Esq., F.R.G.S.

Harrowby, The Earl of, K.G.
Houghton, Lord
Hamilton, Sir Robert N. C., Bart., K.C.B.
Holland, Edward, Esq., M.P.
Halifax, The Mayor of
Hardy, Duffus, Esq.
Hall, S. C., Esq., F.S.A.
Harding, W. J., Esq.
Heath, R. C., Esq.
Hodgson, Joseph, Esq., F.R.S.
Holbech, The Rev. C. W.
Hoskyns, Chandos Wren, Esq.
Hugo, Mons. Victor
Hume, The Rev. Dr., F.R.S., D.C.L.

Ingestre, Viscount, M.P.

Jaffray, John, Esq.
Jephson, H., Esq., M.D.
Jones, J. C., Esq., F.S.A.

Kaye, J. W., Esq.
Knight Charles, Esq.

Lichfield, The Earl of
Leigh, Lord, Lord-Lieutenant of Warwickshire
Lyttelton, Lord, F.R.S.
Leigh, Hon. E. Chandos
Langton, G., Esq., M.P., F.G.H.S.
Ledger, Frederick, Esq.
Leigh, P A., Esq.
Leigh, J. W. Boughton, Esq.

Liverpool, The Mayor of
Lloyd, Sampson S., Esq.
Lucas, Samuel, Esq., M.A.

Manchester, The Duke of
Masson, Professor
Mordaunt, Sir Chas., Bart., M.P.
Moon, Sir F. Graham, Bart., F.S.A.
Machen, John, Esq.
Macready, W. C., Esq.
Manchester, The Mayor of
Martin, Theodore, Esq.
Mellon, Alfred, Esq.
Meyrick, Lieut.-Col. Augustus
Mommsen, Herr
Moore, The Ven. Archdeacon
Mordaunt, J. Murray, Esq.
Morrison, Alfred, Esq.
Muntz, P. H., Esq.

Northumberland, The Duke of, K.G.
Newport, Viscount, M.P.
North, Lieut.-Col. J. Sidney, M.P.
Newcastle, The Mayor of
Nichol, Professor John
Nichols, J. Gough, Esq., F.S.A.

Owen, Professor
O'Hagan, The Right Hon. T., Q.C., M.P.

Palk, Sir Laurence, Bart., M.P.
Padmore, R., Esq., M.P.
Paxton, Sir Joseph, M.P., F.L.S.
Powell, John, Esq., M.P.
Pears, A. H., Esq.
Philips, Mark, Esq.
Philips, R. N., Esq.
Planche, J. R., Esq., *Rouge Croix*
Prichard, The Rev. R.
Plumptre, E. J., Esq.

Ranelagh, Viscount
Rochdale, The Mayor of
Russell, W. W., Esq., LL.D.

Shrewsbury and Talbot, The Earl of, P.C., C.B.
Sherborne, Lord

Salt, Thomas, jun., Esq., M.P.
Scholefield, William, Esq., M.P.
Sheridan, R. B., Esq., M.P.
Shirley, Evelyn P., Esq., M.P., F.S.A.
Smith, Gustavus T., Esq.
Smyth, Admiral W. H., K.S.F., D.C.L., F.R.S., &c.
Stack, J. Herbert, Esq.
Stanley, The Very Rev. Dr., Dean of Westminster.
Starkey, J. F., Esq.
Staunton, Howard, Esq.
Staunton, J., Esq.
Sudeley, Viscount
Swansea, The Mayor of

Talbot de Malahide, Lord
Taylor, P. A., Esq., M.P.
Thornhill, W. P., Esq., M.P.
Tamworth, The Mayor of
Taylor, Tom, Esq.
Temple, The Rev. Dr., *Rugby.*
Tennyson, Alfred, Esq., D.C.L., Poet Laureate
Townsend, The Rev. Henry
Trinity College, Oxford, The President of
Tite, Wm., Esq., M.P.

Vernon, Lord
Vizetelly, Henry, Esq.

Warwick, The Earl of
Wrottesley, Lord, F.R.S., F.R.A.S.
Worcester, The Right Rev. the Lord Bishop of
Wyld, James, Esq., M.P., F.R.G.S.
Warwickshire, The High Sheriff of
Webster, Benjamin, Esq.
West, J. R., Esq.
Wilmot, Sir J. Eardley, Bart.
Worcester, The Mayor of
Worcestershire, The High Sheriff of
Wright, Wm. Aldis, Esq., M.A.

York, The Lord Mayor of

LOCAL COMMITTEE.

Sir ROBERT N. C. HAMILTON, Bart., K.C.B., *Chairman.*

The Rev. G. GRANVILLE, Vicar, } *Vice-chairmen.*
E. F. FLOWER, Esq., Mayor, }

Adams, Mr. E.
Archer, Mr. J.
Atkinson, Mr.
Bellew, The Rev. J. C. M.
Bennett, Mr. J.
Bird, Mr. R. M.
Bolton, Mr. W. G. F.
Bracebridge, C. Holte, Esq.
Chance, T. H., Esq.
Colbourne, Mr. W. G.
Conolly, Dr.
Cox, Mr. James
Craig, J. S., Esq.
Flower, C. E., Esq.
Flower, Edgar, Esq.
Gibbs, Mr. Edward
Gibbs, Mr. William
Greener, W., Esq.
Hansard, The Rev. Septimus
Hobbes, Robert H., Esq.
Harding, W. J., Esq.
Hartley, Mr. E. R.
Hunt, W. O., Esq.
Kingsley, Dr.
Kendall, F., Esq.
Knights, Mr. W.
Lane, H., Esq.
Langford, J. A., Esq.
Leaver, Mr. J. S.
Lowry, Mr.
Loggin, Mr. C. F.
Lucy, Mr. M.
Mathews, Mr.
Morgan, Mr. John
Morton, The Rev. W.
Nason, J. J., Esq., M.B.
Norris, Mr. W. L.
Philips, Mark, Esq.
Puttick, J. F., Esq.
Salaman, Charles, Esq.
Samman, Mr. H.
Stephenson, Mr. W.
Stewart, J., Esq.
Thomson, Dr.
Thompson, Mr. W.
Warden, Mr. J. C.
Young, The Rev. Julian C.

Robt. E. Hunter, *Secretary.*

MONUMENTAL MEMORIAL COMMITTEE.

The Earl of Carlisle, K.G.
The Earl of Somers, F.R.G.S.
Sir Robert N. C. Hamilton, Bart., K.C.B.
Sir Coutts Lindsay, Bart.
Robert Bell, Esq., F.R.S.L.
C. Buxton, Esq., M.P.
C. L. Gruneisen, Esq.
Theodore Martin, Esq.
Gambier Parry, Esq.
John Ruskin, Esq.
Tom Taylor, Esq.
Alfred Tennyson, Esq., D.C.L., Poet Laureate.
William Stirling, Esq., M.P.
Austen H. Layard, Esq., M.P.
J. Beresford Hope, Esq.

GRAND FANCY DRESS BALL.

LADY PATRONESSES.

The Countess of Aylesford
The Countess of Lichfield
The Countess of Warwick
Lady Willoughby de Broke
Lady Vernon
Lady Wrottesley
Lady Conyers
Lady Gwendoline Petre
Lady Charles Paulet
Lady Mordaunt

Lady Steele Graves
Hon. Mrs. Adderley
Mrs. West, *Alscot*
Mrs. Wise, *Woodcote*
Mrs. Hamilton Yatman
Mrs. Keighley Peach
Mrs. Eyton
Mrs. Dickins, *Cherington*
Mrs. Flower

PATRONS AND STEWARDS.

Lord Leigh, Lord-Lieutenant of Warwickshire
The High Sheriff of Warwickshire
The Earl of Lichfield
The Earl of Craven
The Earl of Warwick
The Earl of Aylesford
The Earl of Shrewsbury and Talbot
The Earl Delawarr
The Earl of Coventry
Lord Wrottesley
Lord Dufferin
Lord Northwick
The Hon. E. Chandos Leigh
Col. the Hon. H. H. Clifford
Sir N. W. Throckmorton, Bart.
Sir M. Steele Graves, Bart.
Sir J. Eardley Wilmot, Bart.
T. Bazley, Esq., M.P.
W. Scholefield, Esq., M.P.
Attwood, T. Aurelius, Esq.
Atty, James, Esq., *Rugby*
Arkwright, J. T., Esq.
Bill, John, Esq., *Coventry*
Caldecott, C. M., Esq., *Rugby*
Clarke, Colonel, Scots Greys
Flower, E. F., Esq.

Galton, Darwin, Esq.
Greenway, Kelynge, Esq.
Granville, Major
Hartopp, Major
Hamilton, Captain
Harding, W. J., Esq.,
Hodge, Maj.-Gen., C.B., *Aldershot*
Lucy, H. Spencer, Esq., *Charlecote*
Machen, Major
Mason, Lieut.-Col.
Muntz, P. H., Esq., *Edstone*
Minster, R. H., Esq., *Mayor of Coventry*
Musgrave, C., Esq.
Parker, Francis, Esq., *Worcester*
Philips, R. N., Esq., *Manchester*
Peach, Captain Keighley
Peel, A. Robert, Esq., *Worcester*
Starkey, J. F., Esq.
Smith, Gustavus T., Esq.
Thomson, Dr.
Vaughton, R. Dymock, Esq.
West, J. R., Esq., *Alscot*
Wise, H. C., Esq.
Wright, T., Esq., *Tidmington*
Yatman, W. Hamilton, Esq.

ACTING STEWARDS.

Lord Willoughby de Broke
The Hon. Hugh Somerville
Sir Charles Mordaunt, Bart., M.P.
Sir R. N. C. Hamilton, Bart., K.C.B.

Child, W. Henry, Esq.
Flower, Edgar, Esq.
Kingsley, Dr.
Lomax, Captain
Mordaunt, J. Murray, Esq.

PRELIMINARY PROGRAMME.

In accordance with the expectations manifested throughout the country, that the ordinary marks of respect and rejoicing with which the birthday of Shakespeare is annually commemorated in his native town should, on this, the three hundredth anniversary, be extended to a national celebration, a Committee was formed in the early part of 1863 to suggest and carry out a scheme which might, so far as possible, meet the requirements of the occasion. After many months of unceasing exertion, rendered more onerous by their entire inexperience, and by the difficulty of selecting amongst the vast number of suggestions which have been offered from all parts of the world, the Committee are now in a position to announce the general features of their programme.

Although the festival will only extend over a few days, a spacious pavilion has been erected of a character unusually substantial, decorated in the Elizabethan style, with stage and orchestra for the dramatic and musical entertainments, and with ample accommodation for the banquet and ball. Many of the most eminent dramatic and vocal artistes have given their gratuitous services, and have heartily joined in the earnest endeavour to make the entertainment as attractive as possible.

The substantial objects to which the pecuniary results of the festival will be devoted, are—1st. The erection of a National Monumental Memorial to Shakespeare in the town of his birth. 2nd. The extension of the educational advantages of the Free Grammar School of King Edward VI., Stratford-upon-Avon, at which Shakespeare was educated, and to found one or more Scholarships or Exhibitions to the Universities of the United Kingdom, open to the competition of those who have received their education at that school.

THE FESTIVAL WILL COMMENCE AT NOON
On SATURDAY, April the 23rd.

The President, Vice-presidents, Committee, and others officially connected with the proceedings, will meet at the Town Hall, and should the arrangements of the monumental Committee be sufficiently advanced, they will proceed to the site fixed upon for the erection of the national memorial, and the ceremony of laying the first stone will take place.

At three p.m. there will be a BANQUET in the pavilion, at which the EARL OF CARLISLE will preside, supported by many members of both Houses of Parliament, and others eminent in literature, science, and art. Ladies are particularly invited to attend, and the tickets issued will be strictly limited to the number of guests that can be accommodated with comfort.

In the evening there will be a grand display of Fireworks, by Mr. Darby, the celebrated pyrotechnist.

On SUNDAY, April the 24th,

Sermons will be preached in the Parish Church in the morning and afternoon, and a collection will be made at the close of each service, for the purpose of restoring and beautifying the chancel, where the poet's remains are interred.

On MONDAY, April the 25th, at noon,

Handel's Oratorio of the "MESSIAH," will be performed in the pavilion, by an orchestra and chorus of five hundred performers, conducted by Mr. Alfred Mellon, the Musical Director of the festival, the solo parts will be sustained by Mdlle. Tietjens, Madame Sainton-Dolby, Mr. Sims Reeves, Mr. Santley, &c.

IN THE EVENING, at Seven o'clock,

There will be a GRAND MISCELLANEOUS CONCERT of Music associated with the Works of Shakespeare.

Artistes:—Mesdames Parepa, Sainton-Dolby, Arabella Goddard; Messrs. Sims Reeves, C. Santley, G. Perren, and full Orchestra.

On TUESDAY, April the 26th,

There will be an EXCURSION to CHARLECOTE, and other places of Shakespearian interest. Carriages will be provided for those who apply for tickets before April the 9th. H. Spencer Lucy, Esq., has consented to open the grounds and house of Charlecote on that day to holders of tickets.

IN THE EVENING, at Seven o'clock,

There will be a representation of Shakespeare's Comedy of "TWELFTH NIGHT," or "WHAT YOU WILL," by the Company of the Theatre Royal, Haymarket, London, including Mr. Buckstone, Mr. Compton, Mr. Chippendale, Mr. Howe, Mr. W. Farren, Mr. Rogers, Mr. Walter Gordon, Mr. Braid, Mr. Weatherby, Mr. Cullenford, Miss Louisa Angel, Miss H. Lindley, and Mrs. E. Fitzwilliam. After the Comedy, Mr. Sothern (Lord Dundreary) has promised to appear in a short one-act Entertainment of a peculiar construction.

On WEDNESDAY, April the 27th,

In the morning, there will be a Reading or other Entertainment of a similar character at the Shakespeare Rooms.

IN THE EVENING, at Seven o'clock,

Shakespeare's Tragedy of "HAMLET" will be performed by the Company of the Royal Lyceum Theatre.

The part of *Hamlet* by Mr. Fechter, who will be supported by Messrs. J. Brougham, Emery, Widdicomb, G. Jordon, Shore, Mmes. Elsworthy, K. Terry, &c.

On THURSDAY, April the 28th,

In the morning, at the Shakespeare Rooms, there will be a CONCERT of Instrumental Music, and Glees from Shakespeare's Plays.

IN THE EVENING, at Seven o'clock,

Shakespeare's Comedy of "AS YOU LIKE IT" will be produced. The part of *Rosalind* by Miss Ellen Faucit. The other characters will be sustained by Mrs. Keeley, Mr. Creswick, Mr. W. Farren, Mr. Compton, Mr. Chippendale, Mr. James Bennett, &c.

The DROP CURTAIN will be painted by Mr. W. Telbin.

Assistant Musical Director, Mr. Coote.
The Scenery will be under the direction of Mr. O'Connor.
The Fireworks by Mr. Darby.
These gentlemen, as well as the Vocal and Dramatic Artistes, have given their gratuitous services.

On FRIDAY, April the 29th,

There will be a GRAND FANCY DRESS BALL in the pavilion, to which no one will be admitted except in fancy dress, court dress, or uniform. (Although costumes will not be strictly limited to those of a Shakespearian character, yet it is requested that so far as possible they may be adopted.)

No masks, dominos, or pantomime characters will be admitted.

Coote and Tinney's Band has been engaged.

Dancing will commence at nine o'clock.

Tickets (not transferable) will be issued only on production of a voucher, or letter, signed either by the

President, one of the Vice-presidents, or local Committee, or by a Lady Patroness or Steward.

During the festival there will be an EXHIBITION in the Town Hall of many of the well-known portraits of Shakespeare, and eminent actors of his plays, under the superintendence of Mr. Hogarth, Haymarket.

THE PRICES OF ADMISSION TO THE VARIOUS ENTER-
TAINMENTS WILL BE AS FOLLOWS:—

SATURDAY, April the 23rd.

	£	s.	d.
Banquet (including wine)	1	1	0
Spectators (to the Gallery)	0	5	0

MONDAY, April the 25th.

	£	s.	d.
THE " MESSIAH."—Reserved Seats, Area... ...	1	1	0
,, Gallery ...	0	10	6
Unreserved Seats	0	5	0

EVENING.

	£	s.	d.
MISCELLANEOUS CONCERT.—Reserved Seats, Area	0	10	6
,, Gallery	0	5	0
Unreserved Seats ...	0	2	6

TUESDAY, April the 26th.

	£	s.	d.
Charlecote Excursion Tickets	0	5	0

EVENING.

	£	s.	d.
" TWELFTH NIGHT."—Reserved Seats, Area ...	1	1	0
,, Gallery	0	10	6
Unreserved Seats	0	5	0

WEDNESDAY, April 27th.

	£	s.	d.
MORNING READING.—Reserved Seats	0	5	0
(Shakespeare Rooms.) Unreserved	0	2	6

EVENING.

	£	s.	d.
" HAMLET."—Reserved Seats, Area	1	1	0
,, Gallery	0	10	6
Unreserved	0	5	0

THURSDAY, April the 28th.

		£	s.	d.
MORNING CONCERT.—Reserved Seats	... ...	0	5	0
(*Shakespeare Rooms*). Unreserved	... ...	0	2	6

EVENING.

" As You Like It."—Reserved Seats	Area	1	1	0
" "	... Gallery	0	10	6
Unreserved	... ...	0	5	0

FRIDAY, April the 29th.
GRAND FANCY DRESS BALL.

Tickets (including Refreshments and Supper)   1   1   0
(Issued on production of a voucher).

Spectators in the Galleries (Evening Dress), 10/6 and 5/-

Tickets for the reserved places may be had, and plans of the pavilion seen, at the Ticket Offices, New Place, Stratford-upon-Avon, and at No. 2, Exeter Hall, London. Office hours from 11 a.m. to 2 p.m. An early application is earnestly requested.

All orders for tickets must be accompanied by a remittance for the amount. Cheques and P. O. Orders should be made payable to Mr. John Dickie, Stratford-upon-Avon, or Mr. John Carmichael, No. 2, Exeter Hall, London.

Early in April, a detailed programme will be issued, giving the names of all the performers, words of the songs, arrangements for visitors, times of trains, police and other arrangements, with plans and description of the pavilion.

In order to afford accommodation for visitors at moderate charges, registers of lodgings at Stratford-upon-Avon and the neighbouring towns will be opened at the undermentioned places :—

Stratford-upon-Avon......... Mr. MORGAN, High Street.
Warwick........... Messrs. COOKE & SON, High Street.
Leamington.............. Mr. GLOVER, Victoria Terrace.
Birmingham...... Mr. THOS. HARRISON, Colemore Row.
Worcester....................

K

It is requested that, in order to prevent excessive charges being demanded, all applications from a distance may be made at either of the above offices.

Special trains will start at the close of the performances each night to London, Birmingham, Worcester, Leamington, &c. Return tickets will be available for any day during the continuance of the festival.

The following appointments have been made in connection with the festival:—

Messrs. Mulloney and Johnson, and Mr. Browett, of Coventry, have manufactured a badge and ribbon, which the Committee recommend should be worn on the occasion.

Professor Miller, of the Government School of Design, has produced a bust of Shakespeare, which has the approval of the Committee. Copies may be obtained from the publishers, Messrs. Howell and James, Regent Street, London, or their agents.

Messrs. Burton and Sons have been appointed photographers during the festival.

Messrs. Simmons and Sons, No. 4, Tavistock Street, Covent Garden, London, are appointed costumiers for the ball.

A medal has been struck by Mr. Brown, Crystal Palace, Sydenham, which the Committee recommend should be worn.

The banquet and refreshments will be supplied by Mr. J. H. Mountford of Worcester.

Architects of the pavilion—Messrs. Thompson and Colbourne, Stratford-upon-Avon.

Contractors—Messrs. Branson and Murray, Birmingham.

Decorator—Mr. Charles Brothers, Leamington.

On SATURDAY, April 30, and MONDAY, May 2,
AND THE TWO FOLLOWING DAYS,

There will be a series of Popular Entertainments in the pavilion, the particulars of which will be announced in a further programme, and arrangements will then be made for excursion trains from the neighbouring towns.

" The best laid schemes of mice and men gang aft a gley," or as *Hamlet* puts it in more exalted terms—

> " There is a divinity that shapes our ends,
> Rough hew them how we may."

The scheme of the Committee was not exactly realised. But before adverting to the departures from the preliminary programme it will be necessary to notice the discontent which arose in the minds of the tradespeople and working classes as the plans of the Committee became developed and published. This large and respectable section of society had subscribed their shillings towards a general festival, and they found no provision for them in the bill of fare. The people went in for a pageant and the Committee came out against it. So early as the 22nd of January the *Stratford Herald* pronounced for the people and the time-honoured pageant: —" Much dissatisfaction," said our respected contemporary, " is daily manifested by a large portion of our townspeople, in consequence of the *one* idea of a jubilee festival—a procession of some of the principal characters of Shakespeare's plays—being entirely ignored by those who have taken upon themselves the onerous duties of carrying out the forthcoming festivities in this town. Without intending any doggerelism, we all know that both high and low are fond of show, and the arguments in opposition to this popular view appear to us to be of the very weakest. In the pride of assumed intellectual superiority, some persons assert that a pageant would not be in accordance with the spirit of the age. If, as we believe, the spirit of the age is manifested by the prevailing taste of society, then pageantry has nothing in common with spirit-rapping, sensational dramas, and perhaps what is felt to be, in the domestic circle, worse than all, sensational novels of the most questionable morality. Others say that the Committee would not be justified in spending any part of the public money for such a purpose; but we have heard rumours of torchlight processions, fireworks, rural sports, &c., to which the Committee appear disposed to give countenance; and if the general festival fund can be taxed for these, what tangible reason can be advanced for not supporting a

pageant, the distinguishing characteristic of all Shakespearian festivals of any extent since the days of Garrick.
* * * Should the first stone of a monumental
memorial be laid, a procession of some sort will be inevitable; but who cares to go out of their way to see a
procession composed of the body Corporate, the 'Odd-
Fellows,' 'Becher,' or any other friendly society? If we wish
to present to the popular mind an idea of the vastness of
Shakespeare's genius, we know of no better method than
to produce, on such an occasion as the laying of the first
stone of a monumental memorial to his honour, an embodiment of the characters through whom he imparted to
this benighted world such a blaze of intellectual light."

Still the Committee could not see the philosophy or
propriety of a pageant; and furthermore they expected
such a tremendous influx of genteel visitors that they
apprehended a boxing night crush must take place in every
street of Stratford if any strong attraction were held out
to the million on the first week of the celebration. But the
upper ten did not come in the numbers expected, and the
second week's entertainments, got up that the gentry might
not be incommoded, protracted the festival and entailed
pecuniary outlay, the amount of which has not yet been
published, or perhaps ascertained. The preliminary programme, which promised popular entertainments in the
pavilion on the second week, induced the admirers of the
pageant to hope that their favourite spectacle would also be
got up under the auspices of the Committee; but when the
official programme appeared, without any announcement of
out-door amusements except the ascent of Mr. Coxwell's
new balloon, the people found that they must depend upon
themselves, and they did so successfully, at the eleventh
hour, as will appear in the sequel.

Returning to the preliminary programme, no less than
six thousand six hundred and fifty copies of it were
put into circulation from the 23rd of February to the
24th of March, and during this time alterations were
being made in it almost daily, as changes took place in
the arrangements or additions were made to the *corps*

dramatique. At last an event occurred which caused a serious change, and spread general consternation. Mr. Fechter, the dramatic sheet-anchor, gave way! He now refused to play *Hamlet!* Mr. Phelps had been lost under the circumstances fully stated in the correspondence. Mr. Webster declined on the same or somewhat similar grounds; and no doubt the Committee were at the same time deprived of the services of my friends Paul Bedford, John Lawrence Toole, and others, who would have been forthcoming if required. Mdlle. Tietjens retired on some misunderstanding which I never heard clearly stated; Mrs. Keeley could not appear in consequence of delicate health; and then—*et tu brute*—Mr. Fechter abandoned the labouring barque and left her to the Fates. It was "too horrible for reality." Few could credit the news for a time, but it proved too true; and as there lay no power in the tongue of man to change the Frenchman's determination it became necessary to make the public aware of the misfortune. Accordingly the following correspondence was published:—

" *Shakespearian Tercentenary at Stratford-upon-Avon.*
" *To the Editor of the* MORNING STAR.
" Sir,
"It is with sincere regret that the Stratford-upon-Avon tercentenary festival Committee are compelled to announce to the public that Mr. Fechter has broken faith with them by declining to put the play of 'Hamlet' upon the stage on the 27th inst., and to take the part of *Hamlet*.

"At this late period it is totally impracticable for the Committee to place any tragedy upon the stage, as forming part of the tercentenary celebration, which they much deplore, both on account of the public and the occasion.

"The Committee, however, deem it right that the public should be made acquainted with the circumstances attending Mr. Fechter's breach of his engagement, entered into with the Committee in December last.

"The announcement in the preliminary programme was drawn up by Mr. Fechter himself, and most expensive preparations made, and the stage enlarged under his directions, expressly to allow of the scenic effects which he required; and up to the day of his unfortunate accident he was in most friendly communication with the Committee.

"Judge then of the consternation and surprise of the Committee, when, on the 26th of March last, they received the letter from Mr.

Barnett (No. 1), dated the 23rd, and posted at Vetnor, in the Isle of Wight, on the 24th. The Vice-chairman, Mr. Flower, wrote at once in reply the letter (No. 2).

"On Monday morning (the 28th) a paragraph appeared in one paper only (the *Star*), stating the withdrawal of Mr. Fechter from Stratford, whereupon a meeting of the Committee was held, and the resolution (No. 3) was passed, and forwarded to Mr. Fechter through Mr. Barnett.

"This has produced no alteration in his determination, and now, at the eleventh hour, we are placed in our present difficulty, without any fault of our own; and are driven to the necessity of offering to those who have already taken tickets for the performance of 'Hamlet' a return of their money or an exchange of tickets for other entertainments.

"I have the honour to be, Sir,

"Your obedient servant,

"HENRY KINGSLEY, M.D.

"Hon. Sec. of the Stratford-upon-Avon tercentenary Committee.

"Committee Room, Town Hall, Stratford-upon-Avon,

"April 4th, 1864."

(No. 1.)

"March 23rd, 1864.

"To the tercentenary Committee, Stratford-upon-Avon.

"Gentlemen,

"Mr. Fechter, prevented by his accident from writing himself, requests me to inform you of the painful necessity your late resolution has placed him under, namely, declining the honour of appearing at the Stratford celebration.

"The said resolution giving the force of truth to the false and injurious statement spread about by one of your members, and published by unfriendly papers, viz., that Mr. Fechter, by 'undercurrent and trickery ways, forced on the choice of his *Hamlet*.'

"Mr. Fechter would have felt proud to serve in his humble way to the celebration of the immortal master, but he cannot afford to lose his reputation as loyal artist and honest man through thoughtless resolutions or personal vanities, over which he cannot, nor will not, have any control.

"I am desired by Mr. Fechter to add, that the scenery is at the disposal of the Committee, he having no wish to prevent the carrying out certain proposals so honourably made by the already-mentioned member still sitting in your Committee, and simply retires, forced to such decision by your own will and resolution.

"I am, Gentlemen, your obedient servant,

"H. BARNETT."

(No. 2.)

"The Hill, Stratford-upon-Avon, March 26th, 1864.
" Dear Sir,
        " A letter received from you this morning, dated the 23rd
inst., addressed to the Committee, and opened by me, as Vice-
chairman, is most incomprehensible to me.

"Should Mr. Fechter break his engagement, after his repeated
pledges to the Committee, he would be doing us a wrong, which, at
this late hour, would be irreparable, to say nothing of the still greater
wrong Mr. Fechter would do to himself.

" Your letter has not been shown to the Committee, but to a few
members of it, privately, for I cannot imagine that Mr. Fechter, after
having in so straightforward a manner acceded to the request of the
Committee, will really break faith with them at the eleventh hour;
now that they have pledged themselves to the public, and have, with
great exertions, made their difficult and expensive arrangements to
suit his views and many of them under his own directions; besides
which we have in the country sold largely of tickets, with a prospect
of speedily selling the whole.

" It is my opinion that the Committee cannot accept Mr. Fechter's
resignation, or in any way be a party to such a breach of faith with
the public, the consequences of which must rest with him alone.

" Mr. Fechter's engagement with us is not, and cannot be affected
by gossip and ' unfriendly papers,' and there is not the slightest
foundation for saying that the Committee have by resolution, or in
any other way, given any sanction to the false reports to which you
allude; in fact, we are quite at a loss to know to what resolution you
refer, or who are the members of the Committee meant in your letter.
Do lay this letter before Mr. Fechter at once, and let me have a reply
by return of post, as I hope that, upon reconsideration, he will prevent
the matter going before the Committee.
                                        " Yours truly,
                                                " (Signed)   E. F. FLOWER.
" H. Barnett, Esq."

———

(No. 3.)

" That the reasons assigned by Mr. Barnett for the withdrawal
of Mr. Fechter from the part of *Hamlet* are wholly unintelligible to
this Committee, who have hitherto worked with cordiality and in
harmony with him. The Committee, who cannot be parties to any
breach of faith with the public, are still prepared to co-operate with
Mr. Fechter in the same spirit, and under these circumstances they
trust that Mr. Barnett's letter may be withdrawn, and Mr. Fechter's
engagement for the performance of *Hamlet* fulfilled."

"P.S.—It now appears that the following resolution, passed by the entertainments Committee on the 22nd of February, is the one referred to by Mr. Fechter as his reason for breaking his engagement with the Committee:—'That Mr. Bellew be requested not to make any more arrangements on behalf of the Committee until further communicated with.' The Committee, however, cannot see how a resolution affecting a third person can bear upon the subject, or in any way excuse or palliate Mr. Fechter's forfeiture of his own written and oral engagement, confirmed as that engagement was by words and acts of his both before and after the passing of such resolution. Neither can it be said that Mr. Fechter himself, at the time the resolution was passed, placed any such construction upon it, for, after its adoption, he was in Stratford, and personally gave directions for an extension of the stage to meet his own peculiar views and requirements; and up to the 12th of March, when his accident occurred, he was in friendly communication with members of the Committee upon that and other matters.

"It may be necessary to add, in explanation, that there has been no other resolution bearing upon the same subject, except one, on the 2nd of March, confirmatory, by the general Committee, of that which had been unanimously passed by the entertainments Committee, namely, that 'Mr. Bellew be requested to desist from acting further on behalf of the Committee.'

"H. K."

The following letter appeared in the *Star* of April 8th :—

"Sir,

"The grossly unfair statements embodied in a letter from the Secretary of the Stratford-upon-Avon tercentenary Committee, which appeared in your paper of Tuesday, would have been brought at once under the notice of Mr. Fechter if the state of his health had permitted him to attend to any kind of business. But the severe shock which his system sustained from his late accident, aggravated in its effects by the annoyance to which he has been most undeservedly subjected by those with whom he loyally co-operated until secession became the only course compatible with honour, has brought on so serious an illness that his medical advisers have forbidden his reappearance on his own stage for at least a month to come. It is, therefore, no longer a question whether he will or will not play *Hamlet* at the approaching festival. It would be impossible for him to act, even if he saw reason for abandoning the resolution which he has already communicated to the Committee. But that resolution rests upon grounds so substantial that the public will, I am satisfied, feel that no other course would have been consistent with the maintenance of his own self-respect.

" First, however, allow me to point out some passages in the letter of the Secretary to the Committee which are calculated grievously to mislead the public. 'The announcement in the preliminary programme,' he says, 'was drawn up by Mr. Fechter himself.' This is not true; Mr. Fechter merely had one of these documents handed to him for perusal in common with all other interested parties. 'Most expensive preparations,' he asserts, 'were made' for the representation of 'Hamlet.' This is true, but surely it would have been only honest to add that the outlay was incurred, not by the Committee, but by Mr. Fechter himself, who has laid out more than £300 on scenery, dresses, and properties for the occasion—all of which he offered to place at the disposal of the Committee when he avowed his own inability to appear. Mr. Fechter, it is averred, 'had the stage enlarged under his directions, expressly to allow of the scenic effects which he required.' This, again, is not true; in fact any one at all conversant with such matters must be aware that it would be absurd to dream of producing any scenic effects whatever in such a structure. When Mr. Fechter went down to Stratford, by invitation, to see the temporary theatre, he found that it had been so constructed that a large proportion of the audience could not possibly see the performance, and the stage was advanced and the proscenium widened at his suggestion in order to remedy this defect. So little, indeed, were Mr. Fechter's special requirements kept in view in these arrangements that the stage and grooves as at present constructed are fitted to the scale of the Haymarket scenery and would have had to be altered to fit the larger Lyceum scenery for the night of Mr. Fechter's performance. Lastly, it is alleged that the Committee 'are driven to the necessity of offering to those who have already taken tickets for the performance of 'Hamlet' a return of their money or an exchange of tickets for other entertainments.' It is impossible to understand how this can be, since Mr. Fechter's determination not to play was made known to the Committee before the definitive programme was issued.

" It now remains for me to state the reasons which induced him to form this resolution. On the 21st of January Mr. Phelps addressed a letter to the Rev. Mr. Bellew, then Secretary to the Stratford Committee, declaring that this body had insulted him by asking any man in this country to play *Hamlet* at the festival without first giving him the refusal of the part. On the 2nd of March the Committee dismissed the Rev. Mr. Bellew from his office, and Mr. E. F. Flower, the proposer of the resolution to that effect at the same time wrote to him a letter imputing to him responsibility for the affront offered to Mr. Phelps, and adding that the evil springing from having incurred the enmity of that artist 'far more than outbalances any advantages that could accrue to us from the most zealous advocacy of yourself or any other person.' The contents of this letter remained unknown to Mr. Fechter for some little time, which will account for his not having taken immediate action in the matter; but when its purport was communicated to him it appeared to him that he had but one course to pursue. The Committee had by this act, the motive of which was plainly avowed by its instigator, recognised the justice of Mr. Phelps' complaint that he had been insulted, and the only insult of which that gentleman complained was the assignment of *Hamlet* to Mr. Fechter, who did not choose the part but was asked to play it, and consented to do so. Under these circumstances Mr. Fechter felt it to be his duty to himself as well as to the Committee, to relieve that body from the responsibility of an act of which its members avowedly repented, by removing his name from the programme. There is one curious fact connected with this transaction which ought not to escape notice. Mr. Fechter's withdrawal was communicated by me to the Committee on the 26th of March. On the evening of the 4th of April the Rev. G. J. Granville, Chairman of that body and Vicar of Stratford-upon-Avon, called upon Mr. Fechter, in London, to make an effort to induce him to reverse his decision. They remained in conversation until past midnight, and when the Rev. Mr. Granville found that his efforts were fruitless, his parting words to Mr. Fechter expressed the hope that this affair would in no wise affect their mutual esteem and friendly relations. The Chairman of the Committee clearly did not think that Mr. Fechter had acted dishonourably or in bad faith. But the strangest circumstance has yet to be told. The letter addressed to you by the Secretary of the Stratford Committee, denouncing Mr. Fechter for having violated his pledge, was dated April 4th, and must have been posted early on that day, as it appeared in your paper of the 5th. It must, therefore, have been signed and despatched some hours before the Chairman of the Committee saw Mr. Fechter and was made aware of his final determination. No one who is aware of the high reputation and noble qualities of the Rev. Mr. Granville will suppose that he was aware of this proceeding ; but the mystery is one which certainly calls for a solution.

"Apologising for the unavoidable length of this letter, I have the honour to be, Sir, your obedient servant,

"H. BARNETT, Acting Manager.

"Lyceum Theatre, April 7th."

"*To the Editor of the* MORNING STAR.

"Sir,

"The letter in the *Morning Star, signed* by Mr. Barnett, and dated April 7, contains allegations and imputations so inaccurate that the Stratford Committee feel bound in self-justification to answer them *seriatim*.

"In the first place, the Committee regret sincerely that the effects of Mr. Fechter's accident should have been aggravated by any additional cause, but must attribute such effect to his own keen susceptibility to an imaginary wrong, rather than to any act of theirs.

" Secondly. The fact of Mr. Fechter's having 'drawn up the announcement in the preliminary programme' is denied. It is true that he did not originate the programme, but it is equally so, that when it was submitted to him he added to it, then approved of it, and thereby virtually adopted it as his own.

" Thirdly. That the Secretary's statement that the ' most expensive preparations were made' for the representation of ' Hamlet' was disingenuous, inasmuch as it implied that the outlay was the Committee's, whereas it was Mr. Fechter's. Now the phrase used by the Secretary did not apply to ' scenery, dresses, and properties,' but to the enlargement of the stage in the first instance, under the direction and dictation of Mr. Bellew (to whom great latitude of action was conceded by the Committee under the impression they were led by him to form of his influence with Mr. Fechter), and, secondly, under the suggestions of Mr. Fechter himself.

" Fourthly. It is denied by Mr. Barnett, in Mr. Fechter's behalf, that Mr. Fechter 'had the stage enlarged under his directions, expressly to allow of the scenic effects which he required;' and the very idea of 'producing any scenic effects whatever in such a structure' is indignantly scouted. In answer to that, the Committee can only say that experienced actors who have seen the theatre have pronounced the stage to be one inferior to few in England; and if the production of scenic effects was never contemplated, why was it ever attempted ? Will Mr. Fechter, under his own sign manual, deny that he announced to the members of the Committee that he would put the play on the Stratford boards as it had never been put on any stage before ?

" Fifthly. The Committee's assertion that ' they are driven to the necessity of offering to those who have already taken tickets for the performance of 'Hamlet' a return of their money, or an exchange of tickets for other entertainments,' is broadly denied, on the plea that ' Mr. Fechter's determination not to play was made known to the Committee before the definitive programme was issued.' It is perfectly true that the only programme as yet issued is called on the title page ' Preliminary,' and really is, as Mr. Barnett styles it, ' definitive,' for it is the one on the faith of which our tickets have been selling since the 3rd of March; and the programme about to be published, with the exception of some expansion of details, will be essentially identical with it; and the proof that it is not true that Mr. Fechter's determination was made known to the Committee rests on the fact that the programme was issued on the 22nd of February, whereas Mr. Fechter's determination was not known till the 26th of March.

" Sixthly. And now to meet the reasons advanced by Mr. Fechter for his breach of faith. It is stated that on 2nd of March Mr. Bellew was ' dismissed' from ' office,' and that ' Mr. E. F. Flower, the proposer of the resolution to that effect, at the same time wrote

him a letter imputing to him responsibility for the affront offered to
Mr. Phelps, and adding, that the evil springing from having incurred
the enmity of that artist, 'far more than outbalanced any advantages
that could accrue to the Committee from the most zealous advocacy of
himself or any *other person.*'   It would seem- that Mr. Fechter
appropriates to himself most mistakenly the impersonation of the
imaginary 'other person.'   Now the letter from whence these expressions were cited was one addressed by Mr. Flower to Mr. Bellew, in
answer to an apology tendered by Mr. Bellew to Mr. Flower, for a
false charge preferred by him against Mr. Flower; and the plain purport
of the passage is, that nothing that Mr. Bellew could say, or any
other skilful advocate advance, could make the Committee amends
for the loss of the services of Messrs. Phelps and Webster.   What has
all that to do with Mr. Fechter ?

" Seventhly.   There is an insinuation thrown out that there was
an unseemly interval allowed to elapse between the announcement
of Mr. Fechter's withdrawal on the 26th of March, and the visit of
Mr. Granville, on the 4th of April, to Mr. Fechter.   Now, on the 26th
of March, and on the 2nd of April, letters were written to, and interviews subsequently obtained of Mr. Fechter, with the view of
disabusing his mind of the erroneous impressions which had been
instilled into it.   Moreover, on the 29th of March, the following
resolution was passed by the Committee and forwarded to Mr.
Fechter through Mr. Barnett:—

' That the reasons assigned by Mr. Barnett for the withdrawal of
Mr. Fechter from the part of *Hamlet,* are wholly unintelligible to this
Committee, who have hitherto worked with cordiality and in harmony
with him.   The Committee, who cannot be parties to any breach of
faith with the public, are still prepared to co-operate with Mr. Fechter
in the same spirit; and, under these circumstances, they trust that
Mr. Barnett's letter may be withdrawn, and Mr. Fechter's engagement for the performance of *Hamlet* fulfilled.'

" Finally.   The mystery which Mr. Barnett says requires solution
is easily cleared up.   The letter, which he says must have been posted
early on the 4th of April, was not sent to the papers till the morning
of the 5th, after the interview of Mr. Granville with Mr. Fechter;
and, as a reference to the files of the *Morning Star* itself will show,
did not appear on the 5th in that paper, but on the 6th.

" The Committee, in drawing up this bare statement, have confined
themselves strictly to facts, and leave their case with confidence to the
discernment of the public at large.

" I have the honour to be, Sir,
" Your obedient servant,
" H. KINGSLEY, M.D.,
" Hon. Sec. to the Stratford-upon-Avon
" Tercentenary Committee.
" Committee Room, Town Hall,
" Stratford-upon-Avon, April 8th, 1864."

" P.S. As soon as the Committee are relieved of the heavy pressure which their preparations for the forthcoming festival entails upon them, they will, if necessary, publish *in extenso* the whole correspondence with Messrs. Bellew and Fechter."

" *To the Editor of the* STAR.

" Sir,

" But that I have been until now too ill to write I should have sooner addressed these few lines to you on the subject of Dr. Kingsley's letter, on behalf of the Stratford tercentenary Committee, published in your paper of Monday, the 11th instant.

" Any unprejudiced person who will compare that letter with Mr. Barnett's, published in your paper of Friday, the 8th, I think can hardly fail to see that Mr. Barnett's statements remain untouched.

" But, as Dr. Kingsley asks, ' Will Mr. Fechter, under his own sign manual, deny that he announced to members of the Committee that he would put the play of ' Hamlet ' on the Stratford boards as it had never been put on any stage before ?' I beg to state that Mr. Fechter does ' under his own sign manual ' most positively deny it.

" If Dr. Kingsley were to substitute the Lyceum stage for the Stratford boards, he would be nearer the truth.

" Dr. Kingsley offers, when the Committee shall be quite disengaged, and, ' if necessary,' to publish ' *in extenso,* the whole of the correspondence between Messrs. Bellew and Fechter.' These words (so far as I know English) should lead your readers to suppose that there has been some correspondence ' between Messrs. Bellew and Fechter ' on this subject.

" There is no such thing on the face of the earth, and there never was—not a line, not a word.

" I required the Stratford Committee, when they had passed a resolution expressive of their regret for giving offence to Mr. Phelps, to do me the plain justice of declaring that it was not the offence spread about, and nightly set forth by Mr. Phelps on the bills of Drury Lane Theatre—namely, the having allowed me to be foisted, by some intrigue or other, into the character of *Hamlet.*

" I required them to do me the justice of declaring that they, themselves, without any friendly interference, had proposed to me to play *Hamlet,* and that I had readily consented to do so, and to place the tragedy on their stage at my own cost. Upon their refusal to withdraw the resolution, and thus evading their duty, I withdrew, and they placarded most of the chief railway stations with my ' breach of faith.'

" I now leave my case with confidence to the discernment of the public, and beg to remain, Sir, your obedient servant,

" C. FECHTER.

" 18, Marlborough Place, St. John's Wood,
April 15, 1864."

I have not undertaken the responsibility of giving the complaint of the Committee or Mr. Fechter's defence in my own words for obvious reasons. Doubtless the whole case could be stated in much shorter time than is required to read the foregoing correspondence; but as the subject has been so warmly discussed, and may be still further and more minutely overhauled in time to come, I have preferred to place on record the facts, allegations, and entire controversy, as published by the parties themselves, so that those who hold with one or two of the morning journals, that under the circumstances Mr. Fechter had no other course open to him than that which he adopted, may have before them all that he has been able to write or get written for him in justification of his *coup d'état;* whilst, on the other hand, the large section of society who sympathise with the Committee, and regard Mr. Fechter's conduct as utterly indefensible and inexcusable, may see their view of the matter put forth *in extenso* by the parties aggrieved.

Shortly before the occurrence of this disaster one of national importance took place in the bursting of the great reservoir at Sheffield. Hitherto the Committee had been most fortunate in not having their great undertaking interfered with by the existence of war, famine, pestilence, or any general trouble of protracted consequence in the land. The distress in Lancashire had been relieved, and the trade returns indicated increasing prosperity; but the calamity at Sheffield, occurring as it did, almost on the eve of the celebration, threatened to absorb public sympathy, divert from Stratford-upon-Avon the current of contributions, and cast a cloud over the festival. That it had to some extent this effect there can be no question. Happily, however, the drawback was not of the magnitude originally apprehended.

But the Fechter apostacy was felt like a blow irrecoverable as regards the night in question. The closing of the pavilion on that evening was at first contemplated as unavoidable, but subsequently wiser counsels prevailed. Offers of substitutes and assistance came in from various quarters, and the advice of Mr. Buckstone, who, from his first interview at Birmingham with me as a delegate from Stratford, early in October, had been the warm friend of the Committee, was sought in the dilemma. A deputation, composed of Sir Robert Hamilton, the Rev. G. Granville, the Rev. Julian Young, and Dr. Kingsley (who on my retirement had consented to resume his position as Honorary Secretary), waited upon him at the Haymarket. Mr. Buckstone felt as a member of the Committee, and the result of the interview was a determination to get up the best possible performance in lieu of "Hamlet," and at this crisis Mr. Vining, of the Princesses' Theatre, came nobly to the rescue, and by his generosity and energy the Committee were enabled to produce two of Shakespeare's plays on the night in question, and that too with attractive histrionic talent which embraced the greatest novelties of the season. Miss Stella Collas in *Juliet*, and the Messrs. Henry and Charles Webb in the *Dromios*. On returning to Stratford the proceedings and arrangements of the deputation were fully approved by the Committee, and a vote of thanks, proposed by Mr. William Greener, and seconded by Mr. Norris, was passed by acclamation to the gentlemen whose mission had been so successful.

But the Committee's troubles in stage management were not quite at an end. Mrs. Theodore Martin, who had only given a conditional promise to play *Rosalind*, declined to appear. The accepting of Mdlle. Collas as *Juliet* was said to be connected with her declinature; and as Miss Faucit (Mrs. Martin) is the *tragédienne par excellence* of the British stage, whose delineation of *Capulet's* fair daughter must be ever remembered by those who have witnessed that exquisitely graceful and terribly grand piece of tragic acting, one cannot be much surprised by the view she took of her own professional position and dignity. It was not for the Siddons of the age to come forth in comedy, after a French lady had played *Juliet*—and—but the lady requires no justification of her withdrawal at my hand, nor am I aware that the Committee make any complaint in the matter. The very handsome contribution made to the funds by Mrs. Martin, evinced the interest she took in the success of the festival.

About the period at which I have arrived in this narrative, the services of Mr. Creswick had been fortunately secured for the part of *Jaques;* and that excellent actress Mrs. Hermann Vezin (late Mrs. Charles Young) took the place of Miss Faucit as *Rosalind.* Ultimately, the Committee found themselves in calm water, and might have exclaimed with *Iago—*

> " If consequence do but approve my dream,
> My boat sails freely, both with wind and stream."

" The last meeting," says the *Stratford Herald,* of the 22nd April, " of the commemorative Committee previous to the coming off of the event which has absorbed their time and attention for a period of nearly three years, took place on Wednesday last. The heavy labours which have been undertaken by the Committee, if they cannot command success, eminently deserve it. Very few of the outer world can form an idea of the labours which have been gone through ; and although natural anxiety may be felt at this period as to the result, there is no lack of confidence that the public will come forward and generously support the commemorative festival."

And now, before " ringing up" for the performance, let us take a peep, as stage managers and nervous *bénéficiaires* will do, at the house, *alias*

THE GRAND PAVILION.

This structure was, early in the business, a matter of serious concern to the Committee. After careful examination, a special meeting being called for the purpose, they accepted the plans of Messrs. Thompson and Colbourne, Architects, Stratford-upon-Avon. Tenders for the erection of the building having been advertised for, the following were received on the 18th November :—Messrs. Branson and Murray, of Birmingham, £1,300 ; Messrs. James Cox and

Exterior of the Grand Pavilion.

STRATFORD ON AVON.

Son, of Stratford-upon-Avon, £1,475 ; Messrs. Clarke and Son, Wootten Wawen, £1,799 ; Messrs. Eassie and Co., Gloucester, £2,449. These proposals were fully discussed and then Mr. Cox arose, and in a very honourable manner proposed that the tender of Messrs. Branson and Murray be accepted. The motion was seconded and carried unanimously.

The builders selected got their engagement perfected, and set to work. The alteration on, and additions to, the original plan (no fault of the architects) were so extensive, that it is believed they will cost as much as the amount of the original tender. But the work was remarkable no less for the rapidity of its execution than the substantiality of its character. Within five months from the laying of the foundation stone the pavilion was erected, fitted up internally, and completely decorated.

The building thus rapidly erected challenged general admiration. It was a duodecagon on the plan, 152 ft. in diameter, and constructed of timber on foundations of masonry, with galleries, orchestra, and stage.

The area or pit was 100 ft. diameter, the floor of which was carefully laid down for the dancing. The orchestra was constructed to accommodate five hundred and thirty performers, the lower part of which was removed during the theatrical performances ; and the stage was 74 ft. × 56 ft. deep, with nine dressing rooms, green room, and other rooms. The stairs leading to galleries were 10 ft. in width, with quarter spaces. They were placed outside the building, not to interfere with the floor entrances. The main roof over area, or inner hall, was constructed of twelve trussed principals bolted to the upright timbers, which supported the same, and had a strong wrought iron band round the whole circumference to resist " the thrust," and was surmounted by a lantern 15 ft. diameter, the lower part of which was filled in with perforated zinc for ventilation. The height from the floor to the top of the lantern was 74 ft. The whole of the roofs were covered with asphalte felt, on one-inch deal boards. The vestibule and covered entrances were 20 ft. wide, with

refreshment rooms, cloak rooms, stalls for opera glasses, &c.,
on each side. Twenty thousand cubic feet of timber, twelve
tons of wrought iron, and upwards of four tons of nails were
used in the construction of this building, which no one
could have entered without a feeling of regret that an
edifice so spacious, handsome, and substantial, was so soon
to be demolished. By reference to the annexed plan and
subjoined note, a pretty clear and correct notion may be
formed both of the internal arrangements, and of the
approaches to the building.

The Committee voted £300 towards the decorating of
the building. Advertisements for tenders were widely
published. The proposal of Messrs. Brothers, Leamington,
was accepted. Nothing could have been in better taste or
more effective than the decorations, the Elizabethan style
prevailing throughout. The principal seats were covered
with scarlet cloth, the ledges being cushioned, and covered
with silk velvet. An ingenious monogram of Shakespeare's
name formed a prominent feature in the beautifully painted
canvas on the back wall. The front of the boxes was
decorated with scroll work, interspersed with Shakespearian
medallions and quotations; and the well known passage in
the "Tempest," "The cloud-capped towers, &c.," was
inscribed around the building, sadly suggestive of the
temporary existence of the structure.

EXPLANATION OF GROUND PLAN OF PAVILION.

1 The Stage.
2 Lower part of the Orchestra, removed during theatrical performances and ball.
3 Gentlemen's Retiring Room during oratorio and ball, but used for spectators during the theatrical representations.
4 Ladies' ditto, ditto, ditto.
5 Retiring Room.
6 Ladies.
7 Gentlemen.
8 Stairs to Gallery.
9 Refreshment Rooms.
10 Offices for Opera Glasses.
11 Cloak Rooms.
12 Stairs to Orchestra.
13 Committee Room.
14 Ladies' Dressing Rooms.
15 Gentlemen's Dressing Rooms.
16 Stairs to Ladies' Dressing Rooms.
17 Stairs to Gentlemen's ditto.
18 Green Room.
19 General Dressing Room.
20 Entrance to Ground Floor of Building.
21 Covered Vestibule and Corridors to various entrances of building.
22 Carriage Platform.
23 Office for Sale and Exchange of Tickets.
24 Covered Way.
25 Church Street Approach to Pavilion.
26 Burton and Son's Photographic Studio.

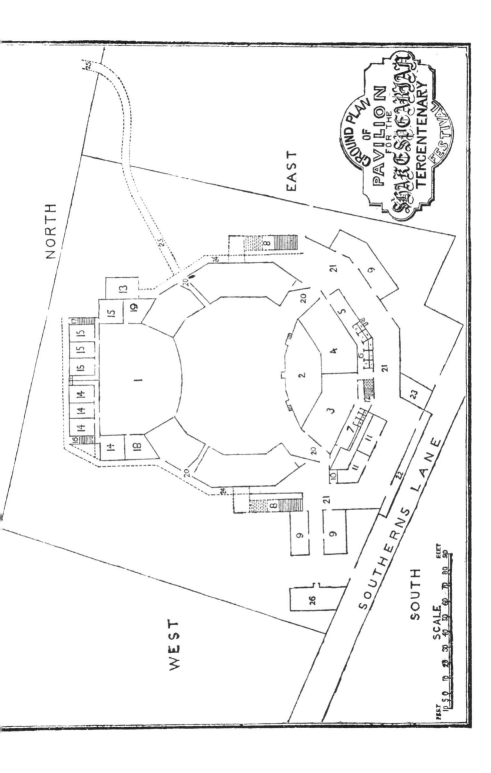

The lighting by a large centre gasalier, branches, and the foot and wing jets, was very complete, and to their credit it must be here recorded, the local company supplied the gas free of charge.

The stage, than which there never was a better constructed for histrionic purposes, was fitted up under the direction of Mr. Wales, stage carpenter of the Haymarket; the scenery, which had been painted principally by Mr. O'Connor, of the same establishment, was under his superintendence. Mr. Fenton painted the proscenium, and Mr. Telbin the drop curtain—a representation of the statue of Shakespeare in a sort of vestibule, surrounded with pillars and curtains, the Stratford church appearing in the distance. Some of these artistic works, although effective, were hurriedly executed, and conveyed no adequate idea of the talent possessed by their authors.

PREPARATIONS OF THE TOWNSPEOPLE.

Whilst the building was receiving the finishing touch at the hands of the artistes, the town of Stratford-upon-Avon was undergoing a complete overhaul and renovation; masons, plasterers, painters, glaziers, and paper-hangers were at work all over it. The front of nearly every house in the town was painted or in some way improved, and specially decorated for the auspicious occasion; vacant houses were taken and fitted up as temporary hotels; the historic old White Lion was resuscitated and filled with furniture; and it is much to be regretted that the inhabitants should have thus taken a great amount of unnecessary trouble in preparing for the reception of a multitude who never arrived. In point of the numbers who visited Stratford on the occasion the festival was a failure, that is compared with anticipations; and this I largely attribute to bad management in the advertising. The first "poster" was necessarily small, in order to have it placed in the railway stations; but for the second there was no such excuse. It was well enough printed on a mere four-sheet bill, crammed with announcements of

eight entertainments, and all their details. As an advertisement for such an occasion it was about as useful as an
old newspaper on the walls ; and in dimensions looked no
better than an ordinarily fortnightly concert room or casino
placard. Such a poster was scarcely magnetic enough to
attract a visitor from Shottery, much less to arouse the
attention of the world to the fête at Stratford-upon-Avon.
It was, in short, inconceivably shabby, and of itself sufficient to account for the failure which took place in the
attendance.

THE SHAKESPEARIAN PICTURE GALLERY.

As already noticed the Town Hall had been for some
time undergoing an extensive enlargement and re-decora-
tion. It was turned to good account by being put in
requisition for the display of a splendid collection of
Shakespearian and theatrical portraits, collected by Mr.
Hogarth, of the Haymarket, in pursuance of an arrangement entered into some time previously with the Committee.
There were nearly three hundred of these pictures,
comprising some of the happiest efforts of the most
eminent masters ; including Sir Thomas Laurence's portrait
of John Kemble as *Hamlet*, the property of the Queen,
who had been obliged (as Col. Phipps stated in a letter to
the Mayor) for some time past to decline to accede to the
numerous applications made for the loan of pictures from
the Royal Galleries, but her Majesty was " graciously
pleased to consider this very remarkable occasion as one in
favour of which an exception might be made." There
were other works by Sir Thomas ; an interesting collection
of pictures by the Sketching Club, and another lot by the
Etching Club ; twenty-five portraits of Shakespeare,
including the Jansen and Hunt pictures ; portraits of
celebrated actors, by Finlayson, Dixon, Faber, Watson,
and Stothard; many well-painted scenes from Shakespeare ;
some admirable specimens of Sir Joshua Reynolds's portraits,
and of the works of artistes of our own age, as Maclise,
O'Neill, Frith, &c., forming altogether the most admirable

exhibition ever seen in a town so small as Stratford. There was also an exhibition of Shakespeare relics, comprising the mask of Shakespeare, in plaster, alleged to have been taken immediately after death; a miniature in oil, painted from the mask; Shakespeare's walking stick and jug, accompanied by histories to establish the authenticity claimed for them. There were moreover busts of eminent actors; the famous Kean testimonial was exhibited, and a variety of other articles highly interesting to the dramatic amateur. The lower part of the Town Hall was let out in stalls for the sale of photographs, medals, badges, ribbons, statuary, and such wares as form the stock of fancy bazaars, but all having some attraction for visitors to the festival. The trade done, however, was anything but lively, and those manufacturers who had speculated in the production of these seasonable commodities must have shared in the general disappointment produced during the first week by the paucity of visitors.

THE FESTIVAL:

FIRST DAY.

It now becomes my duty, as the lawyers say, to enter at last upon a record of the festival, for which preparation so ample had been made. Perfect success seemed ultimately to depend on but one contingency, the weather; and never was gala or festival so specially favoured in this respect as that at Stratford-upon-Avon in 1864. The morning of the 23rd of April, the day of "our warlike champion, thrice renowned St. George," and of our no less renowned Will Shakespeare, dawned in splendour, and the day continued throughout brilliant with the "universal blaze" of the summer sun; and thus did the propitious sky smile on the festival, from its commencement to its termination.

Flags of greater or less dimensions were hoisted from nearly every house of business, and from many private residences in Stratford. The union jack, royal standard,

the red cross, and Shakespeare's heraldic insignia were to
be seen floating on the gentle zephyr in all directions—the
display of bunting was superb. Ribbons, medals, busts,
pictures, trinkets, all Shakespearian, filled the shop windows,
and attracted the attention of the visitor at every step.
The town, beautifully clean as it invariably is, never looked
better, and presented a genuine holiday appearance. And
yet there was a degree of ominous quietude throughout the
streets, which on such an occasion was most remarkable.
There were no cannon, bands, or bells to be heard, but on
the contrary "a dread repose" pervaded the town until
two o'clock, when the bells of the Holy Trinity Church
advertised visitors and inhabitants that the festival had
really commenced. At that time old Stratford presented an
aspect of unusual excitement and gaiety, but the crowd of
visitors was still not nearly so great as had been anticipated,
and whilst the principal hotels were doing a flourishing
business, "lodgings to let" stared you full in the face at
more than one respectable residence.

A few minutes after two o'clock a carriage drawn by four
grey horses drove up to the Town Hall. It contained Lord
Leigh and his honoured and distinguished guests, the Earl
of Carlisle, K.G., and his Grace the Archbishop of Dublin.
They were saluted by the Volunteers, who were drawn up
in Chapel Street, and received at the entrance to the Hall
by the Mayor and members of the Corporation, who, in
addition to their official robes, also wore ribbons, badges,
and medals, prepared for the festival. The noble visitors
were thence conducted up to the picture gallery, where,
for a short time, they inspected with considerable interest
the splendid exhibition just opened, and subsequently drove
to the pavilion. But before the Mayor and Committee
proceeded to the banquet an interesting ceremony took
place, in the reception of the deputation from Germany.

FOREIGN SYMPATHY.

The expressions of sympathy with the objects of the
festival which have been received by the Mayor from

foreign countries formed an interesting feature of the proceedings. Late on Saturday evening a telegram was received from Moscow, of which the following is a copy :—

"The Imperial University of Moscow, recognising the great influence of Shakespeare on the Russian literature and stage, this day publicly celebrates the three hundredth anniversary of the birthday of that great genius, equally dear to the whole civilised world, and hereby congratulates his countrymen on the occasion."

From Kharkov, in the south of Russia, came the telegram:—

"Sympathising with your festival, we forward our congratulations."

The deputation from the German Hochstift afforded additional evidence of the interest felt in the occasion. The Hochstift is an association which has purchased the house of Goethe with the view of preserving it from destruction, just as in this country the house of Shakespeare has been secured. In connection with the duty of preserving the house the Hochstift has also established lectures and other means of instruction for the youth of Germany. The deputation from this body consisted of Professor Max Müller, Taylorian Professor of Modern Languages at Oxford; and Professor G. W. Leitner, Professor of Arabic, &c., at King's College, London. These gentlemen called at once on the Mayor, and made him officially acquainted with the purport of their visit. The Mayor immediately proceeded to convene the Corporation of Stratford at the Guildhall, and as soon as a sufficient number was present to form a quorum Professor Max Müller said :—" Mr. Mayor and gentlemen of the Town Council, the city of Frankfort, the birth-place of Goethe, sends her greeting to the town of Stratford-upon-Avon, the birth-place of Shakespeare. The old town of Frankfort, which, since the days of Frederick Barbarossa, has seen the Emperors of Germany crowned within her walls, might well at all times speak in the name of Germany; but to-day she sends her greeting, not as the proud mother of German emperors, but as the prouder mother of the greatest among the poets of Germany : and it is from the very house in which Goethe lived, and which has since become the seat of the ' Free German Institute for Science and Art,' that this message of the German admirers of Shakespeare has been sent across, which we are asked to present to you—the Mayor and Council of Stratford-upon-Avon. When honour was to be done to the memory of Shakespeare, Germany could not be absent ; for, next to Goethe and Schiller, there is no poet so truly loved by us, so thoroughly our own, as your Shakespeare. He is no stranger with us, no more classic like Homer, or Virgil, or Dante, or Corneille, whom we read and admire and then forget. He has become of ourselves, holding his own place in the history of our literature, applauded in our theatres, and in our cottages studied, known, loved, ' as far as sounds the German tongue.' There is many a student in Germany who has learnt English solely in order to read Shakespeare in the original, and yet we possess a translation of Shakespeare in German with which few translations of any work can vie in any language. What we in Germany owe to Shakespeare must be read in the history of our literature. Goethe was proud to call himself the pupil of Shakespeare. I shall at this moment allude to one debt of gratitude only which Germany owes to the poet of Stratford-upon-Avon. I do not speak of the poet only, and of his art, so perfect because so artless ; I think of the man with his large warm heart, with his sympathy for all that is genuine, unselfish, beautiful, and good ; with his contempt for all that is petty, mean, vulgar, and false. It is from his plays that our young men in Germany form their first ideas of England and the English nation ; and in admiring and loving him, we have learned to admire and to love the people that may proudly call him their own. And it is right that this should be so. As the height of the Alps is measured by Mont Blanc, let the greatness of England be measured by the greatness of Shakespeare. Great nations make great poets ; great poets make great nations. Happy the nation that possesses a poet like Shakespeare. Happy the youth of England whose first ideas of this world in which they are to live are taken from his pages. That silent influence of Shakespeare's poetry on millions of young hearts in England, in Germany, in all the world, shows the superhuman power of human genius. If one looks at that small house in a small street of a small town of a small island, and then thinks of the world-embracing, world-quickening, world-ennobling spirit that burst forth from that small garret, one has learnt a lesson and carried off a blessing for which no pilgrimage would have been too long. Though the great festivals which, in former days, brought together people from all parts of Europe to worship at the shrine of Canterbury exists no more, let us hope, for the sake of England more than for the sake of Shakespeare, that this will not be the last Shakespearian festival in the annals of Stratford-upon-Avon. In this cold critical age of ours the power of worshipping, the art of admiring, the passion of loving what is great and good, are fast dying out. May England never be ashamed to show to the world that she can love, that she can admire, that she can worship the greatest of her poets. May Shakespeare live on in the love of each generation that grows up in England. May the youth of England long continue to be nursed, to be fed, to be reproved, and judged by his spirit. With that nation, that truly English, because truly Shakespearian nation, the German nation will always be united by the strongest sympathies; for, superadded to their common blood, their common religion, their common battles and victories, they will always have in Shakespeare a common teacher, a common benefactor, a common friend. Mr. Mayor, Professor Leitner, Professor of Arabic at King's College, London, has the address from the German nation, and will present it to you."

Professor Leitner then presented the address, in the name of the Hochstift, to the Corporation of Stratford. He said it had been suggested to him that since the Hochstift represented on this occasion the nation of Goethe, and the Mayor and Council of Stratford the nation of Shakespeare, it would be right to present this document in a more public, though less formal, manner. With that suggestion he saw no difficulty of complying, and would therefore take the opportunity at the banquet of presenting it to the Corporation before the assembled public. Till then he would have it thoroughly understood that the Hochstift, proprietors of the house of Goethe, looked to the Stratford Corporation, trustees of the house of Shakespeare, as the most worthy representatives of the nation of Shakespeare on the present occasion. Professor Leitner then conveyed the greeting of the Hochstift to the Corporation, and amid considerable applause formally deposited the address, without reading it, in the hands of the Mayor and the Corporation.

The following is a translation of the address :—

" The Free German Hochstift for the spread of Sciences, Arts, and General Enlightenment, from their seat in the House of Goethe, sends its voice to the whole German nation by congratulating on the tercentenary of Shakespeare's birth, through this document, and addresses this letter to the Mayor and Council of the town of Stratford-upon-Avon.

" Once, as their blood, so was the language of the nations of the Saxons on this and that side of the German Ocean, the same. Sprung from one stem, two separate branches have developed into a separate and perfect growth. On the one side was formed that English tongue which enabled the greatest poet and painter of the human heart and of its passions, whose cradle stood on the banks of the Avon, to give expression to the creations of his mind ; on the other side grew that German mother tongue in which Goethe, the greatest among the host of admirers of Shakespeare, described with graphic touches, as before him no mortal, the macrocosm the universe, together with the microcosm man. Once our country sent to Britain's shores that heroic youth which came as deliverers and successfully established a new Saxon nationality against the invasion of Latin races and influence. Shakespeare's poems, in return, restored to us the mothers' travail of Germania, at a time when, in a century of civil revolution, they were almost forgotten in their own country. Old Teutonic virtues gained their footing as emancipators and expellers of Latin corruption, and, establishing themselves victoriously, gave birth to a new heroic youth; but this time one of the intellects which forced its way through storm and oppression into light, and grouped the brilliant host of our writers round the bold forms of Schiller and Goethe. As England's sons, wherever they be on this globe, so do all Germans thankfully praise the one and only William Shakespeare. May the kindred of blood once more assert its power by uniting into one fellow-feeling all the members of the race of the Saxons on this or that side of every sea. This we wish by our greeting :—

"Hail to the memory of William Shakespeare!
"Hail to the town of Stratford-upon-Avon!
"Hail to the people of England!
(Signed by the Executive of the Hochstift.)

"VOLGER, President.
"KRELS,   } Vice-presidents.
"HEYDEN, }
"SCHIDECK, Secretary.

"Given in Goethe's House on Sunday Jubilate."

The address was tastefully illuminated, the vignette displaying a medallion of Shakespeare in gold and blue; at the foot is a scroll, at either end of which is a wreath, enclosing a sketch of Goethe's house, and another of Shakespeare. On the scroll at the foot is inscribed a sentence from Kückert—"This is my people, the great people, which out of its bosom daily sends its sons. They carry back to its bosom the nations of every tongue; and at the banquet mingle, in wonderful oneness of song, the varied languages of the world."

THE BANQUET.

This appropriate commencement of a series of holidays entitled the " Festival Week," took place pursuant to arrangement in the pavilion. On the floor, or central part of the building, there were placed ten rows of tables ; of these one was a cross or head table, at which the President and more distinguished of the guests were seated. Three other rows of tables were arranged on the stage, and these, set off with the wings and side scenes, made a very pleasing picture. In the lower tier, or what might be called the "pit boxes," tables were also placed, at which, as in other parts of the building, ample justice was done to the " Shakespearian dishes." The upper galleries were occupied by spectators, who looked on with all that gratification that is to be derived from witnessing enjoyments which one is not permitted to share. The decorations of the pavilion were in good taste, but several of the mottoes around the building were not very happily selected. The following from " Julius Cæsar," for instance, were somewhat ominous and apologetic :—

> " O that a man might know
> The end of this day's business ere it come."

And—

> " In such a time as this
> It is not meet that every nice offence
> Should bear its comment."

The tables were, however, very beautifully decorated with flowers mentioned by Shakespeare, and there were also a number of busts and statuettes which formed appropriate and agreeable objects of decoration. On one was placed a bronze representing *Ophelia* in her "brainish apprehension" distributing flowers for " thoughts and remembrance." Another was occupied by the pendant to this, a figure of *Hamlet*—a thoroughly artistic representation of the character. *Romeo* and *Juliet*, the details of the dress, jewels, &c., being most minutely carved, were on a third table. On the centre was placed the beautiful memorial bust of Shakespeare—a copy in bronze the exact size of the original having been expressly produced for this occasion. This bust is the work of Mr. Felix M. Miller, professor of sculpture, Government School of Art, London, and is believed by many to be one of the most successful likenesses ever produced. It formed, together with the *Ophelia*, *Hamlet*, &c., above-named, a portion of the collection illustrative of Shakespeare's plays, which Messrs. Howell, James, and Co., of Regent Street, London, had arranged for exhibition during the festival.

Lord Carlisle, accompanied by Lord Leigh and several others, arrived as above stated, at Stratford-upon-Avon shortly after two o'clock. On his entrance to the town, and when on his way to the pavilion, Lord Carlisle was enthusiastically cheered. Within the pavilion a very hearty reception was also given to his lordship, and on his taking the chair he was cheered by repeated rounds of applause.

Amongst the company present, who numbered seven hundred and fifty, the following were observed :—The Earl of Carlisle, K.G., Lord-Lieutenant of Ireland (the President), his Grace the Archbishop of Dublin, the Lord Bishop of St. Andrews, the Earl of Shrewsbury, Lord Leigh (Lord-Lieutenant of Warwickshire), the Earl of Warwick, Lord Wrottesley, the Hon. F. Byng, the Earl of Harrowby, the Right Hon. C. B. Adderley, M.P., Mr. C. N. Newdegate, M.P., General Ainslie, Mr. J. C. Ewart, M.P., Sir Charles Mordaunt, M.P., Sir R. N. C. Hamilton, Bart., Mr. E. F. Flower (Mayor of Stratford), Dr. Brockhaus, Professor Max Müller, Dr. Leitner, Sir William Fraser, M.P., Hon. Chandos Leigh, Lord Houghton, Sir J. Paxton, M.P., Sir Lawrence Palk, M.P., Hon. F. Ponsonby, Mr. C. M. Caldecott, Mr. W. Holliday (Mayor of Birmingham), the Lord Mayor of York, Mr. Charles Swain, Mr. Martin F. Tupper, Sir N. W.

Throckmorton, Bart., Mr. E. A. Cook, R.A., Dr. Ward, Mr. S. Muntz, Colonel Tomlinson, Rev. G. Granville, Rev. W. Morton, Mr. P. H. Muntz, the Mayor of Tamworth, Dr. Kingsley (Hon. Sec.), the Mayor of Coventry, Mr. T. Gillow (Foxcote House), Mr. Philip H. Howard (Corley Castle, Carlisle), Mr. Geo. Eyston (Overbury), Mrs. and Miss Bellasis, Mr. C. Holte Bracebridge, Mr. C. W. Hoskyns, Mr. J. Staunton, Sir A. Hallam Elton, Bart., Mr. J. R. West, Sir Maxwell Steele Graves, Bart., and Lady Graves, Mr. M. Philips, Mr. R. N. Philips, Mr. Creswick, Rev. Julian Young, the Mayor of Evesham, Mr. F. T. Dinsdale (Leamington), Rev. John Lucy, Mr. W. H. Child, Mr. W. J. Harding, Rev. T. R. Medwin, Rev. G. Bourne, Rev. J. Cadogan, Mr. J. F. Tempest, Mr. G. F. Muntz, Rev. G. St. John, Sir J. Anson, Bart., Rev. W. Barnard, Dr. Thomson, Sir Eardley Wilmot, Bart., Dr. John Tibbits, Mr. F. Tibbits (Warwick), Mr. J. Wright, (Leamington), Mr. H. O. Hunt, Mr. T. Hunt, Mr. H. S. Lucy (Charlecote Park), Mr. Joseph Glover (Leamington), Mr. J. J. Watkin (Leamington), Mr. S. Gwinnett (Warwick), Mr. R. Chambers, LL.D. (Edinburgh), Mr. C. Redfern (Warwick), Mr. Elihu Burritt, the Rev. W. C. Tompson (Alderminster), Mrs. Granville, Mr. P. C. Cleasby (Worcester), Mr. J. Gamble, Mr. John Baldwin, the Rev. H. B. Faulkner (Budbroke), Mr. Leigh (Birmingham), the Rev. C. E. Kennaway, the Rev. A. H. Lea (Loxley), Mr. T. H. England (Snitterfield), Mr. and Mrs. J. J. Nason, Mr. Nason (Nuneaton), Mr. R. M. Bird, Mr. R. Colbourne (Great Marlow), Mr. G. Fosbroke (Bidford), Mr. T. S. Ashwin (London), Mr. Thomas Slatter, Mr. and Mrs. Hobbes, Mr. Albert Hobbes, Mr. W. Flower, Lieut. Flower (S.R.V.C.), Mrs. Charles Flower, Mr. T. Starkey (Rhine Hill House), Mr. W. J. Harding (Baraset), Mr. Fielding Harding (The Elms), Major Machen (Leamington), Mr. D. Deighton, Mr. Amery (of Worcester), Mr. E. Gibbs, Mr. Cox (Kineton), Dr. Fayrer (Henley-in-Arden), Mr. J. B. Freer, Mr. Holroyd (Worcester), Mr. Summerfield (Leamington), Mr. Elvins (Warwick), the Rev. J. Knipe (Wellesbourne), the Rev. H. L. Freer, Mr.

and Mrs. W. Knights, Mr. W. Dickie, Mr. T. Croft, Mr. H. Sanman Wyman (Alcester), Mr. and Mrs. Henry Lane, Mr. John Tarleton (Wootten Wawen), Mr. John Morgan, Mr. E. Adams, Mr. James Rose (Warwick), Mr. William Lane (Warwick), Mrs. Handley (Warwick), Mr. Thomas Lane (Edgbaston), Mr. W. Lane (Warwick), Mr. John Archer, Mr. Bentley (Worcester), Mr. and Mrs. Beale (Worcester), Mr. R. Wolff, Mr. and Mrs. Adcock (Worcester), Mr. and Miss Wilson (Worcester), Mr. Grierson (London), Mr. Frederick Ferrar (London), Mr. W. Hetherington (Lancashire), Mr. Buxton Morrish (London), Mr. W. Greener, Mr. James Cox, Mr. W. L. Norris, Mr. Atkinson, Mr. W. Gibbs (Alveston), Mr. E. R. Hartley, Mr. F. Kendall, Mr. H. Lane, Mr. C. F. Loggin, Mr. M. Lucy (Malvern), Mr. H. Samman, Mr. W. Stephenson, Mr. J. C. Warden, Mr. William Thompson and Mr. William Colbourne (architects of the building), Mr. Branson and Mr. Murray (contractors), &c.

Mr. Mountford, of Worcester, the purveyor, had very little time allowed him to make his extensive preparations. It was only a few days previously that he got an approximate idea of the number for whom he was to provide. His bill of fare contained nearly all the good things necessary for the sustainment of the earthly tabernacle; and as a rare specimen of *cuisine* literature, thrown off for the occasion, may be here recorded :—

" Ladies, a general welcome."—*Henry VIII.*, I., 4.

" Pray you bid these unknown friends to us welcome; for it is a way to make us better friends, more known."—*Winter's Tale*, IV., 3.

ROAST TURKEYS.

"Why here he comes swelling like a turkey cock."—*Henry V.*, v., 1.

PEA FOWL.

" A very, very peacock."—*Hamlet*, III., 2.

ROAST FOWLS.

" There is a fowl without a feather."—*Comedy of Errors*, III., 1.

CAPONS.

" Item, a capon, 2s. 2d."—*I. Henry IV.*, II., 4.

DUCKS.

" O dainty duck ! "—*Midsummer Night's Dream*. v., 7.

BOAR'S HEAD.

" Like a full-acorn'd boar."—*Cymbeline*, II., 5.

YORK HAMS.

" Sweet stem from York's great stock."—*I. Henry VI.*, II., 5.

TONGUES.

" Silence is only commendable in a neat's tongue dried."—*Merchant of Venice*, I., 1.

FRENCH RAISED PIES.

" They are both baked in that pie."—*Titus Andronicus*, V., 3.

MAYONAISE OF SALMON.

" Epicurean cooks sharpen with cloyless sauce his appetite."—*Anthony and Cleopatra*, II., 2.

MAYONAISE OF LAMB.

" Was never gentle lamb more mild."—*Richard II.*, II., 1.

BRAISED LAMB AND BEEF.

" What say you to a piece of beef and mustard ?
A dish that I do love to feed upon."—*Taming of the Shrew*, IV., 3.

ROAST LAMB.

" Come you to seek the lamb here ? "—*Measure for Measure*, V., 1.

GALANTINES OF TURKEYS AND FOWLS.

" The Turkish preparation."—*Othello*, I., 3.

LOBSTER AND MAYONAISE SALADS.

" Sallet was born to do me good."—*II. Henry IV.*, IV., 10.

DRESSED LOBSTERS AND CRABS.

" There's no meat like them; I could wish my best friend at such a feast."—*Timon of Athens*, I., 2.

POTTED MEATS.

" Mince it sans remorse."—*Timon of Athens*, IV., 3.

POTTED LAMPERNS AND LAMPREYS.

" From the banks of Wye and sandy-bottom'd Severn."—*I. Henry IV.*, III., 1.

ASPICES OF EELS, SOLES, AND SALMON.

" Cry to it, nuncle, as the Cockney did to the eels when she put them i' the paste alive."—*Lear*, II., 4.

DESSERT CAKES, JELLIES, AND CREAMS.

" The queen of curds and cream."—*Winter's Tale*, IV., 3.

TOURTES, MERINGUES, AND CHARLOTTES DE RUSSE.

" They call for dates and quinces in the pastry."—*Romeo and Juliet*, IV., 4.

BEE HIVES.

" For so work the honey bees."—*Henry V.*, I., 2.

FRUIT.

" Hercules did shake down mellow fruit."—*Coriolanus*, IV., 6.

DINNER ROLLS.

" The roll! where's the roll?"—*II. Henry IV.*, III., 2.

DRESSED POTATOES.

" Let the sky rain potatoes."—*Merry Wives of Windsor*, V., 5.

BITTER ALE.

" And here's a pot of good double beer, neighbour :
Drink, and fear not your man."—*II. Henry VI.*, II., 3.

CHAMPAGNE, HOCK, CLARET, PORT, AND SHERRY.

" He calls for wine; 'A health,' quoth he."—*Taming of the Shrew*, III., 2.

Grace before meat was said by the Rev. G. Granville, Vicar of Stratford. Part of his prayer was in the words of Shakespeare, " May good digestion wait on appetite and health on both."

The cloth having been removed,

The noble President (Lord Carlisle) rose to propose the first toast, and was received with loud cheers. He said:—Ladies and gentlemen, I give you "The health of the Queen." [Cheers.] It will, I am sure, be received with all the feelings which invariably attend the mention of that name. [Renewed cheers.] I am unwilling even in giving this toast to diverge from the immediate purpose of the day. But Shakespeare, as is his wont, supplies the most fitting words to be used on this as on almost every other occasion. [Applause.] Speaking of the Queen of his day, he says:—"She shall be a pattern to all princes living with her, and those that shall succeed. [Cheers.] All princely

M

graces, with all the virtues that attend the good, shall still
be doubled on her. Truth shall nourish her ; holy and
heavenly thoughts still counsel her." [Applause.] Ladies
and gentlemen, let us drink "The health of her Majesty
the Queen." [Loud cheers.]
    " The National Anthem."
    The noble President again rose, and said : Ladies and
gentlemen, the next toast is that of "The health of the
Prince and Princess of Wales, and the rest of the Royal
Family." [Applause.] With respect to the illustrious
couple who are the subject of that toast, it is not inappro-
priate to resort to the court of Denmark for a description
of them. [Applause.] We shall characterise them as

> " The expectancy and rose of the fair State,
> The glass of fashion and the mould of form—[applause]—
> The observ'd of all observers." [Cheers.]

Let us drink "The health of the Prince and Princess of
Wales, and the rest of the Royal Family." The toast,
which was drunk with much applause, was followed by the
new song by B. Richards—"God bless the Prince of
Wales."
    The noble President next gave "The Memory of
Shakespeare." His Lordship said—I come now to what
we here call "the toast of the evening"—yes, and the toast of
the year ; and I may with truth call it the toast of my life.
[Great cheering.] This may give a hint to me before I say
one word more, that I ought in some way to account for
being where I am. I will make no excuse for my own un-
worthiness, because if we come to that, who can be deemed
worthy to speak in behalf of Shakespeare ? [Cheers.]
Plato might write of Socrates, but who could be the
interpreter of Shakespeare ? I believe that I am wholly
indebted for the signal honour I am now possessed of, to
the circumstance of my having filled the office of Chief
Commissioner of Woods and Forests when some negotiations were being carried on respecting the purchase of
Shakespeare's house in this town, which apparently established a kindly feeling between me and the inhabitants of

Stratford-upon-Avon, which may have naturally led to their recurring to their previous recollections in connection with the present celebration. In my case, it is a distinction which, as it was the last I should have anticipated for myself, I also thought it the last that ought to be declined. I pass on to worthier themes. I heartily approve the idea of this festival. I think the leading events, epochs, persons of this our earth, require their occasional commemoration. [Cheers.] Life is stagnant enough—men and women are commonplace enough to avoid the risk of such disturbances cropping up too frequently. Least of all can the nation which boasts of Shakespeare fear to misplace her homage ; and as I think it right that such a celebration should be held, I am not less clear that the right place to hold it in was Stratford-upon-Avon—his own Stratford-upon-Avon—that Stratford-upon-Avon around which all we know of Shakespeare—all except his undying works, is exclusively clustered —here, on about the most central ground of his own fair England, where I cannot but fancy that the whole impress of the scenery and rural life around is so unmistakably English, that we like to be reminded how home-like, and special, and insular was the cradle of that poet for whom we claim the mastery over the universal heart of man, the pass
word over the earth, and the many worlds beyond it. [Cheers.] We are following, too, the good English rule of precedent, which was set for us by the celebration at Stratford in the last century, mainly under the auspices of him who seems to be universally acknowledged out of the long line of illustrious players of either sex, dead or living, who have distinguished, and in some instances identified themselves with the leading characters of Shakespeare, to have held the foremost place as the interpreter of Shakespeare, David Garrick. [Cheers.] But since that well-timed homage of the England of the 18th century to the memory of Shakespeare, with what colossal strides has his fame advanced in the estimation of mankind. In our own country, at the previous period, the public taste still allowed the representation of his plays to be overlaid by the clumsy alterations and tinsel additions of Dryden, of Cibber, and of Garrick

himself—*Et tu brute!* [A laugh.] I need not point out the gratifying contrast which the reverential and affectionate retention and restoration of the original text, and let me add the scrupulous attention to the whole keeping and chronology of the minutest accessories of the representation, supplies in our days. Then abroad, the middle of the last century was the time when fast and fierce flew the arrows against the alleged barbarism of Shakespeare, aimed from the sarcastic armory of Voltaire, which did not spare higher things than Shakespeare himself; consult the first living names in the brilliant literature of France, and mark not how altered, but how reversed the tone now is in which Shakespeare is now spoken of and judged. As to Germany, I believe her boast is that she reveres, understands, and fathers him even more thoroughly than ourselves. [Cheers and laughter.] I believe I may cite Goethe as the most representative name in the varied and teeming range of German literature. How does he designate Shakespeare ? As the greatest traveller in the journey of life. Happily, any endeavour to define or gauge the genius of Shakespeare would be as much beyond my mark as it would be beyond the limits and requirements of a scene like this. I think he would be a very clumsy worshipper at his immortal shrine who would not admit that his merits and beauties, while they are transcendent, are still unequal, and that in the whole range of his thirty-six admitted plays in some of these he not only falls below his own level, but that of several of his contemporaries and successors. But take him in his height, and who may approach him ? Presumptuous as the idea may appear to classify, there would seem to be few great tragedies which occupy summits of their own—" Macbeth," " Hamlet," " Lear," " Othello ;" I feel we may take our stand within that unassailable quadrilateral, and give our challenge to all the world. [Cheers.] I feel, indeed, tempted to upbraid myself when I think of all the outlying realms of strength and comeliness which I thus seem to leave outside ; the stately forms of Roman heroes, the chivalry marshalled around our Plantagenet kings, the wit of *Mercutio, Beatrice,* and *Falstaff*, the maiden grace of *Imogen* and *Miranda*, *Ariel*, the dainty sprite, *Oberon*, and his elfin court, the memories which people the glades of the Ardennes, the Rialto of Venice, the garden of Verona, giving to each glorious scene and sunny shore a stronger lien upon our associations than is possessed even by their own native land. It is time that I should call upon you, in the right of all the recollections which must throng in your own breasts far more copiously and vividly than I could hope to present them to you—by the thrill you have felt in the crowded theatre, amid all the splendour of dramatic pageantry—by the calmer enjoyment of your closet leisure —by the rising of the soul you must have known that the lines which breathe and warm have led you to recognise and adore the Giver of such gifts to men, to join me in drinking, not with the solemn silence which a more recent death might have enjoined, but with the reverential love and the admiring fervour due to the day and the man— " The Memory of Shakespeare ! "

The toast was drank with repeated rounds of cheering, and was followed by the choir singing Arne's fine composition, " Thou soft-flowing Avon."

Sir L. Palk then rose and said:—I have been requested to propose a toast, one which gives me great pleasure in offering to your notice. It is "The health of the Arch-bishops, and the Bishops and Clergy." [Applause.] My lord, I know of no occasion when the presence of arch-bishops, the bishops, and the clergy, at festive meetings, and where ladies and gentlemen congregate, can be un-welcome—[hear, hear]—but perhaps there never was an occasion when their presence was more welcome than at this moment—[hear, hear]—when they come to render their homage and their praise to that great name which has been made illustrious by the noblest sentiments that can emanate from the heart or the mind of man, clothed in the finest language that the English tongue is capable of supplying. Upon such an occasion, when we are met together to honour the memory of our greatest man and our greatest poet, who has illustrated the history of

England as no other man has done, and whose works alone would make her great and illustrious name known to all the nations of the world—[applause]—no one can be more welcome than the archbishops, the bishops, and the clergy of this country. [Hear, hear.] My lords, ladies, and gentlemen, I ask you to drink their health and thank them for their presence upon this occasion. [Much applause.]

His Grace the Archbishop of Dublin responded to the toast, and said:—My lords, ladies, and gentlemen, neither I nor my brethren here regard even for an instant this toast merely as a formal one, for we do feel that there is a most intimate connection between all true art—and, therefore, before all, between the art of Shakespeare—and that Christian faith whereof we are ministers. But, seeing the special purpose for which you are assembled here to-day—seeing as I do around me the many distinguished guests who have gathered around his Excellency in the chair, and for my own part remembering that I shall have to challenge your attention for some little time before very long, I feel that I shall act wisely if I refrain from occupying time to-day, which you may better employ in listening to others. I shall satisfy myself, therefore, with thanking you in the name of my brethren and myself for the honour you have done us, and the kindness you have shown us. I heartily thank you in their name and my own.

The Hon. F. Byng proposed "The health of the Army, Navy, Yeomanry, and Volunteers." He said, as he was addressing an assembly of people who were acquainted with the history, the achievements, and the gallantry of the army and navy, and therefore even had he the eloquence of the noble lord in the chair, it would be unnecessary for him to speak of all the admirable qualities they possessed. He might say that they were now in a state of efficiency which had never been excelled. [Hear, hear.] It was gratifying to know that such was the case; but still he thought the nation's volunteer force was essentially the means of preserving the peace of the country. [Hear, hear.] They were an important auxiliary force, and he

had no doubt that they as well as the army would be ready
in turn of time to seek—not so much "the bubble reputation" as the safety of their country, "in the cannon's
mouth." [Applause.] He wished to state that the reason
why that toast was intrusted to him was the very melancholy one that he was supposed to be the oldest volunteer
in the three kingdoms. [Laughter and applause.] He hoped
the toast would be cordially responded to. He coupled
with it the names of General Ainslie and the Earl of
Shrewsbury. The toast having been duly honoured,
General Ainslie rose and said he wished the three services,
for which he had the honour of returning thanks, were
represented on that occasion by some one who could more
adequately express their gratitude for the honour that had
been conferred upon them. He returned thanks for the
army, the yeomanry, and the volunteers ; and he assured
the meeting that those services valued very highly such
marks of regard as that which had just been paid to
them.

The Earl of Shrewsbury said he should be wanting in
the respect which he felt was due to that occasion and also
to his own feelings with regard to the service in which he
was brought up, did he not on the part of that service
return his most grateful thanks for the honour which
had been done the navy. Without any disparagement of
the other three services—of which the country was very
proud—he flattered himself that the navy was the popular
service in England. [Hear, hear.] Our wooden walls were
disappearing, and being replaced by iron, but the same
spirit animated the seamen of the present day which
made them the darlings of the people in years gone by.
He felt that the time of an assembly like that was too
valuable for him to occupy a great portion of it, but he
could not forbear saying these few words with respect to
the gallant and noble service in which he was brought up.
[Hear, hear.] He might add one word of a personal
character. As an Englishman, and still more as a Talbot,
he could not forbear taking advantage of the request that
was kindly made that he should become a member of the

Committee. The immortal bard whose birth they had met that day to commemorate had inscribed in his pages the name of Talbot in a way that was honourable to him who bore that name in generations past. [Hear, hear.] As a descendant of that illustrious man, who well deserved the honour that had been done him in the immortal pages of Shakespeare, it was with a feeling of great pride that he took part in that celebration. In conclusion, he had a task to perform which was of a very agreeable nature. It was to propose the health of his noble friend the Lord-Lieutenant of Warwick. [Cheers.] He was sure that toast would be received as it always was, with acclamation, and it would not be drunk with the less pleasure because he should give in conjunction with it the health of the magistrates of the county. [Hear, hear.] In the neighbouring county, in which he had the honour and pleasure of living, he knew the way in which the duties of the magistrates were performed, and he was sure they were performed in Warwickshire in a not less honourable and creditable manner. [Hear, hear.] He could not forbear speaking of his noble friend for a moment in his individual capacity. [Hear, hear.] When great distress prevailed in a neighbouring town, his noble friend distinguished himself by his kindness, his sympathy, and his liberality in the cause of charity—[hear, hear,]—and he was happy to say that his labours had not been in vain—[hear, hear,]—but the fruit of those exertions was already reaped. [Cheers.]

Lord Leigh, in acknowledging the compliment, said :—Lord Carlisle, ladies, and gentlemen, in the name of the magistrates of the county and in my own name I beg to tender you my best thanks for the very kind manner in which you have drunk our health, and to thank my noble friend, the noble earl on my left, for the very kind manner in which he proposed it. I feel it out of place on such an occasion as this to inflict upon you a long speech, and I intend, therefore, simply to return thanks for myself and my brother magistrates. I am quite sure you are all anxious to listen to the eloquence of the many distinguished speakers whom I am happy to see around this table, and therefore I shall be as brief as possible. I am quite sure my brother magistrates would blame me if I did not, in common with the Mayor and Corporation and the inhabitants of the old town of Stratford-upon-Avon, express my own thanks and the thanks of the magistrates of the county to the noble earl who presides at this banquet for having honoured this festival with his presence, and thereby lent additional lustre to the brilliant meeting assembled in Stratford-upon-Avon to celebrate the tercentenary of Shakespeare's birth. [Applause.]

Sir William Fraser then proposed "The Drama." He said:—My Lord Carlisle, ladies, and gentlemen, when this toast was placed in my hands an hour ago by your worthy Secretary I confess I felt considerable apprehension with respect to the ground I was treading on, for the toast is one upon which a man might reflect for ten years before making a speech of ten minutes. [Laughter.] I was, however, induced to take charge of the toast by the assurance of your Secretary that the audience which I would have the honour of addressing would be lenient enough to make allowances for my shortcomings, seeing that I came into town yesterday evening, and have not had time for reflection. The toast which I have the honour to propose is "The Drama," not the British Drama, but "The Drama." Not to speak of what I have already acknowledged, that I have not had much time to reflect upon what I should say on the occasion, I feel that I cannot so far disregard your feelings as to detain you on a hot summer's afternoon with a speech of an hour's length on the drama. If you have not studied for yourself nothing that I can say about the drama will quicken your apprehension of its beauties. I have heard people, but can hardly believe them, who say that their early associations are connected with green lanes, violets, primroses, and honeysuckles. For my own part, I have all my life been an enthusiastic playgoer, and all my earliest reminiscences are of the theatre ; and whatever other people may think, to me the perfume of the honeysuckle is not half so sweet as the smell of the orange peel in the pit of a theatre. [Laughter.]

The toast having been drunk amid great applause,

Mr. Creswick (*tragedian*, London) rose to reply, and was received with hearty cheers.   When silence was obtained, he addressed the assembly as follows:—My lords, ladies, and gentlemen, upon this never-to-be-forgotten day, when the memory of the drama's great high priest is receiving the heart homage of not only a nation, but almost an universe—when the eyes and hearts of all are turned towards his birth-place, his home, and his grave— I find myself, an humble professor of the poet player's art, in the absence of more distinguished merit, called upon to discharge a duty requiring the most gifted eloquence to do it justice.   The knowledge of that truth cannot but seriously and almost painfully impress me with the weight and importance of the task your kindness has imposed upon me.   There is, however, the happy and gratifying circumstance in connection with this toast, that in these days of liberal enlightenment it is not necessary to advance or defend the claims of the drama.   [Cheers.]   They are now generally and generously admitted ; but such was not the case when the first wailing of an infant's voice was heard in the yeoman's house in Henley Street, when the mother thanked her Maker that a man-child was born into the world.   [Cheers.]   The drama of England was then oppressed by dense clouds of ignorance and prejudice. The sun arose in the small, and then almost obscure, town of Stratford, which has dispelled those clouds, and which has given to the drama of England its strength, its vigour, and enduring brightness.   [Cheers.]   Then who can forget or cease to be grateful for the glorious work that man-child has done for the world?   Who can forget that kings, princes, conquerors, mighty wielders of the pen and of the sword, have entered with reverence that lowly house ?   Or that the neighbouring chancel which holds his sacred dust, equally with the room which echoed his first cry, have been transformed to fanes and altars where the world doth worship ?   [Loud applause.]   We remember these things with a grateful spirit of loving admiration, and this wonderful gathering to-day speaks trumpet-tongued to that truth. [Cheers.] You will therefore pardon, I am sure, at such a time as this, a confession of a little extra feeling of honest pride in his profession from one who in its pursuit has had the happy privilege of making the study of Shakespeare's matchless works the pleasant labour of his life. [Cheers.] Indeed, I feel that such an emotion will this day fill the hearts of all my brother students; for though having practised my profession for full thirty years, concerning Shakespeare I proudly own I am but a student still. And, believe me, this pride is not a vain or useless thing, for I do assure you from experience, that whatever crosses, neglects, disappointments, vexations, or rebuffs the true-hearted actor may meet in his chequered career, he finds his great refuge, consolation, and strength, next to that which religion teaches—[cheers]—in the knowledge and remembrance that his art is the one for which great Shakespeare wrote— that his art is the one which gentle Shakespeare practised —and his art is the one by which good Shakespeare lived. [Renewed cheering.] To the unreflecting mind it doubtless seems strange and curious that the great Ruler should inspire the greatest genius, humanly speaking, the world has known—not to advise men from the senate, not to judge men from the bench, not to dictate to them from the closet, not to admonish them from the pulpit, but to touch, soften, mould, and instruct them from the stage—[cheers]— to pierce their hearts with glowing eloquence, to fire them with ambition, to warm them into love, to move them with the soft presence of beauty and goodness, to place before them the true nobleness of virtue; to establish the strong, to sustain the weak, to fright the guilty, and uphold the free; to thrill their hearts with new delights, and to gently chide them to repentant tears. [Great cheering.] It is a proud, a happy and fortunate circumstance for me, that I can make Shakespeare himself answer for the drama; that I can invoke his glorious memory to vindicate, if it were necessary, that which he has ennobled and immortalised, to answer the cavil of the formalist and the sneer of the hypocrite; and to prove by an appeal to Him

without whom not a sparrow falleth to the ground, and by
whom the arm of the warrior, the limb of the peasant, and
the brain of the poet equally are made, that there is an
eternal fitness of things, from the cedar which binds the
mountain with its giant roots to the hyssop that hangs upon
the wall; so, for his own wise and good purposes, he caused
a poet-prophet to be born amongst us, whose voice should
be heard, not in the chapel or the wilderness, but where
it could most reach great masses, mixed multitudes of men,
and stir them to good and gentle thoughts, and to the
noble deeds which good and gentle thoughts produce.
[Cheers.] Ladies and gentlemen, I thank you for the
drama, and in the name of my profession, I beg to thank
the people of Stratford for what they are so nobly doing,
and the Committee of the festival for the honourable
position they have accorded in their programme to the
actor's art—that art which, rightly understood, is a calling
to be proud of, and, when nobly practised, repays a portion
of man's obligation to his fellow men. But we actors shall
best show our appreciation of the honour you have done us
by our deeds—by the conscientious and honourable fulfil-
ment of our mission. When Shakespeare first drew
breath, we had barely escaped from the miracle plays of
Coventry and the mysteries of the travelling monks; now
we have passed through three centuries of glorious names,
and perhaps for both dramatic author and actor we have
culminated. If so, the drama may languish, as it has done
before; but can it ever die? No. For while glorious
Shakespeare lives, it will endure until

> " The cloud-capt towers, the gorgeous palaces,
> The solemn temples, the great globe itself,
> Yea, all which it inherit, shall dissolve,
> And like this unsubstantial pageant faded,
> Leave not a wreck behind."

The close of the speech was followed by the most rapturous
applause. The admirable manner in which the address was
delivered was worthy of the noble sentiments which it embodied, and it fairly divided with the speech of the Earl of
Carlisle, the honour and applause of the evening.

Professor Leitner, in formally presenting the address (above mentioned), said:—Mr. Mayor, ladies and gentlemen, when great responsibilities are publicly undertaken by constituted bodies it is both right with regard to the public feeling, and fitting in itself, that the reason of the assumption of these responsibilities should be publicly given. It therefore remains to be explained why we consider you as the representatives of the nation of Shakespeare, and ourselves as not unworthily addressing you in the name of the nation of Goethe. Mr. Mayor and Council, between us there has been a community of action; we have both felt the influence of the same associations; we are therefore driven to the expression of a fellow feeling. [Cheers.] With you, the highest civic body in the town which has given birth to your greatest poet, as with us, an eminent body in that town where was born our greatest poet, the associations connected with Goethe or Shakespeare's life, labours, and name (whilst with all our respective fellow-countrymen they evoke intense admiration) call forth, because speaking to the hearts of fellow-citizens, the most pronounced forms of enthusiasm and worship. It were vain that great men should bequeath a legitimate source of pride to their countrymen for all succeeding ages by their name and life, if, in their own native towns, they were not regarded with the deepest national veneration, personal affection, and personal gratitude. The birth-place of Goethe fitly therefore sends its greeting to that of Shakespeare. You again, as we, have rescued the house of our respected greatest poet from falling into the hands of the stranger, and what has been successfully acquired by private energy has in both instances been ratified by public approval. The house of Shakespeare is national property delivered into your trust. [Cheers.] The Hochstift have their seat in the house of Goethe, and throw its many appliances open to every teacher or student of literature. We have chosen you, in addition to the above reasons, because of the permanence of your Corporation; we have chosen you because we consider that your antecedents have shown you to possess every qualification for national representation, and we address you because, for the reasons stated, we believe that the Hochstift can worthily speak in the name of the nation of Goethe on the present occasion. [Cheers.] Consider this address, therefore, as a tribute of respect from a kindred race to your and the world's greatest poet. [Cheers.] We almost grudge you the accident of his birth. With us he is a national poet. Shakespeare's writings first roused the Germans to a consciousness of their powers, and made us enter the lists with you in a race of literary emulation. [Cheers.] We have read Shakespeare, we have criticised Shakespeare, we have perused everything bearing on him and his times, till, when we thoroughly understood him, we fell down and worshipped. Our missionaries for Shakespeare have proselytised the whole civilised world for him, until, wherever intelligence has any voice in the education of men, admiration for Shakespeare and a knowledge of his writings have become synonymous for the possession of mind, of judgment, and of qualities of the heart. Yet have we not neglected the development of our specific national literature. We have entered a race against you, and we have not disgraced either you or ourselves by want of energy, want of candour, or want of success. [Great applause.] We believe that in the distribution of national duties the one specially assigned to Germans is the empire over the thought and literary labours of the whole of this globe. Whenever any nation from one pole to the other exhibits dawnings of literary development, German scholars will investigate them, and add the results of their labours to the general stock of information for the common property, the common knowledge, the common good, of the whole of the civilised world. The statutes of the Hochstift again bind every one of its masters and members to the advancement of his speciality, and of knowledge irrespective of prejudice, favour, or emolument. Whatever treasures we may, however, find in other quarters, deserving as the labours of other nations may be, they will in our estimation —unless we degenerate—be necessarily always subordinate to the giant form and overwhelming genius of William

Shakespeare. At any rate, in our House of Goethe Shakespeare will be considered to be what Goethe confessed him to be, "his great teacher," and the Hochstift will never change in their loyalty to both Shakespeare and Goethe. The two united we consider not as English and German poets respectively, but as the "most perfect embodiment of the highest aspirations of Saxon poetry." Let Frankfort also occupy a place in your minds. A free city, the cradle of our emperors, the possible capital of a future united Germany, whose noble and enlightened citizens are the pride of our country, is worthy to speak through its Hochstift to the free, progressive, and yet—God be thanked for it—conservative and Saxon people of England. [Great applause.]

In reply to this address,

Mr. Flower, the Mayor of Stratford, said:—I regret that pressure of business has been so great with me that I have not had five minutes to arrange a few sentences in order to properly acknowledge this gift. We have all of us been busy doing, and have had no time to think of words. This token of a great nation's sympathy for us I receive with satisfaction, pleasure, and pride—satisfaction at receiving this proof of the love of the German nation for a kindred race; pleasure at receiving such a deputation as this; and pride that the Corporation of Stratford should be the recipients of and trustees for such a gift. Yet we receive it not for ourselves only; it is for the whole English nation that we intend to keep it in trust. This document will become the nation's property. This morning it was formally presented by Professors Max Müller and Leitner from the Hochstift at Frankfort to the Corporation of Stratford; now it is formally presented to the nation of Shakespeare by the nation of Goethe. [Cheers.] This most artistically elaborated address is not only valuable because it proves how thoroughly Shakespeare is appreciated and understood in Germany, but because it shows that there is a sincere fellow-feeling between the two countries, because it may be prophetic of a still warmer fellow-feeling, and because it gives our own worship of Shakespeare a stimulus of foreign

example.   And it is not Germany only—although wherever
Shakespeare is spoken of the name of Germany should be
heard with respect—which pays a tribute of respect to our
Shakespeare.   From another foreign source a similar grateful compliment has just reached me.   A gentleman of the
name of Hartenowski telegraphed to me a few hours ago in
his own name and that of his fellow-citizens and admirers
of Shakespeare, from Kharkov, in south-eastern Russia,
to the following effect:—"Sympathising with your festival,
we forward you our congratulations."   [Cheers.]   Gentlemen of the deputation, assure the illustrious body which
you represent that every care will be taken of their valuable
address.   We, indeed, the members of the Corporation, are
getting old, and are liable to decay, but the Corporation
itself, which has already existed for six hundred years, bids
fair, as far as certainty in things human is attainable, to last
for many hundred years more.   The address from the German
nation, will, therefore, be scrupulously handed down through
the agency of our Corporation from one generation to
another, will foment the sympathies of each successive age
which sees it between England and the Fatherland, and will
prove to posterity that on the tercentenary of Shakespeare's
birth English and Germans united in one fellow-feeling.
[Loud cheers.]   I am also glad that you represent a body
which has its seat in the free city of Frankfort.   Yes, it is
indeed that appreciation of free cities—of guilds, and of
corporations, which has stamped the Saxon civilisation of
the world.   We thank the Hochstift, and we hope that
through them our thanks will reach the whole German
nation, for the address.   We thank them for having chosen
men known in both countries to represent them ; and I now
promise, in the name of the Corporation, that the document
will be deposited in Shakespeare's house, and there religiously preserved. [Cheers.]   And, lastly, I must say that
the English nation are indebted to the two spokesmen of
the deputation, Professor Max Müller and Professor
Leitner, for speaking English so well, which they evidently
owe to their studies of Shakespeare, "that Saxon poet,"
whom all Saxons, whether of English or German homes,

are agreed in placing on the loftiest pinnacle ever attained by man in poetic grandeur. [Cheers.]

To render complete the element of German devotion to Shakespeare, as evidenced on the occasion, I may add that Professor Leitner, in reference to the toast of "The Poets of all Nations," made some fitting allusions to the country which he represented. He said:—

"Invidious distinctions are both morally wrong and logically erroneous when they are sought to be established between national excellencies in their varied, and yet of its kind, perfect character. Yet the application of antiquity in the estimate of a poet, though in itself absurd, at any rate gives us a hint towards the right step in forming an estimate; for the superstition of antiquity represents the confusion of the term between the greater experience gained by age, and the veneration paid to the distant and unknown. Not the ages in which man was in his child-hood are the ancient ages; it is each successive century and year as it rolls on, that gathers the hoary hairs of experience from the dying head of the preceding one; and those are the ancient writers who, either from their genius or from the experience they gathered by tradition, study, or actual labour, have shown us an intimate ac-quaintance with the workings of the world and of man. Now, as a German, I ought perhaps not to say it, but in due honesty I must deliberately and emphatically declare that, according to that definition, Shakespeare would be the first poet that the world has ever produced, Goethe the second, and Homer the third. [Cheers.] And, now, when you have had abundant proof of the readiness of Germans to pay their debt of gratitude to Shakespeare, may I ask you to devote something of the literary determination and acumen, something of the same enthusiasm for our Goethe, which we have shown for your Shakespeare. [Great cheer-ing.] We would draw the bonds of fellowship even closer than they are now. We are already connected by every possible tie of common descent, language, religion, and feelings, which can bind men and nations together. We read each other's works with profit and pleasure; but we

N

should see, hear, and read more of one another. The friendship of our more than forty millions of Germans for the kindred English ought never to be shaken. We love one another, and in every way are necessary to one another. Perish, therefore, all attempts that would sever the nation of Goethe from that of Shakespeare." [Cheers.]

Sir R. N. C. Hamilton, Bart., said he had to propose the next toast, and it was one which he was satisfied would be received by the meeting with the loudest acclamations. It was the health of their noble President, the Earl of Carlisle. [Applause.] He might truly say that they were greatly indebted to him for the admirable address with which he had favoured them, and in which he had, as an eminent scholar, alluded to the various points in the works of the great poet to the honour of whose memory they were assembled that day. England had great reason to be proud that she had men like Lord Carlisle, who, while they shared the toils and the cares of office, were equally eminent in council and in literature. On the part of the Committee, he thanked Lord Carlisle for presiding, and for the intellectual treat with which he had favoured the meeting. [Cheers.]

Chorus—" Come thou monarch of the vine."—*Bishop.*

The President:—Ladies and gentlemen, I thank you very sincerely for the honour you have done me in drinking my health. After the indulgence with which you have already listened to me, I should not think of making any further trespass on your patience. But I would not have you believe that I am not deeply impressed with your kindness, and more especially for showing me that you have not thought my presence in my present capacity so much out of place as I thought might have been the case. [Applause.]

Sir Charles Mordaunt proposed " The Poets of England." [Applause.] After some remarks he coupled with the toast the name of Lord Houghton. [Cheers.]

Lord Houghton in replying said:—Lord Carlisle, ladies and gentlemen, I am very grateful to Sir Charles Mordaunt for the kind manner in which he has mentioned me personally. I am the more so because when I looked at this toast list I saw that the toast of the poets of England, Ireland, and Scotland, was to be followed by a glee, " Ye spotted snakes." [Laughter.] I did not think the connection was altogether flattering. [Laughter.] The kindness with which Sir Charles Mordaunt has spoken has taken away all the bitterness from my mind, and I am willing to tell you that I am delighted to appear on this occasion, and am much obliged to the Committee for inviting me to this great festival. [Hear, hear.] I only wish that the poets of England could have been collected around this table; but we must take things as they are, and as my name has been connected with this toast, I would have been glad if I could at an earlier time have occupied your attention, that I might in some degree have illustrated the relation in which Shakespeare stands to the poetry of this country. But I must say I am perfectly conscious that whatever time I had been allowed, the result must have been unsatisfactory. You remember the Arabian tale of the great Genie who came out of a small bottle and spread over the whole heavens; but the wonder of the beholders was greater when he returned into the bottle than when he emerged from it. Now, if I attempted to treat in the short time at my disposal, the subject on which I am expected to speak, to show how the genius of Shakespeare has influenced the literature of this country and made itself felt all over the world, it would be like trying to get into a bottle. [Laughter.] I might have done it, although imperfectly, in an hour or even half an hour's lecture; but to concentrate it within an after-dinner speech of a few minutes' duration is quite impossible. What are called the poems of Shakespeare are a portion of his works less known to the public than his dramas. They are wonderful works, with a riot of fancy, a gaiety, and an ingenuity unsurpassed. They are very interesting in themselves from the biographical facts connected with them; but nevertheless they would have never made Shakespeare what he was. The world of poetry, as poetry, was not enough for him, and so he took to dramatic life, where he could produce in a tangible form on the stage the qualities and the characteristics which he would illustrate.   The immense influence which Shakespeare has had on the literature of this country it is difficult to estimate.   Dear old Goethe said that the reading of Shakespeare was most dangerous to any man who had any productive genius.   Let any man know Shakespeare thoroughly well he said, and he will despair of doing anything himself; and he ventured the extravagance of recommending men who had any productivity not to read more than one play of Shakespeare every year.   What he meant was that the poetry of Shakespeare had that wonderful power, that it was not the poetry of a man, but the poetry of the human race, the poetry of the world.   Thus it is that the influence of Shakespeare on the language of this country has been most beneficial.   It has given the poetry of England a variety which perhaps no other literature in the world has ever attained.   It has enabled our poets to see that poetry is not a mere talent given to this man or that man which he is to produce occasionally, and which shows itself in a spasmodic and visionary manner, but an enormous power of imagination which is spread over the whole of mankind, embracing every form of society, and all the institutions of the world, and thus enabling the poet, instead of being a visionary somnambulist, to be the one most active and vigilant, amid the contending phantoms of a world of dreams.   [Applause.]   Shakespeare was no visionary in the ordinary sense of the term, but a plain practical man—a simple, godly man.   Spenser said of him—

> " And he, the man whom Nature's self hath made
>   To mock herself, and Truth to imitate,
> With kindly counter under mimic shade,
>   Our pleasant Willie, ah ! is dead of late."

That was all.   He was a graceful, gentle, delightful man— that was the recollection he left behind him.   What did Ben Jonson say of him ?   He said : " I love and do revere his memory, on this side idolatry, as much as any, for he was honest, and of a free and simple nature."   [Applause.] These are the things which make the memory of Shakespeare so dear to Englishmen—on the one side his cosmopolitan variety, and on the other his intense personal reality. These are the things that make his poetry as true to-day as it was 300 years ago, and as it will be 300 years hence. Now and 300 years hence the boy and girl who make love will make it in the spirit of "Romeo and Juliet." Great tragedies will occur like that of "Lear;" the states-man and the politician will learn wisdom from the tragedies of "Coriolanus" and "Julius Cæsar"—the wisdom which teaches how politics should be self-contained and yet sympathise entirely with the people. [Hear, hear.] I thank you for the patience with which you have listened to me. I thank you for drinking to "The Poets of England," and I will only add that a thought of the great shade of him, whom our fervent imaginations may picture as here amongst us, should prevent us from naming any other poet. [Applause.]

Lord Wrottesley proposed "The Poets of Ireland." He referred to "Lalla Rookh" and to several other poems by Irish authors ; but after a few observations on this head he said that on that occasion he preferred confining his atten-tion chiefly to one poet. He was unable to express the pleasure which he felt in being present at that year's commemoration. This pleasure was the greater because he had observed that although his countrymen were always ready to award the due amount of praise to warriors and sailors, they were not always so willing to recognise the triumphs of mind. He had no reason to think so any longer, after having seen that great assembly gathered together to commemorate the birth of Shakespeare. If he asked himself which of his countrymen had attained to the greatest eminence, two names presented themselves to his mind, the names of Newton and Shakespeare. To use the words of our immortal poet, they "did not go about to cozen fortune ; they were not honourable without the stamp of merit ; they did not wear a dignity undeserved." He had seen an attempt made to weigh the merits of these two men—Newton and Shakespeare—the one the greatest astronomer and mathematician that ever lived, and the other the prince of poets.

Sir Eardley Wilmot proposed "The Poets of Scotland," and the Right Hon. C. B. Adderley proposed "The Poets of America."

Professor Leitner responded to the latter toast.

The Rev. Julian Young proposed "The Visitors," which was responded to by the Lord Mayor of York.

The Mayor and Corporation of the borough of Stratford were next toasted, and Mr. Flower, the Mayor, responded. This was the concluding toast of the evening, and the proceedings terminated.

THE FIREWORKS.

About an hour after the termination of the banquet, Mr. Darby sent up the first rocket of his pyrotechnic display which had been looked forward to as a grand wind up to the first day's proceedings. The site chosen for the fireworks was a field adjoining the Warwick Road. Thousands assembled to witness the holiday mimicry of fire, and to many of the spectators it must have been a rare and grand exhibition. Two large fire balloons—one inscribed "Stratford"—were sent up with good effect; and after a display, which lasted for upwards of an hour, an illuminated portrait of Shakespeare, surrounded by pyrotechnic devices was exhibited as a grand climax; but the brilliancy of the *finale* was sadly marred by the density of the smoke, which only permitted occasional glimpses of Mr. Darby's *chef-d'œuvre*. In the meantime there was a luminous display overhead to which that of the celebrated pyrotechnist was poor indeed. Cynthia had arisen in her full majesty, the chaste stars became revealed in the dark blue canopy, the nightingale charmed the listener's ear, whilst the full and soft Avon flowed on, paying its bountiful tribute to the gentle Severn; and thus closed without a *contretemps* calmly and beautifully the first day of the festival.

SECOND DAY: SUNDAY.

I have already had the pleasure of noticing the admirable observance of public worship which prevails amongst the

CHURCH OF THE HOLY TRINITY
Stratford-upon-Avon

Published by E. Adams.

people of Stratford-upon-Avon; and if regular in their attendance at church on ordinary occasions, it will be easily supposed there would be a crowded auditory to hear such distinguished orators as the Archbishop of Dublin, and Dr. Wordsworth, the Lord Bishop of St. Andrew's, who were on this day to occupy the pulpit; and accordingly for some time previous to the commencement of the service the Holy Trinity Church was thronged to inconvenience.

There were full choral services at 11 a.m. and 3-30 p.m. Immediately before service in the morning the clergy and choir (about forty in number) passed out of the door in the north transept, and met the Bishops, and Mayor, and Corporation at the end of the avenue, whom they preceded into church—the organ (a fine instrument built by Hill, but lately much enlarged and improved by Mr. T. Hewin's, of Stratford-upon-Avon) playing the National Anthem.

The first part of the service (Tallis's) was chanted by the Rev. C. H. Rice, M.A., Vicar Choral of Armagh Cathedral, and the Rev. W. Morton, M.A., Sub-vicar, sung the Litany; the Rev. G. Granville, Vicar, reading the Lessons, Communion Service, and Gospel; the Bishop of St. Andrew's read the Epistle. The service, morning and afternoon, was Nare's in F. The Anthem in the morning was, "O where shall wisdom be found?"—*Boyce.* The Introit, "Jesu, refuge of my soul," set to a beautiful tune composed by Mr. E. Flood, organist, London. The "Kyrie Eleeson," which was much admired, was set to music by Mr. E. A. Sydenham, assistant organist of Holy Trinity Church.

In the afternoon the first part of the service was chanted by the Rev. W. Morton, the last part by the Rev. C. H. Rice; and the Lessons were read by the Rev. G. Granville. The Anthem, "It came even to pass," was by Sir F. A. G. Ouseley, Bart.; and the Hymn before the sermon, "Holy, holy, holy, Lord God Almighty," was set to an appropriate tune in the possession of the Rev. W. Morton.

After the sermon, during the collecting of the alms, the Hymn used in the morning as the Introit was again sung.

The sermon was preached in the morning by Richard Chenevix Trench, D.D., Archbishop of Dublin.

The Archbishop having entered the pulpit, the sun at the moment breaking with summer brilliancy through the clouds, he selected as his text, JAMES I. 17 : "*Every good gift and every perfect gift is from above, and cometh down from the Father of lights.*" His Grace commenced his discourse with some remarks on the propriety of connecting the services of the day with the celebration of the week— of remembering the Giver whilst they extolled the gift— of especially rendering praise to God for "His most excellent creature man;" and having humbly expressed his desire that on some other, more equal to the occasion, had devolved the task of tracing the connection between the sacred services of the day, and the festal solemnities of the time, he proceeded to the following effect :—

One fitness, indeed, I possess—namely, that I am not wholly unaware of the difficulties of my task. To this I shall address myself now ; only first on one or two points challenging your considerate forbearance.

Thus, if I *preach* about Shakespeare, and that method of treatment sound somewhat novel and unusual in your ears, you will still remember that this is the very thing which I am set to do; which thus in my office as a minister of Christ, and in His holy house, I could alone consent to do. And then, if in so doing I pass over innumerable aspects on which he presents himself to us, and contemplate him only upon one—though that, indeed, the most important of all, namely, the directly moral—it is not because others are indifferent to me, or as supposing them indifferent to you ; but because here I have no right, as certainly I have no desire, to contemplate him in any other aspect than this.

What reason have we then to celebrate with a jubilee the fact that three hundred years ago Shakespeare was born? or, to put the question in the form and fashion which this hour and this house will suitably suggest, Why do we thank God, wherein have we just ground to praise Him, that such a man has been among us? what is there in his writings to render them an enduring benefit to us, a possession for ever; such as we feel makes us richer, wiser, and using it aright, better than we should have been without it? This is the question which I propose a little to consider this morning.

If indeed the literature of a nation were merely an amusement of the cultivated few, the ornament of their idler hours, then indeed what the fashion of it was, or what manner of men they were who bequeathed it to us, would be of very slight importance indeed; could scarcely at the best afford matter of serious thanksgiving. We might desire that it should be graceful, as we should desire that the garniture of our houses or of our persons should be graceful, that it should entertain without corrupting: our desires could scarcely extend further. But a nation's literature is very much more than this. The work of its noblest and most gifted sons, the utterance of all which is deepest and nearest to their hearts, it evokes and interprets the unuttered greatness which is latent in others, but which, except for them, would never have come to the birth. By it the mighty heart of a people may be animated and quickened to heroic enterprise and worthiest endeavour. With the breath of strong and purifying emotions it should stir to a healthy activity the waters of a nation's life, which would else have stagnated and putrefied and corrupted. Having such offices, being capable of such effects as these, of what vast concern it is that it should deal with the loftiest problems which man's existence presents—solve them, so far as they are capable of solution here, point to a solution behind the veil where this only is possible; that, whatever it handles, things high or things low, things eternal or things temporal, spiritual or natural, it should be sound, should be healthy; clear, so far as possible, of offence; enlisting our sympathies on the side of the just, the pure, and the true. Of what supreme concern it is that those who do so much to form and fashion a nation's life, should be men reconciled with God's scheme of the universe, cheerfully working in their own appointed sphere the work which has been assigned them there, accepting God's world, because it is His, with all its strange riddles and infinite perplexities, with all the burdens which it lays upon each one of us—not fiercely dashing and shattering themselves, like imprisoned birds, against the bars of their prison-house, or moodily nourishing in their own hearts, and in the hearts of others, thoughts of discontent, revolt, and despair.

Such a poet, I am bold to affirm, we possess in Shakespeare. For must we not, first of all, thankfully acknowledge a healthiness, a moral soundness in all, or nearly all, which he has written?—that on his part there is no paltering with the everlasting ordinances on which the moral estate of man's life reposes, no challenging of the fitness of these, no summoning of God to answer for Himself at the bar of man for the world which He has created? Then, too, if he deals with enormous crimes—and he could not do otherwise, for these, alike in fiction and in reality, constitute the tragedy of life—yet the crimes which he deals with travel the common road of human guilt, with no attempt upon his part to extend and enlarge the domain of possible sin; and certainly with no desire to paint it in any other colours than its own. He dallies not with forbidden things. All which the Latins, with so just a moral instinct, styled *infanda* and *nefanda*, things not to be spoken of any more than to be done, these, which thus declare themselves un-utterable, remain with rarest exception unuttered by him.

And in his dialogue, if we put him beside those of his age and time, how little, by comparison with them, is there which we wish away from him, would fain that he had never written. There are some of his contemporaries whose jewels, when they offer such, must be plucked out of the very mire; who seem to revel in loathsome and disgusting images, in all which for poor human nature's sake we would willingly put out of sight altogether. What an immeasurable gulf in this matter divides him from them! while of that which we *must* regret even in him, a part we have a right to ascribe to an age, I will not say of less purity, but of less refinement and coarser than our own; and of that which cannot be thus explained, let us at all events remark how separable almost always it is from the context, leaving, when thus separated, all which remains perfectly whole- some and pure. There are writers whose evil is inwoven with the texture of their writings, their very web and woof; writers who defile everything which they touch; for whom, and ere long for whose readers, nothing is pure, one foul exhalation and miasma of corruption presently enveloping them both.

But Shakespeare if he has wrought any passing wrong, or given any just occasion of offence in the matters of which we speak, let us not forget the compensations which he has made—that we owe to him those ideals of perfect woman- hood, which are the loveliest, perhaps the most transcendent, creations of his art. Shakespeare's women—we have but to mention them, and what a procession of female forms, whose very names make music in our ears, move at once before the eyes of our mind. Surely if the woman be in God's intention the appointed guardian of the sanctities of home, the purities of domestic life, we owe him much who has peopled the world of our imagination with shapes " so per- fect and so peerless" as are these. True it is that we want much more than art, much more than the highest which art can yield, to keep us holy, to preserve us from the sin of our own hearts, from the sin of the world around us ; and there is no more fatal mistake than to forget this. Neither dare we affirm of Shakespeare himself that he was always true to those ideals of female loveliness which he had created, that he never broke faith with them. We have evidence—he himself supplies it—evidence, as I think not to be gainsayed, that there was a period of his life when he laid up much matter of after-sorrow and self-reproach for himself, in his own wonderful words, "gored his own thoughts, sold cheap what is most dear;" for what so dear as innocency and self-respect?—he, too, a diamond only to be polished in its own dust ; and, like so many a meaner man, making in one part of his life work of repentance for another. But with all this we dare affirm an habitual delight in the purest, the noblest, and the fairest on the part of one who, in the workshop of his imagination, forged a *Miranda* and an *Imogen*. "Filth savours but itself," feeds, and would fain lead others to feed, on the garbage in which alone it finds pleasure. Of Shakespeare be it said, that he who has painted his long gallery of women holy, and pure, and good, walking in fearless chastity through the world, has painted, in anything like full length, only one wanton woman throughout all the ample range of his art, and her only for scorn and contempt.

Having spoken of Shakespeare's enlarged christian charity towards the church of Rome, and towards the sect of Puritans, despite the excitement of party strife which marked the transition period in which he lived, his Grace proceeded to reply to the charge preferred against Shakespeare of writing without a moral purpose, of making no just distinction of good or evil.

It is, the learned divine said, a shallow view of art, as of life, which could alone have given birth to this accusation. It is true that the moral intention of Shakespeare's poetry does not lie on the surface, is not obtruded; it may and will often escape the careless reader. But it is there, lying deep as do nearly all the lessons which God teaches us through our own lives, or through the lives of others. To no one of the uninspired writers of the world has it been granted, I believe, so strongly to apprehend, so clearly to make visible, that men reap as they have sown, that the end lies in the beginning, that sooner or later "the wheel will come full circle," and "the whirligig of time bring round its revenges." Who else makes us so, and with such a solemn awe, to feel that justice walks the world— "delaying," it may be, but "not forgetting," as is ever the manner with the divine avengers? Even faults comparatively trivial, like that of *Cordelia*, he does not fear to show us what a train of sorrows, for this life at least, they may entail. Certainly we shall look in vain in him, as we look in vain through the moral universe, for that vulgar distribution of rewards and punishments in which some delight; neither is death, which may be an euthanasia, the divine cutting of some tangled knot which no human skill could ever have untied—not death but dishonoured life, is, in his estimate, the worst of ills. So, too, if we would recognise these footsteps of God in the world, this Nemesis of life, which he is so careful to trace, we must watch his slightest hints, for in them lies oftentimes the key to, and the explanation of, all. In this, if I may say it with reverence, he often reminds us of Scripture, and will indeed repay almost any amount of patient and accurate study which we may bestow upon him. Let me illustrate what I say. They are but a few idle words dropt at random, which, in the opening scene of "King Lear," make only too evident that *Gloster* had never looked back with serious displeasure at the sin of his youth, which stood embodied before him in the person of his bastard son; that he still regarded it with complacency, rolled it as a sweet morsel under his tongue. This son, his whole being corroded, poisoned, turned to gall and bitterness, by the ever present consciousness of the cleaving stain of his birth, is made the instrument to undo him, or rather to bring him through bitterest agonies, through the wreck and ruin of his whole worldly felicity, to a true repentance. Indeed for once Shakespeare himself points the moral in those words, so often quoted, but not oftener than they deserve—

> " The gods are just, and of our pleasant vices
> Make instruments to plague us."

But for once that he draws the moral of a life, a hundred times he leaves us to draw it; as indeed is almost always the manner in that Book of books, which, like Joseph's kingly sheaf, stands up in the midst of the field, that even the chiefest among the others may make obeisance to it.

Let me note, in connection with what has just been spoken, that the ideal characters of his art, just as the real characters of actual life, never stand still. They are rising or falling, growing better or growing worse, and ripening thus for their several dooms. Some we behold working out their lives into greater clearness and nobleness, making steps of their dead selves by which they are mounting to higher things. Summoned to the more stern and serious business of life, or brought into the school of adversity, we see them taking shame to themselves that they have played the truant hitherto, learning to look at life as something more than a jest, girding themselves in earnest to its tasks and toil, and leaving for ever behind them the frivolity and the vanity, it may be the folly and the sin, in which hitherto their years were spent. There is no dearer argument with Shakespeare than this, nor one to which he oftener returns.

And then, on the other side, he shows us them who will not use aright the discipline of life, who welcome and allow those downward-dragging temptations which beset us all; these waxing worse and worse, forfeiting what good they once possessed, strengthening in their evil, and falling from one wickedness to another. He shows us a *Macbeth*, met in that most dangerous hour, the hour of his success, giving place to the devil, allowing the wicked suggestion of the Evil One room in his heart, and then the dread concatenation of crime, one ever drawing on, and in a manner rendering necessary, another, till the end is desolation and despair, the blackness of darkness for ever. Where, I sometimes ask myself as I read, where is there a sermon on the need of resisting temptations at the outset, of treading out the sparks of hell before they have set on fire the whole course of nature, like that?

Having spoken of the perfect sober-mindedness of Shakespeare—the man—of the absence of eccentricity or extravagance in his character, and adverted to the opportunity which the occasion afforded of testifying that it was no lip homage which they rendered to his name, by contributing to the restoring and beautifying of the chancel in which the dust of Shakespeare mingles with the common clay, his Grace concluded his splendid sermon in the following terms :—

I will only ask you, as you prepare your offering, each to imagine to himself this England of ours without her Shakespeare; in which he had never lived or sung. What a crown would be stricken from her brow! How would she come down from the pre-eminence of her place as nursing mother of the foremost poet whom the world has seen, whom, we are almost bold to prophesy, it ever will see! Think how much poorer intellectually, yea, and morally, every one of us would be; what would have to be withdrawn from circulation, of wisest sayings, of profoundest maxims of life-wisdom, which have now been absorbed into the very tissue of our hearts and minds! what regions of our fancy, peopled now with marvellous shapes of strength, of grace, of beauty, of dignity, with beings which have far more reality for us than most of those whom we meet in our daily walk, would be empty and depopulated! And remember that this which we speak of would not be our loss alone, or the loss of those who have lived already, but the disappearance as well of all that delight, of all that instruction, which, so long as the world endures, he will diffuse in circles ever larger, as the recognition of him in his unparagoned and unapproachable greatness becomes every day more unquestioned, as he moves in ages yet to come "through ever wider avenues of fame."

But of this enough. Cease we from man. Let no word be uttered by us here, which shall even seem to imply that the praise and honour, the admiration and homage, which a man may receive from his fellows are, or can be, the best, the crowning glory of life. Good they are; but they are not the best. Few, in the very nature of things, can be those illustrious sons of memory, dwelling apart from their fellows on the mountain peaks of their solitary grandeur, and dominating from these their own age, and the ages to come. To very few it can be granted, that their names shall resound through the centuries, that men shall make long pilgrimages to the place of their birth, gather up the smallest notices of them as infinitely precious, chide an incurious age which suffered so much about them, that would have been priceless to us, to perish for ever, or celebrate with secular solemnities the returning period of their birth. All this must be the heritage of the fewest; but because such, it cannot be the best of all; for a righteous God would never have put his best and fairest beyond the reach of well-nigh all among his children. This is not the best. That is the best which all may make their own, those with the smallest gifts as certainly as those with the greatest—faithfully to fulfil humble duties; to follow Christ, it may be by lowliest paths, unseen of men, though seen of angels and approved of God; and so to have names written not on earth, but in heaven, not on the rolls of earthly fame, but in the Lamb's book of life. For, brethren beloved, I should be untrue to that solemn trust which I bear, untrue to those responsibilities from which I can never divest myself, if I did not remind you, above all if I did not remind you on such a day as this, that goodness is more than greatness, and grace than gifts; that men attain to heaven not soaring on the wings of genius, but patiently climbing by the stairs of faith, and love, and obedience; that the brightest crowns, if all their brightness is of earth and none from heaven, are doomed to wither; that there is but one amaranthine crown, even that which Christ gives to them, be they high or low, wise or simple, emperors or clowns, who have loved, and served, and obeyed Him.

This crown they have obtained, the serious and sage poets who have consecrated their divine faculty to the service of Him who lent it. For myself, I am strong to believe that from one so gentle, so tender, so just, so true, as was Shakespeare, the grace to make this highest consecration was not withholden—that we have a right to number him with Dante, with Spenser, with Milton, and that august company of poets

"Who sing, and singing in their glory move."

His intimate, in one sense his profound, acquaintance with Scripture, no one can deny, or the strong grasp which he had of its central truths. He knew the deep corruption of our fallen nature, the desperate wickedness of the heart of man; else he would never have put into the mouth of a prince of stainless life such a confession as this:—" I am myself indifferent honest, but yet I could accuse me of such things that it were better my mother had not borne me, * * * with more offences at my beck than I have thoughts to put them in, imagination to give them shape, or time to act them in." He has set forth the scheme of

our redemption in words as lovely as have ever flowed from
the lips of uninspired man :

> " Why, all the souls that were, were forfeit once,
> And He that might the vantage best have took
> Found out the remedy."

He has put home to the holiest here their need of an infinite
forgiveness from Him who requires truth in the inward
parts :

> " How would you be,
> If He, which is the top of judgment, should
> But judge you as you are ?"

He was one who was well aware what a stewardship was his
own in those marvellous gifts which had been entrusted to
him, for he has himself told us :

> " Heaven does with us as we with torches do—
> Not light them for themselves; for if our virtues
> Did not go forth of us, 't were all alike
> As if we had them not."

And again has told us that

> " Spirits are not finely touched
> But for fine issues;"

assuredly not ignorant how finely his own had been touched,
and what would be demanded from him in return. He was
one who certainly knew that there is none so wise that he
can " circumvent God ;" that for a man, whether he be
called early or late,

> " Ripeness is all."

Who shall persuade us that he abode outside of that holy
temple of our faith, whereof he has uttered such glorious
things—admiring its beauty, but not himself entering to
worship there ? One so real, so truthful, as all which we
learn about Shakespeare declares him to have been,
assuredly fell in with no idle form of words, when in that
last testament which he dictated so shortly before his
death, he first of all, and before all, commended his soul
to God his Creator ; and this (I quote his express words),

o

"hoping and assuredly believing through the only merits of Jesus Christ my Saviour to be made partaker of life everlasting."

Yes, brethren, he has shown us here the one gate of heaven, and there is no other gate by which any man may enter there.

AFTERNOON SERVICE.

At Three o'clock in the afternoon Charles Wordsworth, D.C.L., Bishop of St. Andrews, delivered a sermon to another crowded auditory on "Man's excellency a cause of praise and thankfulness to God," selecting as his text, Psalm cxlv. 10: "*All Thy works praise Thee, O Lord; and Thy saints give thanks unto Thee*"—(Prayer Book version).— The Right Rev. Doctor, after a few preliminary remarks on the order and excellency of creation, proceeded as follows :—The Church of Christ has ever considered it a part of true piety to give thanks for kings and governors ; and rich men have received from the gratitude of posterity a religious commemoration of the benefits which their charity has bestowed.　It needs, therefore, no apology if something be said even in this sacred place respecting one whom God raised up three centuries ago from among the inhabitants of the neighbouring town, to be at once a mighty prince over the thoughts of men, through the pre-eminence of his intellectual powers ; and through the richness of his genius a munificent benefactor, for ages upon ages, not to his own country and nation only, but to the world at large.

And as this place, though consecrated to God's glory, is not unsuitable, so neither is the time, even of this holy day, at all improper for such a commemoration.　For what is it that every Christian Sabbath is designed most especially to bring home to our thoughts and meditations ? It is the resting of the Creator after the making of all His works, man included ; but it is also the rising of Christ out of the grave, and His sending down the Holy Spirit upon His Church, both as on this day ;—in other words, it is not only the creation, but the redemption and the sanctification

STRATFORD UPON AVON CHURCH.

(Architectural view, without the foliage.)

Published by E Adams.

of man. And what would the first, our creation, have availed us unless it had been followed by these other two? What satisfaction could we have had in thinking of ourselves or of our fellow-men? what real or lasting pleasure could we have enjoyed in contemplating the very best and noblest of mankind, unless it had been permitted us to regard ,him, not only as a work of God, but as a work, not created for nothingness, or for woe, but redeemed and sanctified for an immortality of happiness through Jesus Christ?

Entering then upon the subject before us with no mistrust, I shall, in the first place, be fully justified, I believe, in assuming that this celebration would not have taken place—would not certainly have been promoted so generally, or conducted on so grand a scale—unless it had been commonly felt that the works of Shakespeare are plainly on the right side; the side of what is true, and honest, and just, and pure, and lovely, and of good report—in a word, on the side of virtue and of true religion. Nor can it be said, in this case at least, that the popular voice has erred. It is in accordance with the voice of one whose testimony upon such a point will be accepted as of the highest and most unquestionable authority; I allude to the revered author of the "Christian Year." In the lectures which he delivered as Professor of Poetry in the University of Oxford, and which were published twenty years ago, while specifying the notes or characteristics by which poets of the first rank are to be discerned, the distinguishing mark which he requires, first of all, is CONSISTENCY. The first class poet, he remarks, is *throughout consistent, and in harmony with himself.* And where does the critic look for his examples in proof of this proposition? He brings forward two poets, who flourished in the same, that is our own, country, and at the same time. First, he produces Spenser, in whom he sees *everywhere sustained the same very form and look of true nobility*; and next he produces Shakespeare. We need not wonder that the former should have been chosen; but when we consider the disadvantage under which a dramatic- poet lies in regard to a point like this, we may feel well assured that no such example would have

been appealed to except from the conviction that it was
singularly a just one.   And this consistency of character
which, as a first and most decisive test, assigns our poet to
the highest rank, in what is it to be found?   It is to be
found in *the universal impression which his works convey*.
And for this the lecturer confidently appeals to the memory
of his hearers.   " Recollect," says he, " I beseech you, how
you each felt when you read those plays for the first time.
Do you not remember that all along, as the drama proceeded,
you were led to take the part of whatever good and worthy
characters it contained ; and more especially, when you
reached the end and closed the book, you felt that your
inmost heart had received a spur, which was calculated to
urge you on to virtue ; and to virtue, not merely such as
is apt, without much reality, to warm and excite the feelings
of the young, but such as consists in the actual practice of
a stricter, more pure, more upright, more industrious, more
religious life ?   And as for the passages of a coarser sort,
here and there to be met with in those plays, any one may
perceive that they are to be attributed, in part, not to the
author but to the age in which he lived ; and partly they
were introduced as slaves in a state of intoxication were
introduced into the presence of the Spartan youth—to
serve as warnings and create disgust.   We need not
hesitate, therefore, to conclude *illum Virtuti ex animo favisse*
—that he favoured virtue from his very soul; more especially
when we consider how widely different is the case with most
of his contemporaries, who devoted themselves, as he did,
to writing for the stage."

This, my brethren, is lofty commendation ; and I should
not have rehearsed it here unless I had been persuaded that
it is just.   Nor do I scruple to consent to the still higher
praise which the same unexceptionable judge has bestowed
in another part of his work upon the same two poets whom
I just now named ; and which brings the mention of them
still more closely within the legitimate range of a discourse,
delivered upon this holy day, and in this sacred place.
" Not only," he says, " did they measure everything by a
certain innate sense of what is virtuous and becoming ; not

only did they teach to hate all profaneness, but they trained
and exercised men's minds to virtue and religion, inasmuch
as each of them is wont to refer all things which the eye
beholds to the heavenly and the true, whether as occurring
in the actions of men and upon the stage of life, or as seen
in the glorious spectacle everywhere presented in the
heavens and the earth; precisely as does the Church
Catholic, only, as it is her province to do, in a manner
mystical and divine.   And hence it is that the poetry we
speak of led the way, as I believe, to sounder views even
upon sacred things, and to juster sentiments concerning
God himself."

But there is another consciousness no less generally felt,
which has tended to give to this celebration its comprehensive character.   I mean the consciousness of our poet's
nationality.   Like Homer to the Greeks, he is *the poet* of us
Englishmen.   And as we look for no better, so we desire
no other.   *   *   *   *   And now, my brethren, I think it
may be said we see the first rude outline of a character
which, in paying honour to the man, we shall do well to
contemplate.   For it is not (let me repeat), it is not merely
as a poet, or even as a poet who wrote, in a high and genuine sense of the word, religiously, but as a man, a Christian
man, that we, as a congregation of Christians, should be
content to honour Shakespeare.   Let us see, then, what he
was as such.   Undazzled by the world, and coveting nothing
which the world can give, we find him indifferent to the
fate even of the produce of his own immortal mind, and
throwing his pearls with child-like simplicity, into the lap
of time, as if unconscious of their amazing worth.   A man
of a less simple or less sober temper, after he had attained
to prosperity and to fame, would never have chosen, when
not yet fifty years old, to settle down for the remainder of
his days, in rural quietude, and in the place which had
known him, not only in obscurity, but in poverty and distress.   But seeking, as he did, to shun rather than to court
distinction, the fact that " a prophet is not without honour
save in his own country and in his own house," tended
rather to recommend this choice to him the more ;—happy

if only he might be allowed to study nature, and to culti-
vate his own moral being, in order that he might be "ripe,"
in God's good time—which proved to be a very early time
—might be "ripe," I say, for being gathered into a far more
joyful and more glorious abode.

But there is a further point of view, which combines in
one the poet and the man, and which, if we look with a wise
and patriotic interest upon the destinies of our country and
of the human race, cannot fail to raise him still higher in
our esteem.   Born within four years after Francis Bacon,
that gigantic intellect, and worthy to be so reckoned in an
age of giants (such was the bounty of God towards our
land and people in the first half-century after the Reform-
ation!), it was, shall I say, the *vocation* of William Shakespeare to live and to write as if *protesting* against the undue
claims of that physical philosophy which received a new
life from the genius of Bacon, and against the evils to which
an excessive cultivation of it will be apt to lead.   It is impossible to calculate how much we owe to our poet on this
account.   We are pre-eminently a *practical*, and are
becoming more and more a *mechanical* nation; and in
proportion as we become so, the works of Shakespeare
will be to us more and more invaluable.   Not that there is
to be found in his pages any unworthy jealousy of the
powers which physical studies are calculated to evoke, or
of the triumphs which, as time rolled on, they might be
expected to achieve.   Far otherwise.   Not that he has
betrayed any faithless fear of the progress of science, or of
the activity of the human intellect to whatever subjects
it might be applied.   No; to him

> *Ignorance* is the curse of God;
> *Knowledge*, the wing wherewith we fly to heaven.

But what is there in those pages ?   There is the very anti-
dote we need to guard and to strengthen our moral system
against the prevailing epidemic—the epidemic which has
arisen out of devotion to mechanical pursuits, and to the
study of material phenomena in relation to the luxuries
and conveniences of life.   On the one hand, there is every-

thing to refine, to elevate, to enlarge; on the other hand, there is nothing to make us impatient of acquiescence in *imperfect* knowledge, which is a necessary condition of our existence here. In a word, Shakespeare, more than any other writer in our native tongue, gives to Englishmen, who are debarred, as he himself had been, from the higher classical education, what such an education gives still more eminently to those who have enjoyed it, and turned it to its full account. Debarred, I say, he himself had been from direct access to the great intellectual treasuries of Greece and Rome. And yet, how much of the highest and purest sentiment, how many of the noblest thoughts and images, for which the best authors of antiquity are distinguished, lie scattered also over the pages of his works; just as in the vegetable world, specimens of the same plants have been found growing in widely distant regions of the globe, between which no certain channel of communication has been known to exist!

Having adverted to the common topic of complaint—our ignorance of Shakespeare's life—the eloquent Divine said, We know his " unwearied diligence " and the blessing which attended it. We know how he has written. What truth has he not taught? What duty has he not enforced? What relation of life, and of living things, rational or irrational, has he not illustrated? How has he looked *through* nature, and above all into the heart of man, with the intuitive knowledge with which the skilful artisan inspects the mechanism of the watch which he himself has made!

And knowing these things, we know enough to teach us how little true greatness is dependent upon external circumstances. We know enough to shame us, if any of us should complain of the difficulties and disadvantages in which God has placed him. The theatre itself, which received those masterpieces of Shakespeare's genius, what was it but a hovel, all rude, and shapeless, and unadorned? The father of Shakespeare was so little able to instruct his son, that he could not so much as write his own name; so little able to advance his son that, for a time, he could not even appear in this church on the Lord's day, from liability to arrest for debt. Yet Shakespeare lived to make the stage worthy of the utmost contrivance and embellishment of art. Shakespeare lived to relieve his father from distress in his old age. Shakespeare lived to become a teacher of the world, so long as time shall last. And, what deserves to be commemorated more especially in this place, Shakespeare lived to receive, as a benefactor, the blessings of the poor, not forgetting them, we may be sure, while he lived, inasmuch as he remembered them when he died.

Having taken up and expatiated on several other topics in relation to his subject, Dr. Wordsworth concluded his memorable sermon in the following terms:—Shakespeare is one of whom, judged of in the character up to which he grew, the Church of Christ has no need to be ashamed; because in him, *as a poet*, poetry has fulfilled every purpose for which in the mercy of God she was given to our fallen race as, next to Revelation, His most precious boon; and because in him *as a man*, the Gospel has exemplified that truest element of the Christian character, of which it is written—and fulfilled as on this day—"Blessed are the meek, for they shall inherit the earth." And, therefore, though this tercentenary commemoration points confessedly to the *year* of his *birth*, yet it was the *day* of his *death* which we celebrated yesterday; as the Church has ever been wont to celebrate not the birth-day, but the death-day —as being the truer and more glorious nativity—of her saints and confessors.

But, my brethren, if, not having seen, we honour and we love our departed brother for his works' sake, how greatly—how infinitely—more ought we to love and to bless HIM who made our brother what he was, and gave him to us; not to become (as human genius, alas! has sometimes proved) an instrument of desolation, but of culture, refreshment, of fruitfulness; not to resemble the full but faithless reservoir, which, when it has burst its barriers, carries death and ruin in its course, but the varying, yet ever-faithful Nile; which, while it is the grandest of all rivers, and while it is subject no less than the feeblest rivulet to the law which regulates its boundless floods, is at the same time the most beneficent in its influence, and the sweetest in its taste. And as in the surface of that majestic stream the traveller sees a true reflection of the heavens which are above his head, so in the poetry of Shakespeare the reader may behold no uncertain image of the word of God; may behold shining in its depths the starlike truths of the Bible; may behold and may adore the SUN OF RIGHTEOUSNESS, overclouded, we must confess, from time to time, with the mists of earth, but still shedding around His divine rays, and lighting up all with faith and hope, with love and joy.

THIRD DAY: MONDAY.
THE "MESSIAH."

The event of this day was the performance of Handel's "Messiah," in the pavilion, to the enjoyment of which nearly two thousand auditors assembled. The leading artistes who had given their services were Madame Parepa, Madame Laura Baxter (in the unavoidable absence of Madame Sainton-Dolby, who was unfortunately seized with sudden indisposition), Mr. Sims Reeves, Mr. George Perren, Mr. Patey, and Mr. Santley; and Mr. Alfred Mellon as leader. There was a band and chorus of five hundred performers. The chorus had been selected from the following celebrated societies:—The Festival Choral Society and Amateur Harmonic Society, Birmingham; the Sacred Harmonic Society (who sent down entirely at their own expense fifty picked members of their chorus), London; the Festival Choral Society, Worcester; and Holy Trinity Church, Stratford-upon-Avon. The orchestra comprised a hundred and twenty instrumentalists, including Mr. Blagrove as leader, and Mr. Harper, the celebrated trumpeter.

"The 'Messiah,'" the *Times* said on the following day, "went off admirably. A larger assemblage of voices has often been heard, but the magnificent choruses could scarcely have been executed with greater vigour and precision. Mr. Sims Reeves, recovered from his indisposition,

was in excellent voice, and sang to perfection, ' Comfort ye
my people,' and ' Thou shalt break them with a rod of
iron.' The consummate execution of Mademoiselle Parepa,
the steady artistic singing of Mr. Santley, the powerful
organ of Madame Laura Baxter were thoroughly appreciated
by a most attentive audience, and, under the masterly
conduct of Mr. Alfred Mellon, the vast musical machine
moved on without hitch or impediment.

"It might be objected that there is little apparent
connection between Shakespeare and Handel's ' Messiah,'
and that the performance of the latter is, therefore, somewhat out of place at a Shakespearian festival. But it is
always to be borne in mind that among the literary admirers
of Shakespeare are many persons who, from various reasons,
would not choose to attend theatrical performances, and
that in an universal collection it is as well to consult the
greatest number of tastes. Besides, the work which the
English place at the head of musical classics may be
reasonably thought worthy of association with the chief
classic of English literature. At the Garrick jubilee of
1769 the oratorio of ' Judith ' was performed."

MISCELLANEOUS CONCERT.

In the evening there was a miscellaneous concert,
which was more numerously attended than the oratorio of
the morning, the prices being considerably lower, whilst
the vocal artistes were the same as above mentioned, with
the addition of the gifted pianiste, Madame Arabella
Goddard, and Mr. Charles Coote as pianoforte accompanist.
The programme was drawn out with strict regard to the
occasion, the melodies selected being those associated with
the words of Shakespeare. The *Daily Telegraph* noticed
the audience and concert in the following terms :—

"The amphitheatre presented a brilliant appearance from the
strict observance of evening costume by all who entered the area,
and the élite of the county may be said to have graced the concert
with their presence. Macfarren's overture to ' Romeo and Juliet,'

Mendelssohn's expressive overture and incidental music to 'A Mid-summer Night's Dream,'' so wonderfully illustrative of the subject, and Allridge's Shakespearian overture, re-arranged for this festival by Mr. Alfred Mellon, and introducing the airs, 'Soft flowing Avon,' 'Sweet Willie, O,' and 'Ye Warwickshire lads and ye lasses,' were included in the instrumental portion of the programme. Madame Arabella Goddard charmed her hearers with her pianoforte fantasia of 'Where the bee sucks,' and this being enthusiastically encored, the fair executant paid a delicate compliment to the natives of Stratford by showing them the treasures of harmony enshrined in 'Home, sweet home.' Mr. Sims Reeves having evoked an encore by his charming rendering of 'Blow, blow, thou winter's wind,' repeated the last verse; Mr. Santley gave the recitative and aria, 'Pieta rispetto,' from Verdi's 'Macbeth;' Madame Parepa contributed Weber's grand scena, 'Portia,' and, still more to the delight of the company, 'Bid me discourse;' and Mr. George Perren sung in his best style, 'Come live with me and be my love.' The duet, 'I know a bank,' by Madame Parepa and Madame Laura Baxter, and Stevens's glee, 'Ye spotted snakes,' by Mesdames Parepa and Baxter, and Messrs. Perren and Patey elicited the warmest applause. The concert terminated a little before eleven.''

The third day of the festival was thus brought to a close amid universal satisfaction.

FOURTH DAY: TUESDAY.

The programme for to-day comprised excursions to Charlecote in the morning, and a performance of the "Twelfth Night" by the Haymarket Company in the evening. Through the kindness of H. Spencer Lucy, Esq., the Committee were enabled to announce that the picturesque grounds and hall so associated with the deer stealing story, would be thrown open to visitors holding excursion tickets, which were sold at 5s. each. As already observed, the weather was fine throughout the entire festival, and on this day specially brilliant and favourable to the excursionists. A very considerable number consequently availed themselves of the opportunity of inspecting the fine old mansion and park, highly interesting in themselves, and doubly so by reason of the Shakespearian associations. The worn and grey park paling—constructed without an iron nail—the soft winding Avon, the lime tree, the elm, the spreading

oak and sycamore, the herds of deer, " full of the pasture,"
skudding timidly away on the approach of a stranger—
Jaques' " fat and greasy citizens"—attracted the attention
and delighted the excursionists as they drew near to the
venerable mansion. The house itself, an architectural
curiosity, built in 1558—the first year of the reign of
Elizabeth—by the Sir Thomas Lucy, of alleged perse-
cuting memory, contains much to interest the antiquary
and virtuoso. On being ushered into the hall—which
brings at once to mind the olden time of pikes and bows,
and bucklers, profuse hospitality, and hearty revelry—the
strangers inspected a fine collection of portraits of the
Lucy family, who have been settled at Charlecote for nearly
seven centuries. On proceeding to the drawing room, they
found another set of pictures—valuable works of the old
masters—decorating the walls ; the ceilings beautifully
gilded, the floors of polished oak, and the furniture in fine
keeping with the solidity and proportions of the mansion.
The library was next visited, and found stored with the
best and oldest editions of Shakespeare, and amongst the
furniture, a set of nine chairs and two cabinets made of
ebony, inlaid with ivory, which were presented by Queen
Elizabeth to the Earl of Leicester, at Kenilworth, at which
place they had been purchased for Charlecote. After
examining lots of other curious furniture and objects of
interest, and fully satisfying themselves with their visit to
the hall, a number of the party proceeded to view the
magnificent little church of Charlecote, erected by Mrs.
Lucy, on the site of the old one pulled down some fifteen
years ago. Several splendidly executed monuments, in
white marble, are here to be seen, including that of the
famous justice, Sir Thomas Lucy, and of another Sir
Thomas, who was killed by a fall from his horse, in the
time of Oliver Cromwell. The latter, a marvellous work of
sculpture by Bernini, was erected by the widow of the
unfortunate cavalier.

Having " done " Charlecote and the charming neighbourhood, the excursionists found it nearly time to return
to dinner, and prepare for witnessing the performance of

at the pavilion. The curtain was drawn up for this Shakespearian treat, at seven o'clock in the evening, before a very large audience, comprising the Earl of Carlisle, K.G., the Earl of Shrewsbury, Lord Leigh, Lord Wrottesley and the Hon. Mrs. Wrottesley, the Hon. F. Byng, Sir W. Fraser, Sir M. S. Stewart, Sir N. C. Hamilton, Bart., K.G., Sir L. Palk, Bart., and Lady Palk, Sir H. Elton, and the Hon. and Rev. F. Leigh. The piece was cast as follows :—

Orsino . . . . . Duke of Illyria . . . . Mr. HOWE.

Sebastian . . . { A Young Gentleman, brother to Viola } Mr. WEATHERSBY.

Antonio . A Sea Captain, friend to Sebastian . Mr. BRAID.

Roberto . A Sea Captain, friend to Viola . Mr. WALTER GORDON.

Curio . *Valentine* } Lords attending on the Duke { Mr. CLARK. Mr. WORRELL.

Sir Toby Belch . . Uncle to the Lady Olivia . Mr. ROGERS.

Sir Andrew Aguecheek . . Mr. BUCKSTONE.

Malvolio . . . Steward to Olivia . . . Mr. CHIPPENDALE.

Fabian *Clown* } Servants to Olivia { Mr. W. FARREN. Mr. COMPTON.

A Priest . . Mr. CULLENFORD.

First Officer . . Mr. COE. *Second Officer* . . Mr. JAMES.

Olivia . A Rich Countess . Miss H. LINDLEY.

Viola . . . . In love with the Duke . Miss LOUISA ANGEL.

Maria . . Olivia's Woman . Mrs. E. FITZWILLIAM.

Ladies, Priests, Sailors, Officers, Musicians, and other Attendants.

The entire performance was remarkable for that perfect smoothness and harmony which talent, intimate acquaintance with each other on the part of the company, and careful rehearsals can alone ensure. Touching the respective merits of the different portraitures in the comedy, I may adopt the language of the *London Standard's* correspondent, and say—

" I need hardly tell you that Mr. Buckstone played to perfection *Sir Andrew Aguecheek;* that Mr. Rogers was an admirable make-up as *Sir Toby Belch;* that Mr. Chippendale made a very fair *Malvolio;* and that Mr. Howe was a very effective *Duke;* while Mr. Farren as *Fabian* and Mr. Compton as the *Clown* made more out of their part than could have been made by any other members of the company.

But I must tell you that Miss H. Lindley was an exceedingly satisfactory *Olivia*, while Miss Louisa Angel, as *Viola*, charmed every one who had the pleasure of listening to her delivery and watching the well-studied grace of her acting. I was sorry that the song was omitted at the close; for those who can remember its introduction a dozen years ago at the Princesses' can bear witness to its effectiveness, with Hatton's music; but after all the matter is not a great one, and I find that the majority of theatrical folks are in favour of its excision."

After the "Twelfth Night" was performed a Comedietta in one act, adapted from the French of M.M. Pierron and Laferrière, by Mr. Sothern, entitled

"MY AUNT'S ADVICE."

Mr. Charles Arundel	MR. HOWE.
Captain Howard Leslie	MR. SOTHERN.
Mrs. Charles Arundel	MISS NELLY MOORE.
Jane	MISS COLEMAN.

This trifle was not much admired, either for its literary merit, or the acting to which it gave scope, the general opinion being that it was not a happy selection for such an occasion by an actor of Mr. Sothern's distinguished professional position.

The above named were the principal events of the day, but there was a variety of minor amusements got up by private caterers, of which the people partook. There were trips down the Avon to Luddington, and a number of shows in the Market-place, from the renowned but diminutive Punch and Judy, up to the extensive menagerie of Wombwell. The puppet performance only requiring one animal, besides the manager, which entails any expenditure for "wittles"—Toby, to wit—seemed to thrive and prosper by reason of the limited expenditure; but the menagerie found itself in the wrong town, and had to make a speedy *exit*, as the expected multitude had not arrived in Stratford.

FIFTH DAY: WEDNESDAY.

This day it was apprehended at one time would be a *dies non* so far as dramatic performances were concerned, but it proved quite the reverse, being the most important of the week. The proceedings commenced with a dramatic reading in the theatre or Shakespeare Rooms, by Mrs. Macready, who has acquired some celebrity in the art. The attendance was not very large, nor the entertainment remarkably successful. Had it been given in the evening it might have been otherwise, as the programme was judiciously drawn out, and the lady is possessed of more than ordinary ability.

Small excursions to Anne's Cottage, and visits to the picture gallery, and to places in the town and neighbourhood not previously seen, occupied the afternoon, and in the evening the largest auditory which had up to this period assembled in the pavilion was collected to witness the " Comedy of Errors," and " Romeo and Juliet "—the principal characters in these plays being undertaken by artistes who had made something of a " sensation " in them, and obtained the highest patronage in London. The unusual course of playing the tragedy after the comedy became necessary, in order to permit some members of the Princess' Company to proceed early to town. The first piece was announced in the programme and played with the following cast from the Princesses' Company :—

"THE COMEDY OF ERRORS,"

Performed from the text of Shakespeare.

The new and splendid Scenery by Messrs. F. Lloyds, Fenton, Hann, and Gray.

Solinus . . .	Duke of Ephesus . . .	Mr. ROBINS.
Ægeon . .	A Merchant of Syracuse . .	Mr. H. NELSON.
Antipholus of Ephesus	{ Twin Brothers and Sons to Ægeon and Æmilia, but	Mr. J. MELLON.
Antipholus of Syracuse	unknown to each other	Mr. VINING.
Dromio of Ephesus	{ Twin Brothers and Attendants	Mr. HY. WEBB.
Dromio of Syracuse	on the Antipholi.	Mr. CHAS. WEBB.
Balthazar . . Mr. TAPPING.	*Angelo* . . Mr. C. SEYTON.	
A Merchant . Mr. CHAPMAN.	*Dr. Pinch* . Mr. R. CATHCART.	
Officer . . . . Mr. TRESSIDDER.		
Æmilia . . Wife to Ægeon, an Abbess at Ephesus . . Miss STAFFORD.		
Adriana . Wife to Antipholus of Ephesus . Miss CAROLINE CARSON.		

Luciana . . her Sister . . Miss HELEN HOWARD.
Luce . her Servant . Miss SYDNEY. *Lesbia* . Miss EMMA BARNETT.
Officers, Lords, Merchants, Male and Female Citizens, Executioner,
Nuns, Attendants, &c.
Stage Manager . . . . . Mr. GEORGE ELLIS.

The Messrs. Webb, who enacted the *Dromios*, after
playing the parts frequently with success at Mr. Henry
Webb's theatres, in Dublin and Belfast, essayed the
characters in other towns with equally good fortune, and
ultimately obtained an engagement at the Princesses', in
London, where, on their first night, they had the honour of
sustaining the *Twin Brothers* in presence of the Prince
and Princess of Wales. The performance subsequently
drew large audiences and obtained the encomiums of the
press. Indeed, if Mr. Harry Webb was not an actor of
considerable ability, or his brother capable of sustaining
the part as well as he does, the extraordinary resemblance
of the brothers must impart peculiar interest to the revival
of the comedy. It may be fairly questioned whether the
Dromios were ever so correctly embodied as by these
artistes. The audience are for the time completely puzzled,
much diverted, and in the concluding scene thrown into
loud fits of laughter. The *Antipholi* were well made up,
and the comedy altogether creditably put on the stage
and performed to the general gratification of all present.
The cast of

" ROMEO AND JULIET "

was only remarkable for the presence of Miss Stella
Colas. It stood thus :—

Prince Escalus, Mr. ROBINS.	*Friar Laurence*, Mr. FORRESTER.
Paris, Mr. BROOKE.	*Apothecary*, Mr. CATHCART.
Montague, Mr. LICKFOLD.	*Peter*, Mr. D. FISHER.
Capulet, Mr. H. MELLON.	*Balthasar*, Mr. CHAPMAN.
Romeo, Mr. J. NELSON.	*Abram*, Mr. TRESSIDDER.
Mercutio, Mr. VINING.	*Sampson*, Mr. TAPPING.
Tybalt, Mr. C. SEYTON.	*Gregory*, Mr. ALLEN.
Lady Capulet, Miss STAFFORD.	*Juliet*, Mdlle. STELLA COLAS.

Nurse, Mrs. H. MARSTON.

The young French lady had made a very decidedly successful stand at the Princess', in *Juliet*, last summer, and on returning to London, in April, met with a hearty reception. As I have so strong an aversion from hearing the sublime and beautiful language of Shakespeare read with a foreign and broken accent, I cannot say anything of the performance myself. The correspondent of the *Standard* declined entering into any criticism, as he "did not understand Miss Stella Colas." But I have heard no mean judges of acting speak in very high terms of the histrionic capabilities of the young *tragédienne*. Mr. Nelson looked *Romeo* very well albeit a little too stout. Mr. Vining and Mrs. Marston received high commendation in their respective parts, and on the fall of the curtain the Committee felt that, so far as performances in the pavilion could make the festival a success, it was to be a distinct triumph throughout.

SIXTH DAY : THURSDAY.

CONCERT.

The festivities were revived with unflagging spirit to-day in the Shakespeare Rooms, where an excellent concert of instrumental music, and glees from Shakespeare's plays was given, under the conductorship of Messrs. Coote and Stockley, according to the following programme:—

PART I.

OVERTURE . . . "The Merry Wives of Windsor" . . . *Nicolai.*
PART SONG . . . "The Cloud-capped Towers" . . . *Stevens.*
GLEE . . . . From "Oberon" . . . . . . *Stevens.*
INSTRUMENTAL FANTASIA on Shakespearian Airs, with Solos for Pianoforte, Flute, Clarionet, Cornet-a-Pistons, Violin, Violoncello, Contra-Basso, and Euphonium. Arranged expressly for this occasion by . . . . *C. Coote.*
"SHAKESPEARE,"—An Ode, written expressly by John Brougham, Esq., for the Tercentenary Festival . . . *Mellon.*
OVERTURE . . . . "As You Like It" . . . *Harold Thomas.*

PART II.

PART SONG . . . . "When Daisies pied" . . . . *Macfarren.*
PART SONG . . . . "Who is Silvia?" . . . . . *Macfarren.*

P

DUET.—Cornet-a-Pistons, and Euphonium, "Merry Wives of
  Windsor." Performed by C. Coote, jun., and Alfred
  Phasey . . . . *Percy.*
GLEE . . . . . "Hark! the Lark!" . . . . . . *Kucken.*
FINALE . . "Wedding March"—"Midsummer Night's
  Dream" . . . . *Mendelssohn.*

The ode mentioned above, which had been written by
Mr. Brougham, and set to music by Mr. Alfred Mellon, was
as follows :—

> "What shall his crown be? not the laurel leaf,
> That blood be-sprinkled decks the warrior's head;
> Who grasps a glory, as destruction's chief,
> A living monument to thousands dead;
> Bequeathing one vast legacy of grief;
> Some pest incarnate, fed with human life,
> Born of ambition or the lust of strife.
> In regal coronet shall we proclaim
> Him monarch? That would circumscribe his worth;
> A kingly diadem would only shame
> The kinglier thought whose realm is the whole earth.
> Such petty vanities but mock his fame.
> Profane it not! He is all crowns above—
> Hero of Peace, Evangelist of Love."

This was the only production of the kind during the
festival. An application had been made to the Poet
Laureate for an ode, but it was not successful. However,
this concert was, and formed an agreeable item amongst
the other entertainments.

The performance in the evening was the beautiful
comedy of

"AS YOU LIKE IT,"

under the management of Mr. Creswick, who was so
fortunate as to be able to cast it as undermentioned :—

Rosalind . Daughter of the banished Duke { Mrs. HERMANN VEZIN,
  (late Mrs. C. YOUNG.)
Celia . Daughter of Frederick . Miss REBECCA POWELL.
Phebe . . . . A Shepherdess . . . . Miss BUFTON.
Audrey . A Country Wench . Miss CHARLOTTE SAUNDERS.
The Duke . . . Living in exile . . . Mr. JAMES BENNETT.

Jaques ⎱ . Lords attending upon the ⎰ . Mr. CRESWICK.
Amiens ⎰ . Duke in his banishment ⎱ . Mr. W. H. CUMMINGS.
Orlando . Youngest Son of Sir Rowland de Bois . Mr. W. FARREN.
Adam . . Servant to Oliver . . Mr. CHIPPENDALE.
Touchstone . . . A Clown . . . Mr. COMPTON.
Le Beau . A Courtier attending upon Frederick . Mr. BELFORD.
Oliver . . . . . . Mr. ROBERT DOLMAN.
Charles . . . . A Wrestler . . . . Mr. H. PAYNE.
Frederick . { Brother to the Duke, and Usurper of } Mr. NANTON.
his dominions.
Jaques de Bois . Son of Sir Rowland . Mr. SIDDONS.
Eustace, Mr. POYNTER. Louis, Mr. ELDRED. Dennis, Mr. CONCANNEN.
Corin ⎱ Shepherds ⎰ . Mr. WILLIAMS.
Sylvius ⎰ ⎱ . Mr. WARNER.
William . A Country Fellow in love with Audrey . Mr. WORBOYS.
Lords belonging to the two Dukes, Ladies, Pages, Foresters, and other
Attendants.

———

The Play produced under the superintendence of Mr. CRESWICK.
Costumes gratuitously supplied by . . . . . Mr. S. MAY.
Scenery under the direction of . . . . . Mr. O'CONNOR.

No performance gave more general satisfaction than the above, as a glance at the cast will readily explain. "Mrs. Charles Young," said the *Morning Post*, "was warmly cheered during the performance, and enthusiastically called for at its close. Mr. Creswick had full scope for his great abilities in the part of *Jaques*, and did full justice to the character. Mr. Compton, as *Touchstone*, was full of quiet drollery and humour. Miss Saunders', in the part of *Audrey*, was an excellent performance, and the by-play and humour of the country wench created an immense amount of laughter. The piece was in every respect well put on the stage. The scenery of the Forest of Arden left but little to be desired, and the whole of the other portions was highly creditable, considering the difficulties under which the play was produced. The attendance was not quite so large as on the previous night, but all present were well pleased with the entertainment."

SEVENTH DAY : FRIDAY.

FANCY BALL.

The Committee wisely gave their patrons and supporters
a rest during to-day, that they might be more lively and
agile at the ball in the evening. Time was also necessary
to look after dresses, and settle that most arduous undertaking for the novice—the getting into fancy costume and
making up for a character. Young ladies had bored their
friends and relatives for weeks, nay, months, on the important question of " What ought I to go as ?" They had
cudgelled their brains and tortured their ingenuity to discover the characters to be assumed by others, and the
garments to be adopted for the purpose. Young gentlemen
were perhaps equally nervously anxious on the subject. I
know one who changed his mind about the character of his
adoption at least twenty times, ranging through " the
juveniles" from *Romeo* to *Rosencrantz*. Messrs. Simmonds
and Sons were the costumiers to the ball under the
patronage of the Committee, but Messrs. Nathan and May
did a fair share of the business.

The pavilion was put into admirable order, the floor
being waxed and well prepared for the dancers. Nothing
could exceed the efficiency of Messrs. Coote and Tinney's
quadrille band. The programme of the dances and music
was as follows :—

1 ENGLISH COUNTRY DANCE			
2 QUADRILLE	" Cologne"		Coote.
3 VALSE	" Ariel"		Gung'l.
4 LANCERS	" Original"		Hart.
5 GALOP	" Locomotive"		T. Browne.
6 QUADRILLE	" Shakespeare"		Coote.
	(Arranged expressly for this occasion.)		
7 VALSE	" Faust"		Gounod.
8 LANCERS	" Old English"		Coote.
9 VALSE	" Humming Bird"		Coote, jun.
10 QUADRILLE	" Dramatic College"		A. Mellon.
11 GALOP	" Prince Imperial"		Coote.
12 LANCERS			Tinney.
13 VALSE	" Kate Kearney"		Coote.
14 QUADRILLE	" Faust"		Gounod.

15 GALOP . . . . . "Bel Demonio" . . . . *Montgomery.*
16 LANCERS . . . . . "The Cure" . . . . . *Coote.*
17 VALSE . . . . . "Fairy Fountain" . . . *Frewin.*
18 GALOP . . . . . "Tuberose" . . . . . *Balfe.*
19 QUADRILLE . . . . "She Stoops to Conquer" . *Macfarren.*
20 VALSE . . . . . "Village Rose" . . . . *Coote.*
21 GALOP . . . . . "Extravaganza" . . . . *Coote.*

The company were not limited to Shakespearian characters, but in accordance with the recommendation of the Committee they were generally adopted. About nine o'clock, the hour appointed, there was an opening "sound of revelry," and the dancers began to appear upon the floor, and very shortly afterwards "motley was the only wear." The warlike Britannia, with trident, helmet, and shield, was followed by several delicate and dainty Perditas. A North American Indian had happily foregathered on his travels with a fair water nymph, and escorted her to the ball. Hamlet had coted Othello on the way, and both picked up with a party of jolly huntsmen, all of whom, with a sprinkling of Turkish Pachas, and a few Ophelias, keeping naturally in the wake of the Prince of Denmark, got into the room in a ruck. All sorts of characters began to arrive in rapid succession, some very plain, almost divested of any character in their exterior, others fantastic to a degree— heroes of peace and war, heroines ancient and modern, ladies and gentlemen from the Pantheon in sandals—congregated amongst others in the latest court costume. A couple of Shylocks, a Touchstone, and a solemn Egyptian dignitary held a counsel on some grave question—probably of obtaining partners for the first set. "Night," as was observed, entered into confidential conversation with "Morning" touching some rare toilette, doubtless, or the aforesaid question of partners. The pretty innocent Mirandas, and the gentle Desdemonas and fair Ophelias mingled with brigands, Zouaves, and bearded warriors. Benedict, Owen Glendower, a "nutty" little jockey, Edgar of Ravenswood, and Harry the Eighth escorted Cordelia, Rosalind, Ceres, "Spring," Portia, Juno, Mrs. Ford, and Anne Page. In short, as the song says—

"There were warriors, and statesmen, priests, courtiers and pages,
All costumes, all grades, from all climes and all ages ;
And the eye sought in vain to dispel the illusion,
Mid the glitter and glare of that splendid confusion."

Amongst the company the following were observed :—

Lord Leigh, *as Lord-Lieutenant.*
Sir W. Fraser, Bart., M.P., *Garibaldi.*
Sir J. Maxwell Stetch Graves, Bart., *in his Deputy-Lieutenant's Uniform.*
Sir Lawrence Palk, Bart., *in his Deputy-Lieutenant's Uniform.*
Lady Palk, *a Lady of the Sixteenth Century.*
Lady Hampson, *Marie Antoinette.*
Colonel Holdsworth.
The Hon. F. Byng, *in his Deputy-Lieutenant's Costume.*
E. F. Flower, Esq., *Mayor of Stratford, in his Official Robes.*
Colonel Bourne, *Royal Lancashire Artillery Militia.*
Captain Hamilton, *Stratford Rifles.*
Mrs. Stanley Baldwin, *Nerissa.*
Miss Bird, *Spanish Lady.*
Mrs. Brown, *Lady of Louis Quatorze period.*
Miss Badger, Shipston, *a Water Nymph.*
Mr. Bissel, Wolverhampton, *Manrico,* "*Trovatore.*"
Miss Lauri Brown, Leamington, "*Morning.*"
Mr. S. Bird, *Mercutio.*
Miss Baldwin, *Portia.*
Miss E. F. Burbury, *Perdita.*
Mr. G. G. Brown, *Bassanio.*
Mr. G. Baldwin, *Shylock.*
Mr. S. Baldwin, *Antonio.*
Mr. H. H. Burn, *Lord Hastings.*
Miss Bourne, *Rosalind.*
Miss H. Bourne, *Celia.*
Mr. D. G. Bourne, *Court Dress.*
Mrs. Bourne, *Countess de Rosselin.*
Mr. Alfred Baldwin, *Lorenzo.*
Mr. C. H. Bracebridge, *Deputy-Lieutenant.*
Lieutenant Baker, *Birmingham Volunteers.*
Mr. P. Butt, *an Albanian Prince.*
Miss Buller, "*Spring.*"
Miss Booth, *Juliet.*
Mrs. R. Cox, Edinburgh, *Don Cæzar.*
Mr. B. Campbell, *Edgardo of Ravenswood.*
The Miss Clifford, *Perdita.*
Mr. Cumberland, *a Zouave.*
Miss Calcraft, *Cordelia.*
Miss F. Calcraft, *Anne Page.*
Miss M. A. Cook, *Jessica.*

Mr. W. H. Child, *Court Costume.*
Mr. Corston, *Lorenzo.*
Mr. W. Colbourne, *Iachimo.*
Mr. Alexander Carter, *Benedict.*
Miss Corrie, *Lady of the time of King George II.*
Mr. W. Creswick, *Iago.*
Mr. Dowson, *a Brigand.*
Mr. Davis, Bickmarsh, *Charles II.*
Mr. Dighton, *the Duke Vicentio.*
Mrs. Dighton, *Olivia.*
Miss Duke, *Perdita.*
Miss F. Duke, *Helena.*
Mr. Dadley, *Cassio.*
Miss Ellen Dennis, *Titania.*
Mr. Fielding, *Capucious,* "*Henry VIII.*"
Miss Featherstone, *Juno,* "*Tempest.*"
Miss E. Featherstone, *Ceres.*
Mrs. Fielding, *Mrs. Ford.*
Mr. Charles Flower, *Lieutenant of Volunteers.*
Mr. E. Flower, *Longaville,* "*Love's Labour's Lost.*"
Mrs. E. Flower, *Hermione.*
Mrs. Greenway, *Lady Capulet.*
Mr. Kelynge Greenway, *Benedict.*
Mr. C. Durfort Greenway, *Owen Glendower.*
Mr. J. Garner, jun., Tatchbrooke, *Turkish Officer.*
Miss Gibbs, *Miranda.*
Mr. Guy, *Charles I.*
Mr. Wm. Greener, *a Gentleman of the Elizabethan period.*
Mrs. F. Gibbs, *The Princess Catharine.*
Miss Gibbes, *Ophelia.*
Miss Steele Graves, *Jessica.*
Mrs. F. T. Gill, *a Spanish Countess.*
The Misses Guy, *Shepherdesses.*
Mr. Wm. Gibbs, *Court Costume.*
Miss C. D. Greenway, *Beatrice.*
Miss C. M. Greenway, *Mrs. Wisis.*
Miss P. N. Greenway, *Quadrille.*
Mr. Honner, of the King's School, Warwick, *Elizabethan Character.*
Mr. Hobbs, Bickmarsh, *Edward, Page to Charles II.*
Mr. O. Hunt, *a Spanish Mediator.*
Mr. Hammond, *Wm. Shakespeare.*
Mr. Gilbert Hamilton, Leamington, *one of George II's Guards.*
Mr. Handford, *1st Middlesex Artillery.*

Miss Hamilton, *Fancy Dress.*
Mr. Gilbert Hamilton, *Sir Roger de Coverley.*
Mrs. Hamilton, *Countess of Essex.*
Mr. Wm. Hteherington, Manchester, *Captain of Volunteers.*
Mr. Wm. Hartley, *Hamlet.*
Mr. E. R. Hartley, *Mercutio.*
Miss Hartley, *" Night."*
Miss J. Hartley, *" Morning."*
Miss Hartley, Yorkshire, *Helena.*
Miss Hawkes, Tolton, *Flower Girl.*
Miss M. Holbech, *Lady Macbeth.*
Miss Hobbes, *Silvia.*
Miss M. Hobbes, *Scotch Girl.*
Mr. E. W. Jones, *Deputy-Lieutenant.*
Mr. J. Jervoise, Stretton, *Prince Ferdinand.*
Mr. J. H. L. Jones, *Lieutenant, City of Worcester Rifles.*
Mr. Jell, Liverpool, *Malvolio.*
Mrs. Kingsley, *" Night."*
Miss Keating, Birmingham, *Lady Capulet.*
Miss Kendall, *a Shepherdess.*
Mr. T. B. Lucy, *Naval Captain.*
Mrs. T. B. Lucy, *Beatrice.*
Mr. E. J. Lucy, *an Ensign in the Volunteers.*
Miss L. Lowe, *Maid of Honour.*
Mr. Lea, Birmingham, *a Gentleman of the Court of Queen Elizabeth.*
Mrs. Lea, *a Lady of the Court of Queen Elizabeth.*
Mr. H. Lane, *Assistant Surgeon, S.R.V.C.*
Mrs. Henry Lane, *a Lady of the Sixteenth Century.*
Mr. Margetts, jun., *Turkish Pacha.*
Mr. Moore, jun., Warwick, *Sir Walter Raleigh.*
Lady Mordaunt, *Fancy Dress.*
Mr. John Morgan, *an Elizabethan Courtier.*
Mr. E. G. Muntz, Radford, *an Elizabethan Courtier.*
Miss Mills, *Katharine.*
Mr. A. A. March, *a Florentine Noble.*
Mr. Buxton Morrish, *Valentine.*
Miss Newman, *Juliet.*
Mr. Nichol, Brighton, *Charles I.*
Miss D. Neill, *Lucetta.*
Mr. Nason, *Court Costume.*
Mr. Peyton, *Turkish Pacha.*
Miss Peyton, *Lady of Louis Quatorze period.*
Miss Pearce, Grantham, *" Spring."*
Mr. W. Pearce, *one of the Attendants at the Court of Henry VIII.*
Miss Plowright, *Ophelia.*
Mr. John Paget, *Prospero.*

Miss Paget, *a Peasant in Brittany.*
Mr. Guy Paget, *a Neapolitan.*
Mr. R. N. Philips, *Deputy-Lieutenant of Lancashire.*
Mrs. R. N. Philips, *Katharine of Aragon.*
Miss Philips, *a Shepherdess.*
Dr. Porter, Birmingham, *Court Costume.*
Mrs. Prideux, *" Night."*
Mr. D. Rice, *Volunteer.*
Mr. R. Scott, *The Earl of Rochester.*
Miss L. Smith, Bruton, *Perdita.*
Miss M. Sale, Shipston, *Ceres.*
Miss Sharshaw, Guernsey, *a Water Nymph.*
Mrs. Smith, *a Polish Lady.*
Mr. G. Shepherd, *Othello.*
Mrs. G. Shepherd, *Desdemona.*
Mr. Gus. T. Smith, *Uniform W.H.C.*
Mr. T. Smith, *Prince Ferdinand.*
Mr. Sims, Staffordshire, *Lord Leicester.*
Mrs. Sims, *Ophelia.*
Miss Synge, *Anne Boleyn.*
Miss Simpson, Birmingham, *Miranda.*
Miss Schmidt, *a Gipsy Queen.*
The Misses Shelley, *Ladies of the Court of Louis XIV.*
Mr. Spicer, *an Officer in the Militia.*
Mrs. Simpson, Birmingham, *Lady Capulet.*
Mrs. J. Tibbits, Warwick, *a Lady of Queen Elizabeth's time.*
Mr. J. W. Thomson, *a Huguenot.*
Mr. Wm. Thompson, *Charles II.*
Mr. Tanner, *Hamlet.*
Miss Thompson, *a Spanish Girl.*
Mr. G. Unett, Leamington, *The Earl of Essex.*
Mrs. J. A. Tompson, *Gondomar, Spanish Ambassador.*
Mr. Unett, *Henry, Prince of Wales.*
Mrs. Unett, *Portia.*
Mrs. Wood, *Anne Boleyn.*
Mr. C. Williams, *Touchstone.*
Miss A. Watson, *a Lady of Louis Quatorze period.*
Mrs. Washbourn, *Swiss Peasant.*
Miss West, *a Hungarian Peasant.*
Mr. W. Warrilow, *Valentine.*
Mr. Augustus Wise, *an Elizabethan Character.*
Mr. C. Warden, *Henry VIII.*
Mrs. Williams, Hereford, *Britannia.*
Mr. Williams, Hereford, *Indian Chief.*
Master Williams, *Jockey.*
Mr. R. N. Ward, *Manchester Volunteers.*
Mr. R. Walker, jun., *Bassanio.*
Mr. E. C. Webber, *Costume of James II.*
Miss Gertrude Young, *Miranda.*

The entire company numbered between three and four hundred ; but there were more than twice as many spectators in evening costume in the gallery. Dancing commenced about ten o'clock, and the scene became indescribably beautiful—novel—ever varying, as brilliant, gay, and delightful as the hundreds of jets that illumined the pavilion, the rainbow-hued costumes, and the host of gaudy figures could make it.

> " A thousand hearts beat happily :
> And when music arose with its voluptuous swell,
> Soft eyes looked love to eyes which spake again,
> And all went merry as a marriage bell."

Dancing was kept up with indefatigable vigour till five o'clock in the morning, when, as was generally observed, the Shakespeare tercentenary celebration proper had come to a magnificent conclusion.

EIGHTH DAY : SATURDAY.

THE PAGEANT.

Saturday was spent generally in resting after the enjoyments and fatigues of the week, especially by all who had taken part in the scene of the previous evening, but by a number in preparing for the popular entertainments originally intended to commence forthwith, but as the pavilion was not quite ready for the second series of performances, a postponement till Monday became unavoidable.

The programme for the people's week, prepared by the Committee, comprised a promenade concert, a balloon ascent, for which Mr. Coxwell was engaged, a public ball, and the performances of Shakespeare's plays. Still the absence of the pageant appeared to many to be " a mar in the great feast, and all things unbecoming." For some time it was doubtful whether this section of the community would carry their point, and in fact a week before the birthday nothing had been done in the matter. On the 14th of April, however, the often ·discussed question came up again at a convivial meeting in "the Shakespeare." Mr. Ginnett, the equestrian manager, who had just come off a journey in South Wales, happened to be present, and took part in the conversation. Time and money seemed wanting, when Mr. Ginnett made a generous proposal, in relation to both requirements. "If," he said, "you get up a pageant, I'll find you horses, carriages, and all my company to take part in it at my own expense." This settled the question. A provisional Committee was formed at once, and several guineas there and then subscribed. A deputation waited the following day on the Mayor, who, after some discussion of the subject, granted permission for the pageant to pass through the principal streets of the town, and contributed £5 towards the funds. Subsequently a public meeting was held, and a Committee formed consisting of

Mr. John Talbot, *Chairman,*

Mr. J. E. H. Greves,	Mr. James Coles,
,, F. Ginnett,	,, John Louch,
,, W. G. F. Bolton,	,, Russell,
,, Hy. Coombs,	,, Alfred Wilson,
,, Thomas Birch,	,, Wm. Hutchings,
,, Moses Hands,	,, Thomas Robbins,
,, John Court, Church Street,	,, Jelleyman,
,, John Walker,	,, John Inns.

Messrs. J. E. H. Greves, and W. G. F. Bolton were appointed Hon. Secretaries to the Committee, and Mr. John Court, of Church Street, was named as Treasurer. The town was then divided into districts, and duly canvassed for contributions. A sum more than adequate for the purpose was raised.

Posters were then got out and well circulated, and ultimately the following programme was issued:—

" SALUTATION AND GREETING TO YOU ALL!"
As You Like It.—Act 5, *s.* 4.

STRATFORD-UPON-AVON TERCENTENARY FESTIVAL.

A Grand Pageant and Jubilee Procession, in honour of the natal day of Shakespeare, on Monday and Tuesday, May 2nd and 3rd, 1864, and which will start from the Grand National Pavilion, near the Unicorn Hotel, each morning at eleven o'clock.

> " 'Tis well : the citizens have shown at full their royal minds, as they are ever forward,
> In celebration of this day, with shows, pageants, and sights of honour."
> *Henry VIII.—Act* 4, *s.* 1.

PROGRAMME OF THE PAGEANT.

Two Heralds, with trumpets, on horseback; Boy with Union Jack; the Royal Standard of England (borne by two men) ; Boy with Union Jack; Boy with Banner; Bellman; Boy with Banner; Flag; Flag (Red, White, and Blue) ; Boy with Flag; the Band of the Stratford-upon-Avon Rifle Corps; Boy with Flag.

> " The spirit-stirring drum, the piercing fife,
> The royal banner, and all quality,
> Pride, pomp, and circumstance of glorious war."
> *Othello.—Act* 3, *s.* 3.

Banner of the Arms of Stratford-upon-Avon; the Device of Shakespeare; Banner of the Arms of Shakespeare (carried by two men); the Device of Shakespeare; Ginnett's Band in Carriage (drawn by four cream-coloured horses); St. George, on horseback, in full armour; St. George's Banner, borne by his Esquire, on horseback; Page with Prince of Wales' Feather; Banner of the Arms of the Prince of Wales; Page with Prince of Wales' Feather; Melpomene, the Tragic Muse (in a black draped car, drawn by four black and white horses, with four Furies in position on the car); Banner; "King Lear"—*King Lear, Edgar,* as Mad Tom; Banner; "Richard the Third"—*King Richard the Third,* on horseback; Banner; "Macbeth"—*Three Witches,* with cauldron, and many-coloured fires, *Macbeth,* General of the King of Scotland; Banner; "Othello"—*Othello, Iago ;* Banner; "King John"—*King John* (on horseback), *Faulconbridge* (on horseback); Banner; "Hamlet"—*Hamlet, The Ghost;* Banner; Page with Flag; "Romeo and Juliet"—*Romeo* and *Juliet,* in a chariot, drawn by two white ponies, *Friar Laurence;* Page with Flag; Banner; *Anthony* and *Cleopatra,* in a car, drawn by two ponies abreast; Banner; Page with Flag; "Henry the Eighth"—*Henry the Eighth* (on horseback); Banner of the Ancient Arms of England; Page with Flag; Banner of the Prince and Princess of Wales; the Stratford-upon-Avon Brass Band; Boy with Flag; Boy with Flag; Thalia, the Comic Muse, on a car draped with fantastic devices, surrounded by four Harpies, and drawn by four spotted horses; Banner; "The Tempest"—*Prospero, Caliban, Ariel, Miranda;* Banner; "Winter's Tale"—*Shepherd, Autolycus;* Banner; Page with Flag; "A Midsummer Night's Dream"—*Oberon* and *Titania,* in a fairy car, drawn by two ponies abreast, *Bottom ye Weaver;* Page with Flag; Banner; "Merchant of Venice"—*Shylock, Portia;* Banner; "The Merry Wives of Windsor"—*Sir John Falstaff, Mrs. Ford,* and *Mrs. Page;* Banner; "Henry the Fifth"—*King Henry the Fifth* (on horseback) ; Banner of the Ancient Arms of England; Heralds ; *Pistol* and *Bardolph* (on two ponies) ; a Grand Triumphal Car, decorated with armorial bearings and devices, Shakespeare on an eminence, surrounded by *Desdemona, Ophelia, Beatrice,* and *Queen Anne, Cardinal Wolsey, Prince of Wales, Richmond,* and *Benedict.*

> " He was a man, take him for all in all,
> I shall not look upon his like again."
>
> *Hamlet.—Act* 1, *s.* 2.

Banner, the Royal Standard of England; Grand Military Band.

> Ye Warwickshire lads and ye lasses,
> See what at our jubilee passes ;
> Come revel away, rejoice and be glad,
> For the lad of all lads was a Warwickshire lad,
> Warwickshire lad ;
> All be glad,
> For the lad of all lads was a Warwickshire lad.

ROUTE OF THE PAGEANT.

From Ginnett's Grand National Pavilion, near the Unicorn Hotel, along Bridge Street and Henley Street to the Birth-place of the Bard of Avon, where solemn and appropriate Shakespearian music, by Dr. Arne, will be played. It will then proceed round the corner of the Old Post Office, along the Guild Pits, Union Street, High Street, Chapel Street, Church Street, Bull Lane, Sanctus Street, College Street, Old Town, Bree Street, Rother Street, Ely Street, Sheep Street, Upper Water Side, the left side of Bridge Street, Wood Street, Rother Street, Windsor Street, Guild Street, Tyler Street, Payton Street, Warwick Road, to the National Pavilion.

Mr. Ginnett, the celebrated equestrian, has most handsomely placed the whole of his magnificent stud of horses and equestrian troupe, properly caparisoned in appropriate Shakespearian costumes, at the service of the pageant Committee free of charge.

The dresses, armour, &c., for the procession, will be supplied by Messrs. J. Nathan and Winter, costumiers to Her Majesty's court balls, Castle Street, Leicester Square, London; and the procession will be marshalled by Mr. Joseph Tyrrell, stage manager, Liverpool.

Donations received by members of the pageant Committee, and by the Treasurer, JOHN COURT, Church Street.

> JOHN TALBOT, *Chairman.*
> J. E. H. GREVES, } *Hon. Secs.*
> W. G. F. BOLTON, }

Coxwell's monstre Balloon will ascend on Monday, May 2nd.

> "GOD SAVE THE QUEEN!"
> *Richard III.—Act* 4, *s.* 1.

The weather, so long fine, began to show signs of change. Rain fell heavily on Sunday night, but despite this unpropitious appearance the news of the pageant, which had got abroad, had so roused the country people that they crowded in thousands to Stratford-upon-Avon. Every train brought hundreds, whilst vehicles of all shapes and designs poured laden with visitors into the town. Mr. Ginnett had arrived with his circus. A number of other parties were engaged for impersonation of characters in the pageant, and the whole strength of the company, having mustered about ten o'clock, were arranged and marshalled in about an hour afterwards.

By this time it had pleased the aërial potentates to grant fair weather to the people's festival, and amid the crashing of martial music the procession started from "Ginnett's Grand National Pavilion," near the Unicorn Hotel. The streets at the time were crowded to inconvenience; the flags still floated and glittered from the house tops and windows, and the pageant presented no such ridiculous appearance as may have been supposed by those who only read descriptions of it. Of course there is always in the best of such displays something to laugh at, and the cynic, like the jealous, makes the meat he feeds on ; but those who are best acquainted with the getting up of such spectacles are well aware that however absurd they may appear to the grave or sour, the true philosopher knows they amuse the people, and make lasting impressions on their memories and feelings.

Having set out from the Unicorn, the pageant, arranged according to the programme above quoted, passed up Bridge Street, and along Henley Street to the birth-place of Shakespeare, "where solemn and appropriate Shakespearian music" by Dr. Arne was played. It then passed round the corner of the Old Post Office, along the Guild Pits, Union Street, High Street, Chapel Street, Church Street, Bull Lane, Sanctus Street, College Street, Old Town, Bree Street, Rother Street, Ely Street, Sheep

Street, Upper Water Side, the left side of Bridge Street, Wood Street, Rother Street, Windsor Street, Guild Street, Tyler Street, Payton Street, Warwick Road, and so back to the "National Pavilion."

Some of the characters were very fairly represented—the dresses were good, and considering the short time at the disposal of the Committee, their labours were meritorious, and must have been useful to their fellow tradesmen by the crowds which they attracted to Stratford. A funny incident occurred as the procession passed through the town. *Mad Tom*, in "Lear," was personated by a very clever Irish ballad singer, who happened to be amongst the illustrious strangers in Stratford at the period in question. He was representing the character admirably, when one of the police force—who doubtless thought the part ought to be sustained with "all the nice conduct of a clouded cane"—went up to him and cautioned him to "keep step," and refrain from his disorderly deportment in the ranks!

At two o'clock there was a concert at the great pavilion, and a performance at Ginnett's pavilion. The latter, a very large and beautiful tent, was attended by some fifteen hundred spectators. The band of the Royal Scots Greys attracted a good audience at the Committee's pavilion, and several fantasias on the flute by Master J. C. Arlidge elicited loud applause. There was a ball in the evening which was well attended.

TENTH DAY : TUESDAY.

The weather remained steadily fine. The procession again passed through the town by the route above named. As on the previous day the streets were crowded. Indeed, it was said that a greater number of people visited Stratford on these two days than had been present during the whole week before. Equestrian and other performances and entertainments amused the people. The balloon had proved a failure. Gas in sufficient quantity could not be obtained to inflate it, and it had to be taken down, packed up and carried back to London. In the evening the tragedy of "Othello" was played to a very large audience in the pavilion. The principal characters were cast as follows :—

Othello	Mr. CRESWICK.
Iago	Mr. JAMES BENNETT.
Brabantio	Mr. VOLLAIRE.
Cassio	Mr. VANDENHOFF.
Roderigo	Mr. WARBOYS.
Desdemona	Miss BUFTON.
Emelia	Miss A. BOWERING.

This performance gave general satisfaction.

ELEVENTH DAY : WEDNESDAY.

Old Stratford to-day began to resume something of her wonted quietude. The flags and banners had coiled themselves round their staves, as if weary of the fluttering and flapping they had had for nearly a fortnight. People talked of the tercentenary celebration as over at last, but there was still a concluding and very respectable perform-ance to take place.

" MUCH ADO ABOUT NOTHING "

was played at the pavilion this evening.

Benedick	Mr. CRESWICK.
Don Pedro	Mr. JAMES BENNETT.
Claudio	Mr. HERMANN VEZIN.
Leonato	Mr. NANTON.
Dogberry	Mr. VOLLAIRE.
Verges	Mr. WARBOYS.
Beatrice	Mrs. HERMANN VEZIN.
	(Late Mrs. CHARLES YOUNG.)
Hero	Miss BUFTON.

After which the " Trial Scene" from the

" MERCHANT OF VENICE."

Shylock	Mr. JAMES BENNETT.
Bassanio	Mr. HERMANN VEZIN.
Gratiano	Mr. SIDDONS.
Portia	Mrs. HERMANN VEZIN.
	(Late Mrs. CHARLES YOUNG.)
Nerissa	Miss TURNER.

Prices of Admission to these performances were—Lower Tier and Pit, One Shilling; Upper Tier, Two Shillings; Reserved Seats and Area Stalls, Three Shillings. The doors opened at Six o'clock, the curtain rose at Seven precisely. Excursion Trains ran on the Great Western, and London and North Western Railways from Birmingham, Wolverhampton, and Worcester.

For these performances the ladies and gentlemen were engaged professionally, the gratuitous services being confined to the first week. Entrusted to the management of Mr. Creswick, it is needless to say the "mounting" of the plays on the last three evenings was as perfect as possible under the circumstances, or that the characters in which he appeared were sustained in a manner worthy of the position he occupies. Mr. Bennett's *Iago* and *Shylock* have been long favourably known in the provinces; and in the present state of the profession, Mrs. Young can scarcely be said to have a rival. Amongst the other members of the company several well known names bear their own commendations, so that these concluding entertainments, as may be readily supposed, elicited as much applause and proved fully as successful as any of their predecessors during the celebration.

THE FINALE.

With the fall of the curtain over the fourth act of the " Merchant of Venice," the Shakespeare tercentenary celebration terminated. The event of the year 1864 in Stratford was fortunate in many respects. It was favoured with glorious weather; it was a splendid, a peaceful, and most orderly demonstration—a petty squabble implicating but one individual, being the only case during the entire festival calling for magisterial enquiry. But the festival was specially blessed in this, that of the many thousands engaged as promoters or patrons of it not one sustained the slightest personal injury. No widow or orphan associates his or her bereavement with this joyful occasion.

The magnitude of the conception and the indomitable energy with which, despite hindrances and irritating disappointments, the great undertaking was carried out, are

worthy of high and abiding commendation. Stratford-upon-
Avon has certainly earned for itself the lasting admiration
of the country, for never did any town of its size and
resources plan and realise so grand a festival. Some clever
discerning people beheld in the speculative eye of the
Stratfordians nothing throughout the business but self-
aggrandisement ; others charitably thought they were all
mad ! But these legitimate descendants of the old gentleman who " hung out in a tub," never felt a throb of pure
patriotism, and never were gifted with the power of appre-
ciating " the genius of our isle," or they would have known
that no jubilee, however stupendous or magnificent, could
adequately honour the memory of the man whose works
will live when those of kings, emperors, poets, philosophers,
and heroes have faded away like the mirage of the desert.
His works, I am thankful to say, are growing more popular
daily ; and one great result of the late celebration will be
to increase the number of their readers, and, let me hope,
the patrons also of the theatres at which they shall be
worthily performed. For my own part, my knowledge of
them is but limited and superficial. There is employment
for the leisure of my life in reading and studying them,
and at last I shall probably feel with Newton, " I have only
been playing with pebbles on the strand, whilst before me
lay the unexplored ocean." But from what I do know of
his works, I can say with all due reverence, blessed be God
for Shakespeare.

In subjoining a list of the contributors to the late
festival and the ulterior objects contemplated, I regret that
I have not been able to attach the Committee's balance
sheet, although I have detained the issue of this book in
hopes of being able to do so. In the meantime, rumours
have got abroad that there will be a serious deficit in the
exchequer, arising, in some measure, from unexpected
demands on the part of those eminent artistes who were
announced as giving their services gratuitously on the
occasion. I am not aware of a case of the kind, nor do I
think any has occurred—save one, arising out of a supposed
slight or want of appreciation on the part of the Committee,

all of which has been explained away. But the expenses of carriage, of railway fare, board and lodging, workmen, servants, London managers' "costs out of pocket," will form an aggregate amount of startling magnitude. The sum expended in advertising is something which ere now has, in all probability, drawn a few hasty expletives from the Chairman of the finance Committee; and, to descend from great to small things, I know the postage stamps cost, in one quarter of the year, nearly forty pounds. I do not "for a' that, and mickle mair than a' that" believe that the financial condition of the Committee is nearly as bad as it seems. And, furthermore, I believe a national monument will yet be raised to Shakespeare in Stratford-upon-Avon. To make a remark which is quite original—if I have not made it before, as I strongly suspect—"Rome *was not* built in a day." That the aspirations of the Committee deserve to be realised none will deny, and that they shall be so, we are not without reason to believe from the following

LIST OF CONTRIBUTIONS.

	To the School.			To the Monumental Memorial.			To the Festival Fund.		
	£	s.	d.	£	s.	d.	£	s.	d.
The Right Hon. Lord Leigh ...	105	0	0	...			10	10	0
Sir R. N. C. Hamilton, Bart, K.C.B.	25	0	0				10	0	0
The Rev. Granville Granville ...				5	0	0	5	0	0
E. F. Flower, Esq. ...	50	0	0	50	0	0	5	0	0
C. Holte Bracebridge, Esq. ...	10	0	0	...			10	0	0
Robert Hiorne Hobbs, Esq. ...	5	0	0	5	0	0	5	0	0
Mark Philips, Esq. ...	10	0	0	50	0	0	40	0	0
The Rev. J. C. Young ...	...			...			10	10	0
W. O. Hunt, Esq. ...	10	10	0	...			10	0	0
Mr. E. Adams ...	1	1	0	5	0	0	1	0	0
Mr. W. Stephenson ...				5	5	0	1	1	0
Charles E. Flower, Esq. ...	10	0	0	50	0	0	5	0	0
Edgar Flower, Esq. ...	5	5	0	10	0	0	1	1	0
Mr. R. M. Bird ...	5	5	0	5	5	0	2	2	0
Mr. Edward Gibbs ...	...			10	10	0	...		
Mr. W. G. F. Colbourne ...	...			5	5	0	...		
Mr. W. Thompson ...	...			5	5	0	...		
Mr. W. Gibbs ...	2	10	0	2	10	0	5	0	0
Mr. W. Lowry ...				20	0	0	5	0	0
Messrs. J. Cox and Son ...				20	0	0	2	0	0
J. J. Nason, Esq., M.B. ...	5	0	0	5	0	0	5	0	0

Q

	To the School.			To the Monumental Memorial.			To the Festival Fund.		
	£	s.	d.	£	s.	d.	£	s.	d.
Mr. H. Samman ...	10	0	0	5	0	0	3	0	0
W. J. Harding, Esq., Baraset	...			30	0	0	5	0	0
Mr. J. Bennett	...			5	5	0	1	1	0
H. Lane, Esq.	5	0	0	...			5	0	0
Mr. C. F. Loggin	...			10	0	0	1	1	0
Mr. W. L. Norris	...			10	0	0	1	1	0
C. T. Warde, Esq.	10	10	0	52	10	0	10	10	0
W. Greener, Esq.	...			25	0	0	1	1	0
John Lane, Esq.	...			20	0	0	2	0	0
Mr. Robert Walker	...			20	0	0	2	2	0
Mr. John New	...			10	10	0	1	1	0
Mr. John Morgan	...			4	4	0	1	1	0
Mr. John Bachelor	...			10	10	0	1	1	0
John Baldwin, Esq., Luddington ...	...			10	10	0	...		
Mr. Robert Gibbs	...			10	0	0	1	1	0
Mr. M. C. Ashwin	...			10	0	0	...		
Messrs. J. and G. Callaway ...	...			10	0	0	2	0	0
Mr. Charles Thomas	...			10	0	0	1	1	0
J. Cove Jones, Esq.	...			10	0	0	...		
T. S. Burman, Esq.	...			10	0	0	3	0	0
Mr. H. Downing	...			5	5	0	...		
Mr. John Moss	...			5	5	0	...		
Messrs. J. Bebb and Co.	...			5	5	0	...		
Mr. G. Lindsay	...			5	5	0	1	1	0
Mr. F. Winter	...			5	5	0	...		
Mr. H. W. Newton	...			5	5	0	1	1	0
Mr. John Walker	...			5	5	0	1	0	0
Mr. W. Ennals	...			5	5	0	1	1	0
Mr. W. K. Ewen	...			5	5	0	1	1	0
Mr. W. Holtom	0	10	0	5	0	0	0	10	0
Mr. S. Bromley	...			5	0	0	...		
Mr. T. Humphriss	...			5	0	0	...		
Mr. W. H. Haden	...			5	0	0	...		
The Rev. T. R. Medwin ...	5	0	0	5	0	0	2	0	0
The Rev. F. Annesley, Clifford ...	...			5	0	0	...		
Mr. E. H. Hawkes	...			5	0	0	...		
Mr. C. D. Pratt	...			5	0	0	1	0	0
The Rev. W. Morton	...			5	0	0	...		
Mr. R. Lapworth	...			5	0	0	...		
Mr. W. Pearce	...			5	0	0	5	0	0
Mr. Joseph Holtom	...			5	0	0	...		
J. C. Adkins, Esq., Milcote ...	...			5	0	0	...		
The Rev. A. H. Lea, Loxley ...	...			5	0	0	5	0	0
Joseph Townsend, Esq., Alveston ...	...			5	0	0	...		
The Rev. M. C. Tompson, Alderminster	...			5	0	0	...		
Mr. T. Hutchings	...			5	5	0	1	0	0
J. Gamble, Esq.	...			5	0	0	1	0	0
Mr. J. Court	1	1	0	2	2	0	2	2	0
Mr. T. Adams, Birmingham ...	...			5	0	0	...		
Gustavus T. Smith, Esq.	...			10	0	0	...		
Captain Peach, Idlicote	...			10	0	0	...		
Arthur Crowdy, Esq., Billesley ...	5	0	0	5	0	0	1	0	0
H. J. Starkey, Esq.	...			10	0	0	...		
Mr. W. Knights	...			5	0	0	1	1	0
J. R. West, Esq., Alscot Park ...	...			25	0	0	...		
Charles Lucy, Esq.	...			25	0	0	5	0	0
T. B. Lucy, Esq.	10	0	0	...			...		
The Rev. W. Bassett	5	0	0	...			...		

	To the School.			To the Monumental Memorial.			To the Festival Fund.		
	£	s.	d.	£	s.	d.	£	s.	d.
H. D. Dighton, Esq.	...			5	0	0	...		
John Hardy, Esq.	1	1	0	5	5	0	5	5	0
E. P. Shirley, Esq., M.P., F.S.A. ...	...			25	0	0	...		
H. O. Hunt, Esq.	2	2	0	2	2	0	2	2	0
Mrs. G. Holbech	...			5	0	0	...		
The Corporation of Stratford-upon-Avon	50	0	0	50	0	0	50	0	0
Miss Newland	10	10	0	3	3	0	3	3	0
Messrs. Price and Co., Gloucester ...	...			5	0	0	...		
Messrs. Hillhouse and Son, London	...			5	0	0	...		
Mr. Martin Lucy, Malvern ...	...			5	0	0	...		
Sir Charles Mordaunt, Bart., M.P. ...	...			25	0	0	...		
Chas. Gassiott, Esq., London ...	5	5	0	...			5	5	0
J. F. Cosens, Esq., London ...	...			...			5	0	0
Messrs. Willis and Sotheran, London	...			5	0	0	...		
Admiral Smyth, K.S.F., D.C.L., F.R.S., &c.	...			10	10	0	...		
M. T. Bass, Esq., M.P.	...			10	0	0	...		
R. N. Philips, Esq., Manchester ...	...			...			25	0	0
The Hon. Charles Lennox Butler ...	...			10	0	0	...		
Sir Francis Graham Moon, Bart., F.S.A.	...			...			10	10	0
J. G. Nichols, Esq., F.S.A. ...	...			...			10	10	0
T. R. Cobb, Esq., Banbury ...	...			...			10	10	0
Alfred Morrisson, Esq., Fonthill ...	...			...			10	10	0
H. G. Bohn, Esq., London ...	...			...			10	10	0
H. Edwards, Esq., London ...	...			...			5	5	0
W. M. Neill, Esq., Hampstead ...	...			10	0	0	1	1	0
Sampson Lloyd, Esq., Birmingham	10	0	0	10	0	0	...		
Richard Greaves, Esq., Warwick ...	5	5	0	10	10	0	5	5	0
The Rev. R. Prichard, Newbold ...	...			...			5	0	0
The Corporation of Boston ...	...			...			10	10	0
W. Hepworth Dixon, Esq. ...	10	10	0	...			...		
Messrs. Cunliffe, Dobson, and Co. ...	...			...			5	0	0
Charles M. Caldecott, Esq., Rugby ...	5	5	0	5	5	0	5	5	0
R. C. Heath, Esq., Warwick ...	...			...			5	0	0
The Right Rev. The Lord Bishop of Worcester	...			...			10	0	0
Robert Leech, Esq., Leamington ...	...			...			5	0	0
His Grace The Duke of Manchester	...			...			5	0	0
Eaton Hall, Esq., Bebington, Cheshire	5	5	0	...			...		
Joseph Ellis, Esq., Brighton ...	...			...			10	10	0
Mitchell Henry, Esq., London ...	...			...			10	10	0
Frederick Dinsdale, Esq., LL.D., F.S.A., Leamington	...			...			10	10	0
Messrs. S. and W. H. Teulon ...	10	10	0	...			...		
Captain Lomax	...			10	10	0	...		
J. Dugdale, jun., Esq.	10	10	0	10	0	0	...		
J. E. Todd, Esq., Bayswater ...	...			...			26	5	0
The Right Hon. The Earl of Harrowby	15	0	0	10	0	0	...		
H. A. Bowyer, Esq.	...			...			10	10	0
A. Morrison, Esq., London ...	...			...			10	10	0
John Faurie, Esq., London ...	...			...			10	10	0
Edward Wood, Esq.	...			...			10	0	0
Charles Knight, Esq.	...			...			10	0	0
Lord Wrottesley	...			...			20	0	0
Earl of Dartmouth	10	0	0	...			...		
A. Penizzi, Esq.	...			...			5	5	0
Mayor of Liverpool	...			...			10	0	0
W. Tite, Esq., M.P.	...			...			10	0	0
J. Bazley, Esq.	...			...			5	0	0

	To the School.			To the Monumental Memorial.			To the Festival Fund.		
	£	s.	d.	£	s.	d.	£	s.	d.
R. Padmore, Esq. M.P.	...			...			10	0	0
W. Schoefield, Esq.	...			...			10	0	0
Lord Feversham	...			...			10	0	0
Lord Willoughby de Broke	...			...			10	0	0
H. Ewart, Esq., M.P.	...			...			5	0	0
Sir W. Page Wood	...			...			10	10	0
Sir J. Maxwell Steele Graves, Bart.	...			...			10	0	0
Henry Spicer, Esq.	...			...			10	0	0
W. H. Child, Esq.	...			...			10	0	0
P. H. Muntz, Esq.	10	0	0	...			...		
W. Charles Macready, Esq.	10	10	0	...			...		
Hepworth Dixon, Esq.	10	10	0	...			...		
The Earl of Clarendon, K.G.	...			5	0	0	...		
The Earl of Carlisle, K.G.	...			...			50	0	0
Lord Vernon	...			...			5	0	0
Lord Sudeley	10	0	0	10	0	0	...		
Sir J. Eardley Wilmot, Bart.	...			...			5	0	0
Colonel J. Sidney North, M.P.	...			...			5	0	0
J. Hutton Wilkinson, Esq.	...			...			10	10	0
Earl of Delaware	...			...			25	0	0
Earl of Craven	...			...			50	0	0
Sir G. R. Philips	...			...			25	0	0
Alderman Copeland, M. P.	...			...			10	10	0
Rev. H. Incks	...			...			10	0	0
Sir J. Anson, Bart.	...			...			5	0	0
Lord Houghton	...			...			10	0	0
Mrs. Theodore Martin	...			25	0	0	...		
T. Martin, Esq.	...			10	10	0	...		
Dr. Kingsley	...			...			15	15	0
W. Dickens, Esq.	...			...			5	0	0
Sir James East, Bart.	...			...			5	0	0
Hon. F. Byng	...			...			5	0	0

Sums under £5, about £600.

The above list is exclusive of the subscriptions being collected in towns where branch committees are formed.

On the first of June, the *Times* published the following account of the sale at the pavilion :—

"The last act but one of the Shakespearian tercentenary drama was performed on Tuesday in the spacious and beautiful pavilion erected at Stratford for the musical and dramatic specialities of the late festival. On Tuesday, Messrs. Puttick and Simpson, of Leicester Square, sold by public auction the effects belonging to the Committee, consisting of an elegant act drop, painted by Mr. Telbin, of Her Majesty's Theatre; a proscenium, designed by Mr. O'Connor, of the Haymarket; fly-borders of drapery, sky, &c.; stage machinery and appliances of such a perfect and expensive kind that one would have supposed the building was to be permanently used as a theatre, with drawing-room furniture and other et ceteras to match. There was a good attendance of persons engaged in theatrical speculations from Liverpool, London, Leeds, Birmingham, Bradford, &c., bidding for the act drop, which is exquisitely painted, and represents Shakespeare standing before an architectural design, with the church of Stratford in the distance; medallions of Thalia and Melpomene, &c. This was accompanied by the most complete machinery for working the drop. The lot was bought by Mr. Shepherd, of the Surrey Theatre, for £26. The proscenium, with inner proscenium, borders, and wing, with royal arms surmounting the whole, was purchased by Mr. Hobson, of the Amphitheatre, Leeds, for six guineas. The gas-fittings offered for sale were costly, including wing lights, batten lights, shadowless argand burners, brackets throughout the building, and a range of footlights for the stage, having forty-five shadowless burners, with shades and glasses complete; they were knocked down to Mr. Shepherd for £3 15s. The principal item here was the centre chandelier or corona of above three hundred jets, arranged in two rings, with groups of jets and six-star burners, bearing treble lights, &c., and this lot was bought by Mr. Clapham, of the Royal Park, Leeds, for 46s. Among the other purchasers of theatrical properties were Mr. Simpson, Theatre, Birmingham; Mr. Wild, of Bradford; Mr. Day, Crystal Palace Music Hall, Birmingham; Mr. Montague, Secretary to Christy's Minstrels, &c. There were not less than one thousand seven hundred official programmes of the late festival, published at 1s., selling in lots of fifty at about 4s., and about three thousand chairs in sets of six, twelve, and two dozen, ranging from 2s. to 1s. 6d. each. The result of the sale cannot have materially benefited the fund. The last act of the festival is yet to be performed—namely, the presentation of the Committee's balance-sheet. It is discouraging and disappointing to them to know that a very considerable deficiency will be shown; whether from mismanagement, or the local unpopularity of a section of the Committee, with whom the county and resident families would have no connection, it is useless to dwell upon. The Lord-Lieutenant of the County (Lord Leigh) has acted generously, and marked his appreciation of the labours of the Committee and his desire to lessen the deficit, by voluntarily transferring his subscription of one hundred guineas from the scholarship to the festival fund. Lord Leigh's example will, in all probability, be followed by the county gentry and residents of Stratford generally, who are contributors in some form to the threefold objects of the tercentenary, although not to the fund wholly appropriated to the payment of festival expenses, and many Vice-presidents at a distance are only waiting the publication of a balance-sheet to co-operate with the Committee in relieving the latter body from all pecuniary responsibility and loss."

The loss spoken of will not, in my opinion, be of the magnitude apprehended, and time will show that the labours of the Stratford-upon-Avon Committee to do honour to the memory of Shakespeare have not been in any respect in vain.

THE END.

BIRMINGHAM:
MARTIN BILLING, SON, AND CO., PRINTERS, LIVERY STREET.

www.ingramcontent.com/pod-product-compliance
Ingram Content Group UK Ltd.
Pitfield, Milton Keynes, MK11 3LW, UK
UKHW010345140625
459647UK00010B/839